Head Check

WHAT IT FEELS LIKE TO RIDE MOTORCYCLES

Also by Jack Lewis

Nothing in Reserve:
True Stories, Not War Stories

Head Check

WHAT IT FEELS LIKE TO RIDE MOTORCYCLES

by **Jack Lewis**

For Tucker Dog,
who holds a piece of me
for later.

Copyright © 2014 Jack Lewis
Published Dec. 2014, Litsam Inc.
All rights reserved.

ISBN-13: 978-1-935878-08-7
E-book ISBN: 978-1-935878-09-4
LCCN: 2014954856

Litsam
for the books!

Shoreline, WA U.S.A.
http://litsam.com

This is a creative work. Names and stories, fictional and factual, are rendered from the author's imagination. Any resemblance to persons living or dead, or events past, present or future, is coincidental and incomplete. Truth is an unfolding story.

FOREWORD

Band of Brothers

The message from Jack Lewis' "Pretty Wife" seemed innocent enough: "It would be great if you could write a foreword for Jack's book, seeing as how you 'discovered' him."

Yeah, well, somebody discovered the Ebola virus, too, and I don't see him beating his chest about it.

I didn't really "discover" Jack anyway. Truth be told, his was amongst a pile of unsolicited manuscripts left on outgoing *Motorcyclist* editor Mitch Boehm's desk when I got promoted, ca. 2006. (Another in that stack belonged to Ari Henning, who I eventually hired as Associate Editor.) Mitch didn't say much about any of those stories, but allowed that there was "some good stuff in that Lewis guy's work."

Yeah, yeah, sure there was… except when I finally got around to reading "that Lewis guy's work," I did indeed find that it contained "some good stuff." Titled "Riding Home," the story detailed Jack's very personal experiences as a veteran returning from the Iraq War. One paragraph about a souvenir bullet gave me serious pause, and convinced me to publish the piece posthaste.

> *I kept it close as a lover, and it whispered to me for months, chasing me like a ghost. It was my rosary, skeleton key, ballistic lodestone, taunting me with a papery laugh even after its author died in his barri-*

caded window, head-shot by a better soldier than me. Zzzzip.

Clearly "that Lewis guy" could write. Trouble was, the story was too long. As in book-length. And cutting it down to size proved problematic as it quickly became apparent that Jack *does not like* to be edited. Not surprisingly, this book contains the unedited versions of "Riding Home" and some other previously published magazine articles. Consider them the Director's Cuts.

"Riding Home" was as much of a lightning rod as anything ever published in a motorcycle magazine. Some readers hated Jack's nonsense and called him a warmonger and other unflattering names not heard since the Vietnam protests. I politely reminded them that it was perhaps unwise to insult a rifleman who could part their hair from a half-mile out.

Others loved Jack's prose and appreciated his years of military service. I'll never forget *Motorcyclist's* Executive Editor Tim Carrithers, himself a fine writer, walking into my office, shaking his head and proclaiming, "Man, that Lewis guy is *good*." The mere fact that we heard from readers who enjoyed Jack's work boded well, because in this Communication Age people are all too quick to fire off flaming emails and not so forthcoming with the compliments. I duly offered to make him a columnist.

A word about character: Jack and I are about the same age, the first generation to avoid the draft without having to dodge it. When I reached the age of consent, I chased girls, raced motorcycles and played in rock bands. Jack enlisted in the army. Two decades later, when September 11th happened, I marked the occasion by riding a motorcycle cross-country and writing a story that never got published. Jack re-enlisted, making him a better man than me twice over. And he wrote a book about his experiences called *Nothing In Reserve*. Reading that, I learned to respect him as much as I admired him.

I won't ever pretend to know what it's like to be a soldier on the field of battle. But I think motorcyclists — and especially racers — likewise make peace with the fact that we face the very real possibility of serious injury or death on a regular basis. That, in turn, breeds a sense of camaraderie that those who don't share it will never understand. Think *Band of Brothers* on wheels. As someone who has one foot in each of those two worlds, Jack offers a unique perspective. Better yet, he's that rarest breed of writer who is both a clever wordsmith *and* actually has something to say. Too often it's one without the other.

I won't take the credit — or the blame — for "discovering" Jack Lewis. But I am damn glad that I gave him a shot! Enjoy reading *Head Check*. I know I will…

— *Brian Catterson*

Author's Preface

For several years, I've resisted calls to collect up a packet of my *Motorcyclist* ramblings and pack them into a book. For one thing, it seems a bit exploitive: I've already been paid upon publication. Secondly, there is a kind of loyal opposition among readers who write letters. These folks regularly and carefully explain to my Editor (sequentially Messrs. Boehm, Catterson, and Cook) and to me — not, it must be noted, without a certain delight — the precise and manifold reasons why my writing should never again sully a public forum.

More compelling to me is that writing for moto rags — even as eminent a publication as the ancient and venerable *Motorcyclist* — remains nearly as evanescent a form as spoken-word *haiku* over your dozenth round of late-night *saké*. The wheel turns, another month rolls by, and you change out your toilet tank literature for a fresh issue. Think of it as the Great Circle of Bold New Graphics. Anyway, I already had a little Kindle book about motorcycling out, titled "Coming & Going on Bikes," and it was bubbling along.

So when my publisher, Litsam, Inc., inquired about this project, I turned them down. Making a book is far harder than it looks, even if the content is already substantially produced, and anyway I was busy writing things for the magazine.

Then a brass ring dropped into view with the suggestion that a few favorite pieces could be run at their full uncut length, not at the length to which they were edited down to fit available magazine pages. That shiny ring was further burnished with the suggestion that a few previously unpublished items could be included, including an energetic ramble in an ingenious three-wheeler that no proper gearhead could ignore (the rig, that is). Finally, my project editor dropped the tastiest bait, saved for last: the Loyal Opposition would be heartbroken without further opportunity to voice their detailed critiques.

That opportunity is now open. As for those of you who bought this book on purpose, if you'd be so kind as to avail a bit of real estate on your toilet tank, the writing in here represents some of the most fun I've had behind keyboard or handlebars.

There's a rumor floating about that writing for a motorcycle magazine is just about as good as life gets. That rumor, I'm forced to report, is true. What you'll find in this book is as good as it's gotten for me.

I hope you'll enjoy it, too.

— *Jack Lewis*

PROLOGUE

I came out early.

I wasn't a sportbike guy then. It wasn't time yet.

That was the summer I moved from a standard to a factory cruiser. My "new" bike came complete with a fat back tire, sweet chrome highlighting metallic green paint, apehanger bars and a suicide shifter carefully positioned to prevent any future siring of children. Like all the best cruisers, styling was bitchin', brakes crude and suspension proudly hardtail — and hardnosed, for that matter. It was 1971. For the first and last time, I was well ahead of the fashion curve.

Best of all, no training wheels.

I learned many bad habits on my Schwinn Sting Ray, an original lead sled built in Chicago by American union workers. Its slapstick shifter taught me to pick the holeshot gear, and the coaster brake setup was instructive on the subject of countersteering through feet-up skids without flying over the high side. Not every time, anyway.

Unlike today's effete, lavishly priced poseursickles, the Sting Ray was cheap, readily available and a true do-it-all machine. More than just a chick magnet for third graders (I went for older women back then), mine was good for clearing a full three inches of air over dirt bumps, speed trials on Dad's long driveway, popping wheelies and chasing my little brother through the grass.

Other epiphanies included a quick, violent primer on speed wobbles, and an object lesson on the importance of protective gear. Manically chasing my big sister downhill on her big kid bike with five, count 'em, five speeds forward, I got deep into a negative feedback loop and the shoulder-high, glitter-green grips wrenched right out of my undersized paws.

Landing chin first on asphalt at 30 mph started me down a life path of frequent interaction with emergency room medical professionals. Freaked out by needles, I refused treatment, but Dad saw my jawbone peeking out through the red cabbage slaw of my face and pulled rank. Three layers of stitches ensued.

Boy, did I learn a lesson from that. Two more gears and taller tires, and I would have caught her for sure. That's when it dawned on me.

An *engine…*

January 2009, Motorcyclist

Comes Around

Something borrowed, something blue,
Something wicked, something true.

It was 1974 when my cousin barreled into Dad's circular drive and skidded to a stop on 432 pounds of booming black badass, good for a buck and a quarter on a cool day with a tailwind: a Norton 850 Commando, last and greatest dinosaur to stomp out of Druidic folklore, hunting for Harleys and scaring the womenfolk, dripping with primordial chrome. It was all Carl could do to boot that beast, but the roar it made convinced me that my grandma was right about everything except them debbil motorcycles. I wanted that. It was the coolest thing ever.

Bikes became my alternative homework. I sketched dirt bikes with 17-inch suspension in algebra, and spent part of every lunch hour wearing out the library's bike mags. By these one-way correspondence courses I studied motorhead philosophy under Dr. Allan Girdler, racing Italian from *Signor* Cook Neilson and the home economics of fried egg sandwiches from Prof. (emeritus) Ed Hertfelder.

Magazine dreams aside, I came late to the party, finally learning the clutch-throttle dance at the wizened age of 13 on a Harley (Aermacchi) 250 Sprint. It came with all the options: ribbed front tire, knobby rear, and rubber-mounted handlebars. Periodically, it would backfire on startup and blow its muffler tip across the garage, which is how I chipped my dad's ankle that day. That's my story, anyway, and I'm stickin' to it.

My first traffic ticket came at 14, sneaking a ride to freshman two-a-days on a DT175 Yamaha. Two years later, its hairy-nippled cousin, my notorious IT175, administered a Monocross bite in the ass and tore my left leg mostly off. For years I kept a sandwich bag full of stainless orthopaedic hardware, determined to recycle my tibia plate into a beer opener. It's probably around here somewhere, maybe under the Whitworth wrenches behind the 6V battery charger, or under that pile of questionable nitrogen cartridges.

My mom, expressing sharp interest in the survival of her progeny, marched me into Langlitz Leathers for a "Christmas and birthday" present the year I turned 16. The jacket they fitted me for traveled with me for 23 years. After crashing on it four times and growing a prosperous midlife midriff, I passed the brown bomber to my little brother in fine working order. I have another one now, and it may be my last.

Or not.

By my senior year, I was practicing wheelies on a red 1978 RD400 (Gawd, but I loved them two-smokers) with DG expansion chambers dented on their bottoms from landing street jumps on Cornell Boulevard. My buddy Bill bought a blue RD just like mine, and we took many an informal sabbatical from academic endeavors to pursue girls, various contraband (what isn't contraband to a 17 year-old?), and potential victims on Hondas. We were convinced you beat the nicest people on Hondas, but I hear they're actually pretty fast now. And they don't seize hard after the Autolube line comes adrift, 200 miles from home in a leather-loading NW thunderstorm…

The Cool Guys™ at my high school drove hopped-up Camaros, but no matter how much got spent on paint and blowers, those were still Chevys. Big, fat things that worked as well static as moving. The definition of The Edge is that you fall off when you stop paying attention. No car has ever been that kind of test. What good is a vehicle too stupid to kill you when you're drunk?

My best and dumbest moments have mostly been on bikes. Because of that, motorcycles remain part of home, no matter where I am in the world: an international language, a brain-breeze respite, a core competency that — like combat shooting or fire-eating — raises eyebrows and starts the best (or dumbest) conversations.

I've had a slew of bikes now, most good and some better — are there any truly bad motorcycles? — all bristling with lessons I needed to learn. There is no better way to learn humility than by begging your buddy to yank your suddenly porky dirt bike off you, *now-right-now-please-now* before your barbequing leg starts to smell like food. There isn't a finer lesson in the subtleties of international relations than seeing the wiring diagram of a Moto Guzzi 850 T-3 translated into Texican with a roach clip and circuit tester, 180 miles east of Santa Fe. The world's best object lesson in sweating the details is your first lusty leer at the steering head of a new-to-you Ducati. Triumph hardtails, plunger Beezas, RZ350s and single-cam Hondas all had things to teach this slow, hard-headed student.

All I've really learned is that I'm a rider first. I've nailed two degrees, failed at two industries, gone to war and written a book. I've piloted armored vehicles, Class 8 trucks, construction equipment, large yachts, hydroplanes and aircraft, but those are only pieces of my experience.

Motorcycles are a piece of my personality. I still whip my head around to see what kind of bike just went by. Bilateral hearing damage doesn't prevent me telling a Harley from an open-pipe Virago, eight blocks off.

My second wife was too practical to suffer riding. Important things must come before such frivolity. Leaving her to grind away at those important things, I decamped south to work on fine and frivolous things with a pretty girl who learned to ride her KZ440 around the green hills of Eugene.

After a couple of weeks, sister Joy called to tell me that my old buddy Bill is a chicken farmer in (where else?) Eugene. The BMW R1200S I fired up to run out there may not be Commando-cool, but it is a sinister black thunderhead of vicious torque and Wagnerian pathos. One hot spring afternoon I skittered down Bill's steep dirt driveway, ignored the waving 12-gauge and chugged his last beer. In random order, we viewed his chainsaw, glass-blowing lathe and flock of free-ranging guard chickens that lay pastel Easter eggs. Behind his shed door, I spied a flash of blue Yamaha paint.

Bill still keeps his RD400, in sad shape but mostly complete. As my dad still says of every pretty girl, it makes an old man want to try again. With radial-finned heads, maybe, and some Spec II headers off Craigslist…

A long time ago, I thought a Norton 850 Commando was the coolest thing ever.

I was right, too.

December 2007, Motorcyclist

CRASHING VASHON

Readers were as scandalized by this revelation as if Motorcy-clist *had shamelessly pimped the last untainted village of inno-cent pygmies, but the clandestine, inside knowledge of the TT is not its existence. It's the scheduling.*

Join the club, get the dates. Go.

The best-kept secret in motorcycling just got out.

The first thing you need to understand about the Isle of Vashon TT is that this is eyes-only, double-secret-probation stuff. According to the website of sponsoring club Vintage Motorcycle Enthusiasts, "It is the considered opinion of most of the leadership that over-promotion may potentially threaten the future of the event."

There is no event date listed.

First Wednesday is when the VME stages its monthly rollout at a pub in Seattle's retro-hip Georgetown. Over a Velocette Thruxton in the parking lot, I asked a member, "Hey, is the TT this weekend? I've been out of state for a while."

He looked me over narrowly, taking in my fresh haircut, Costco jeans and BMW golf shirt left over from working the motorcycle show.

"Corporate stooge," his expression said.

"I think it was a couple of weeks ago."

Dude, I'm a dues-paying member! Just looking to exploit the event for personal vanity, and gnaw at the thin bone of Motorcyclist *remuneration...* but it was too late. He stalked away to join a group of iron-bearded geezers. They all glared suspiciously. I backed away slowly, then darted inside Planet Georgetown. Next year I'm growing a beard. It's cheaper than paying dues.

Pat, warm-hearted and patient, keeps the VME more structurally integrated than most of its bikes or any of its members. She cross-checked my membership status, then lowered her voice and muttered, "The TT's this weekend."

Hide the women and call out the actors! It's Hollister all over again!

• • •

The very girl of my silken dreams whispered, "Jack, it's eight o'clock."

"Mmmm…eight o'… Hell! I'm supposed to be at the ferry dock!"

Such is the measure of her character that she didn't laugh while I hopped around the room, one leg jammed into my leathers and the other trying to remember where it left its drawers. At least not while I could hear her. I hadn't ridden Honey, my '69 Beemer, in five months. Whipping the cover off, I carefully administered my standard BMW tune-up: tickle her 'til her bowls ooze, crack the throttle and kick 'er in the guts. If it ever takes more than two pokes, I'm selling that sumbitch.

I laid my full-coverage, titanium-gray Arai onto Honey's broad seat. The helmet's tag assures me it was hand-formed in free-fall by body-shaven Japanese *otome* orbiting on their secret shuttle, and coated with liquefied diamond plasma. I watched it vibrate off and pound into the asphalt with the sickening crack of delamination.

Off to a healthy start, then.

Bloated lane hogs, vying for most ostentatious "12th Man" display, breasted down the main line to help the Seahawks enjoy their billion-dollar romper room. Honey and I veered onto the espresso lanes and zapped quietly past, lapping up sunshine. What a great day to be on the road, punching my season ticket for a box seat to summer's grand finale. Wouldn't sit it out for a billion taxpayer dollars.

Judging by the traffic along Admiral Way in west Seattle, I still led the main body of poseurs and punters. The muscular guy slouched curb-side on a '50s Beezer looked too calm to be broken down, and too young for the VME. Wraparound shades and neck tats IDed him as Cogs, the Cretins' lookout man. Hybrid spiritual descendants of Boozefighters and Quadropheniacal Rockers, the beer-pounding bike maulers of the Cretins M/C are precisely the delinquents to make the VME fret.

The ticket window for the Fauntleroy ferry was besieged by a foursome of chic hog-skinners on catalog sleds, brandishing credit cards and practicing factory-fresh sub-vocalization — you get a free grunt with each eagle patch. Every man and bitch of them sported identical roguish stickers on their piss-pots, but I was looking for the old bikes. Had to be around here somewhere...

They were already on the boat. I looked and under the sun saw the requisite Prada Ducatis and Fabergé Harleys beautifully outnumbered by grease-squozin', oil-spittin', chain-slappin', gimpy ol' bikes — the kind of motos you can't get loans for and don't need to, anyway. A mint Honda CB400F looking like a jeweler's screwdriver, a cafe-hacked Yamaha RD400 in the requisite orangey-red, and squadrons more poster girls from my squandered youth whispered alluringly. I couldn't wait to hear them all crank up at once and scream into the echoing belly of the boat.

The ferry ramp dropped at Vashon. Sixty vintage steeds bestridden by 60 tatty old sets of leathers were kicked over — and immediately drowned out by the phat blat of a dozen brand-new Harleys. The 4-inch un-mufflers of the bagger in front of me rippled my jacket with potato-cannon concussions, flexing the temples of my skull like passive subwoofers. I wondered if my Beemer's engine had died. I couldn't hear it, couldn't feel any vibration not rolling off the bike in front of me. Then the bling kings wobbled forward and I moved out, slick and suave.

Dry-nursing through a half-mast petcock, Honey lurched and burped through her Bings. Lightning middle-aged reflexes blazed into action just in time to conk out on the approach ramp and become That Guy.

I hate being That Guy.

Two strapping ferry swabbies sprinted off the boat and pushed me uphill to the parking lot, steps ahead of a baying pack of SUV pilots. I felt like the kid who fell off the chair lift. Happily a BSA Scrambler crapped out simultaneously. "Idiot," I thought, waving cheerfully. Human cortexes turn vintage much faster than good motorcycles. Who let all these damn gummers onto the boat anyway?

Cranked up again, I took off uphill toward the rally proper. Half a mile past the road fork, a gold-sparkle helmet impaled on a mailbox post demarked the Cretins' hideout. I hooked in and linked up with Gator, impromptu road captain for the gang's ride into town. We would serve up a *frisson* of flagrant lawbreaking by non-members to jazz the juices of VME stalwarts into a faint memory of youth. I'm a member of VME, but not a Cretin brother. Tell no one.

"Every year I tell these muf'fuhs," Gator told me before the ride, "don't pull in the bank lot 'less you got bankin' t' do. And every year…," he sighed.

We howled into town with the brethren hunched over their motley gaggle of cut-down Honda 750Ks, aluminum-seated Yamaha XS650's and…uh, a Ducati Paul Smart Replica 1000. Honey was wiggling like Beyoncé in butt floss, and I cussed my laziness for not going through her front end. It's hard to be a badass when your steering head bearings are hammered.

Weaving along at the tail end of the patch-holder crew, I got right into the club identity. We were a Mongol horde, a guerilla uprising, pitchforks and torches marching on the Bastille, Seventh Day Adventists stomping up your walk, armed with the Powah: You'll come to Jesus *now*, mister!

Revving and snorting, we executed a group snap-roll of military precision straight into the bank parking lot. Birds sang, women swooned. Arms crossed, Gator stood across the street, shaking his head and muttering.

•••

The town of Vashon looked like Sturgis Minor — albeit with older bikes, dozens of marques and not a trailer on view. The Isle of Vashon TT is a rider's event, not a posing stage.

There was a Honda CBX with a 6-into-6 aftermarket pipe. I wanted that once, and maybe still do. There were flocks of Ducks, grinds of Guzzis, bevies of Beezas, hundreds of Hondas and veritable Wehrmachts of Bee Ems.

The streets were chrome-plated with history, and generously lubed with roasted Castrol.

Darn if the secret hadn't gotten out again! We VME types will have to be more careful next year…

The TT is actually a pastoral poker run, carefully described in the handout as "NOT a race! Please observe all traffic rules, especially posted speed limits."

The thinking goes that problems ensue only when tuff guys show up on 100-horse sporty bikes, looking to prove something. Old guys on old iron just want a gentle gambol on a sunny day, in the company of like-minded gentlemen, around Vashon Island's forests and along gyrating coastlines to a nice lunch at the Sportsmen's Club.

As a gentleman [*sic*] of a certain age, I cleave to that philosophy resolutely — except for last year when Honey got the bit in her teeth and swept inside a Ducati Pantah on the inside of a curve marked for 25mph. Dunno what got into the old girl…

Then there are the guys who may slow down, but never back down. At the Cretins hideout, Gator and Swage laughed about a vintage fistfight between two beleathered aulde phartes squawking querulously over their shiny scoots until the punches started, uhm, flying.

"One guy must have been 65 and the other was maybe 70," said Swage, shaking his Mohawk. "I never saw a punch so telegraphed."

"Uh-huh," Gator said. "He launched 'at punch 'bout 1972."

The TT is a gamble for the VME. It's a cool event that's fun on any Sunday, but only cuts a fat hog in bluebird weather. This was that day. The lines were long and profitable.

I paid my 20 bucks for the ride and another five for the pin — that'll be cash, please — and threw a dart for my first card. A Jack of Hearts made it already my best hand ever.

The bikes lining Vashon's streets were gorgeously diversified and I knew the pickings would be even richer at the Sportsmen's Club, but the whole point of the exercise is what Freddie Mercury advised fat-bottomed girls to do: "Get on yer bikes and ride!"

I was a little nervous about those steering head bearings, but what the hell. Real men steer with their feet.

The sun was higher than a Rastafarian co-pilot, the spirit was willing and bikes snarled up and down the main drag as Honey and I peeled out of town at a smokin' 30 per. Every year, I nearly miss the hairpin turn onto Cedarhurst Road while I squeeze her sludgy drum brakes awake — imagine a Yamaha FJR1300 rolling downhill, armed with the formidable stopping power of a Sachs moped — but we cheated Death again. One day I'll fail to muster the hand strength to negotiate that turn. That's the day I buy a scooter, and not a Yamaha Vino. Think Rascal with a wire basket.

The real secret of IoV revealed itself again this year. Fresh winds off Puget Sound leavened 78 degrees of sunshine as we laced along brilliant island roads. No rush, no pell-mell squid proving ground, just a sweet ride on a gem-cut day. Hitting the pace on Vashon means skimming the pavement with your outsoles without ever warming the brakes. It's like riding the Cyclone at Coney Island: vintage fun near the salt water, more scary than dangerous, best on a sunny day.

Every year a few bikes wail past at speed, but they usually learn their lesson the first time they fetch up against a rolling road plug led by an AJS hack or parade-float Honda Dream, tiddling along two-up. While the TT is an all-comers' run-what-ya-brung, blasting this vintage rally on a rural island flaunting the 150-hp tattoo on your ass seems to miss the point. It's like hunting roaches in Granny's china cabinet with a Louisville Slugger: it may satisfy some sick, long-suppressed desires, but don't expect repeat invitations.

When the first checkpoint netted me a Jack of Clubs, my best hand ever looked even stronger. That was the last decent card I got, of course.

A little girl sold me lemonade (I am not making this up) at the general store in Burton overlooking Quartermaster Harbor, and her grand-auntie directed me around the road closure. We all briefly channeled the Isle of Man as road closures turned Dockton into a low-rent Mad Sunday, with bikes haring up and down every which way.

My steering felt wobbly, but it smoothed right out when I bullseyed an oil slick just past the ridge.

•••

By the time I reached the Sportsmen's Club after stops for lemonade, pictures, B.S. and the traditional roadside recycling of lemonade, the field was so jammed with Jurassic bikeosauruses there wasn't room to swing a cat.

It was glorious. I could have looked at those bikes all day, and listened to them all night. The chromatographic collage of paint and nickel and alloy and rubber stimulated me straight into overload. Or maybe it was the twin-cylinder herbal exhaust settling over the Sportsmen's Club field. "Damn these hippies and their gray-haired excess!" I mumbled. "I will not be safe to ride!"

Not that it's ever stopped me.

Vashon is the dirty-fingernail cousin to Half Moon Bay. Every bike gets ridden in (a tower-shaft Ducati 900SS tuner special biffed it *en route*), and instead of a Concours d'Elegance, there's a yellow nylon rope and a Magic Marker sign announcing "Concourse [*sic*] Bikes Only."

But it's right on point about riding old bikes. Poetic justice is when $40k Heavily-Blingedsons go invisible next to rows of bleeding, farting, antique gaspers from ye Olde Countrye, *Mama Italia* and *der Vaterland*.

Just when I started to wonder whether we won those wars or not, a ghostly gray 1919 Harley-Davidson Model J swaggered into the parking lot with its second owner kicked back in the sidecar, sucking down a Pabst Blue Ribbon while his son steered the rig. G-d bless America, Hoss! We walk tall, sit low and ride the bikes we want.

I glanced over at Honey — an R69S, U.S. edition — and realized two things: 1) Harley never made a "Deutschland Edition" and 2) a big twin and Levis get you a lot farther in Tokyo (or Moscow or Doha or Milan) than a Honda and Versace will get you in L.A. The übermensch clout of our Team America World Police era hasn't yet scrubbed off the last greasy stains of underdog cool.

Conversations swirling around me personified the mid-life maundering of born-again expertise: "Oh look, honey! A Blister-Worting EB-6! I useta own one. Fastest bike at Humptulips High." The men would trail off wistfully, walk a few feet farther, then brighten up. "Hey, look-a that!"

I smiled indulgently. Everyone has the right to remember themselves cooler than they were, but it's always better to sublimate that revisionist "glory days" nonsense. Hoping their wives wouldn't require surgery to unroll their eyes, I stepped through a line of parked bikes and almost knocked over a Yamaha RZ350.

It was the Kenny Roberts Edition! Man, I used to have one-a those — and that sucker was *fast!*

The sun fell into brownout. My belly and fuel tank were both full. There was tread on the tires, life left in my brake linings, and a faint memory of steering-head bearings. I punched the 2007 Isle of Vashon TT pin through the cover of my triple-waterproofed German Army utility bag and prepared to wobble home at the legal limit.

The MV Augusta pilot howling by as we debarked nearly hip-checked me into the curb. His jerk move would have really pissed me off, but for the ripping howl of that under-slung battery of organ pipes. It was like nearly being killed by some idiot in a convertible, then realizing said idiot is topless, perky and *molto Italiano*. Look for the silver lining.

It was too good a day to go straight home, but six feeble volts of luminescence wouldn't keep me topside of the grave in Seattle traffic. Arcing north onto the Alaska Way Viaduct revealed Seattle's best poor man's view of sunfire over the Olympic Mountains. Pretty close to a perfect day on bikes: sun, ferrying over the fjord, no blood spilled, and hundreds of neat old crocks (and their motorcycles).

I tell ya, I don't know why people live anywhere else. But don't you tell anyone.

It's a secret.

August 2008, Motorcyclist

ADV Boyz

Field soldiers quickly discover that the superhero moon ranger types with all the latest, shiniest, retail tac gear generally spend more money in the PX than time in the field — but you never want to tell them that. They can be a bit touchy.

This short column, with its simple message that you don't need specially selected and rally-prepped bikes to go out and have fun, prompted volumes of outrage on the ADVRider forum.

Not that there's any parallel there.

It usually hits at about 41, on a drizzly day, when a man realizes his fingers are a little stiff in the gloves, and thanks his deity of choice for heated grips and jacket liner. He might even gaze longingly into the heated cab of the porcine Denali one lane over, where someone's trophy wife in Bluetooth headgear grooves in a very restrained way to drive time radio. He hopes for a little warmth, but the ominous gray overhead is anything but encouraging.

Call it the mid-spring crisis. With premium season ("riding season" is properly defined as anytime there's not ice on the ground) right around the corner, logistics still haven't caught up to your dreams. This won't be the year you blitzkrieg *die Schweitze Alpen* on a factory-new Ducati or plonk the Himalayas on a Royal Enfield running a lumpy custom piston sand cast in a hillside village. Watching your fading plans trampled under life's prosaic intrusions, you realize you should count yourself lucky if you can make it out to poker night to BS on a Seussian scale: "O, the places you'll go!" Someday…

There's therapy on offer at the KTM dealership down in the valley, although I try not to go there too often. One more easy payment, I do not need — but they're fun to look at. The "Austrian Harley" (i.e. lifestyler accoutrement with parts that fall off at random and are quickly replaced by a robust aftermarket), along with BMW's GS series (pronounced "Geezerese"), is a Walter Mitty wet dream incarnate, a tangerine tangibility of wanderlust. Park one in your garage and you can spend the gray months waxing, adjusting, poring over catalogs in pursuit of that perfect farkle to transform your Dreamsicle into seven league boots that vault you over the far hills to Shangri-La: bark busters to give you fists of iron, forty cubic liters of aerospace aluminum baggage and a Scott Oiler so your chain can go to the moon and back on a single (dealer-provided) adjustment.

Some guys upgrade their quad arrays of overclocked processors every four months and run Cat. 5e to every bathroom. Other guys rig custom-welded fishing dories with GPS, fish finders and Moby Dick downriggers. My brother and I used to construct plaster of Paris dioramas around HO train sets. At some point, pictures in the magazines you keep stacked on your toilet tank just aren't enough anymore. It's time to build the perfect beast.

It's been awhile now since rebel bikers got commodified, Sturgis got comfy and beer guts got replaced by squid-ink-pasta-and-fusion-sushi guts. Then came the Microsofties' phase-craze for shiny red Ducatis. Nowadays, adventure is spelled "ADV." But where are all those adventurers? Not braving the mid-spring drizzle around here.

I raised my gloved hand to every bike on the road yesterday, all three of 'em: a Nighthawk S, a Twinstar (!) with milk crate top box and a rusty black Shovelhead sporting apehangers. The hog drover wore a "BMW beard" and crusty leathers. Maybe he just never cleans them — or maybe he's been a few places. Maybe a way-cool digital avatar and smartass comments on www.advrider.com aren't actually the moral equivalent of saddling up your swayback Honda for an errant quest two towns over to slay a bag of barbeque for your damsel.

Turns out you don't have to go to Macchu Pichu to find bugs and dust and rain. You don't even need a two-wheeled SUV with titanium armor, RealtorTits™ on the pillion and a sat-link, antilock coffeemaker. Round here, our mountains are twenty minutes away. You can get on your bike — just any old bike — start it up and ride it straight out of suburban desperation, any day you want.

Rain or shine.

June 2008, Motorcyclist

RIDING HOME

This piece is substantially responsible for the existence of the book containing it. In August, 2005, I sat down in an upstairs room, logged onto a mailing list of online friends and fellow riders called Wetleather™, and tried to explain where I came from, where I was calling from, and where I thought I might be headed.

First publication of Riding Home took place in Northwest Cycle News. *Subsequently, an abbreviated version ran in* Motorcyclist *magazine. I've been writing for them ever since.*

"Riding Home" was also anthologized in The Devil Can Ride *(Ed. Lee Klancher, Motorbooks 2010), making this a fourth-hand appearance, but this is the first place the full version has appeared in print.*

The first person to respond to my post on Wetleather™ was my then-future Pretty Wife. Concluding no stranger's essay was worth that much time, she skimmed to the ending and was the first to reply, "Welcome Home."

It was sunny and warm when I stepped off Amtrak's #507 Cascades line in Portland, Oregon, helmet in hand. Paul was waiting on the station's oak pew; he stood and I gave him a hug with my free arm.

"One-arm hug, huh?," he grinned. Mucho macho, we are.

My heavy, black goatskin Langlitz jacket, still squeaky-new, smelled like bad folks wearing good leathers. I got measured in Portland while on R&R, then picked up my custom-cut masterpiece after I redeployed. It has a gun pocket sewn in. People moved away, trying to be subtle.

It's hard to care about scaring the home folks. I'll get used to them as they get used to me.

Twenty miles south, my black beauty lay waiting. We drove straight to the storage unit and pulled boxes off her. Unearthed after 12 years, she had two flat tires and gray layers of dusty crud, but otherwise looked about the way I remembered. It's not always that way, is it?

We aired up the tires with her onboard squeeze pump and I pushed her half a mile in the sun to Paul and Mom's house, sweating happily. There, we worked her over for a day and a half.

As a mechanic, I make a pretty good wheel chock. But Paul, Jedi warrior of the garage, *makes* parts that he can't find, and he's pretty well memorized every last bolt on vintage BMWs. So I immersed myself in his short induction to the mysteries of de-varnishing Bing carburetors and lubricating ignition flyweight arms. We put in a new, vintage-look battery he had stashed: six volts of thundering fury! Ah, well, the magneto will spark even when the thing is dead as a doornail. We adjusted the idle, replaced the right side carb slide when it wouldn't quit sticking (an old habit of this bike), replaced the balding Magura throttle grip (after disassembling the original Hella bar-end winker), adjusted the idle again, checked the timing (slightly retarded to run on crappy, 91-octane "premium"), adjusted the idle some more. We stepped back and looked at her: still dirty, but chuffing away with industrial purpose. Beautiful.

"Some of the that dust is probably from Steen's Mountain," Paul said, referring to a good, long trip we took with passengers and tents, fifteen years, two college degrees, a wife-and-a-half ago.

Then he rolled out his workhorse R90/6, and we went for a shakedown ride, south over the road to the shop of a guy who does boutique restos — i.e. no dust! That guy comped me a petcock liner so I could run in the "AUF" position without running out of gas every two blocks. He's good people.

Our second stop was at the house of Paul's old buddy, Ben.

•••

Ben's a nice guy, practicing engineer and wood technologist. He lives in an octagonal house carefully handmade from recycled and exotic woods, overlooking a pond, with a stream running through and under the place. Once upon a time in Vietnam, Ben was a scout/sniper. We checked out his house, enjoyed the details, took note of the guard tower, scoped rifles at the doors, and the armory and reloading center that are not shown on the plans. He took note of my stained desert boots.

"I used to walk my perimeter with a weapon every night," he said as we were adjusting the idle once more in his driveway. "I don't do that anymore.

"So long, my brother. Be well."

So long. I tightened down the left side mixture adjustment nut, shook his hand, clunked her into gear, rolled around the barn and back up to the road.

"He's kind of, uh … stuck, isn't he?," I asked afterward, through a mouthful of roadhouse Reuben.

"Yes. Ben's good for three or four hours a day, then that's it."

"I don't want to get stuck like that."

Paul smiled his slight smile, dry but warm. "That's what motorcycles are good for."

That night, I bungeed a big CFP-90 rucksack onto the bike, got some last minute tips from its long-term owner, and gave Paul a hug. With both arms.

Then I rolled out my summer bag in his pickup bed, pulled it up against mosquitoes, and slept my series of one-hour periods, startling up to check my water-proof, impact-resistant, scratch-defying, gas-illuminated watch five or six times before finally sitting up and pulling on my boots in the purple predawn, listening for movement, checking for roaming packs of feral dogs.

Hollow, agitated feeling. Got to move. So quiet with no prayer call. Need to go before the neighbors get up and wonder. Familiar heavy feeling of gear and helmet, but no weapon. Just Honey and me, bag and baggage.

•••

This bike and I are old friends reunited. She's an R69S, the U.S.-market model with telescopic forks (Euro bikers of the Sixties got the sidecar-friendly Earles fork arrangement), scrambler-style handlebar and wide, American-style "comfort" seat. I call her "Honey" by default, because it suits the way I talk to her: "Let's go, honey" when we're moving well together or, "Ah, *come on*, honey!" when she's recalcitrant or mysterious.

Her seat's a little wider and softer than I remembered, but isn't that always the way with an old flame? Memories are fickle. A little morning tickle to her Bing buttons, then she started on the second kick and we were off into the fire-born dawn.

Bye, Mom.

En route to Estacada, I stopped for gas, mostly to dry the stinging tears with which the sun was punishing me for riding east at dawn. I bought a Power Bar inside, walked up to the side of the bike and kicked down the start lever *mit* follow-through, which simultaneously started Honey and snapped off her sidestand bolt flush at the frame lug. I wrestled the foundered, sputtering motorcycle back onto her wheels and took inventory: one sprained ankle (my four times-broken left leg, which sprains in a high wind), one busted toe and a dangling sidestand spring, bleating for its mother.

Great start.

The attendant goggled through the glass, but didn't say a word. Scary biker man, I guess, or just good entertainment.

Shut down the bike, sat on the curb, taped up my toe with electrical tape from the tool compartment in the tank, ate the Power Bar. Got warmer. Thought of roads sweeping through the Cascade range. Good to be home. Good to be alive. Good to have a center stand. "Hmm.

"Bet I can still start that bike …"

Yup.

Highway 224 runs two sweet lanes southeast from Estacada through the Mt. Hood National Forest, flowing sinuously along the Clackamas River. I missed my planned turn east at the Oak Grove Fork due to throes of extreme road ecstasy, and ended up 40 miles south in Detroit, Oregon in time for a nice breakfast and a tankful of premium.

A Beemer-mounted couple (R1100RS and F650GS) greeted me as we swapped nozzles at the busy gas station pumps.

"Where're you coming from?," the man asked. Now there's a poser. I settled for where our house is. "Seattle.

"Is there a good spot for breakfast?"

"The place across the highway has great food, but we waited 90 minutes for a table. They said they're putting on another cook, if they can find him."

The place across the highway was surrounded three cars deep. I passed it by, only to find a log roadhouse three blocks further on. It was attended by seven or eight prominently posed Harley-Davidsons, looking new and shiny. I parked off to the side under a shade tree.

Inside, the menu face had a note: "We speak…," followed by a little graphic of a motorcycle. The owner was dressed in a black shirt with stitched-on flames. He held court behind the counter, making eggs and conversation. Allowed as to how he liked old Beemers pretty well, even if they're not Harleys.

My waitress was a blonde girl of maybe nineteen with a sunny-side-up disposition and a startling lack of focus. She shorted the couple ahead of me ten bucks at the till, then overcompensated by handing them a twenty. Then she forgot to hand back my credit card, offering a giggle and a dazzling smile as her apology when I pointed it out.

"You know, I've just been like this all *day*." Longer than that, I imagine, but the eggs were good and the coffee had flowed.

That day was filled with rivers, forests, and roads to make you weep for their beauty. We touched the Mt. Hood, Willamette, Deschutes, Ochoco, and Malheur National Forests, crossed or tracked along the Clackamas River, Oak Grove Fork, Santiam River, Breitenbush River, White Water

Creek, Metolius River, Squaw Creek, Deschutes River, Murderer's Creek, Crooked River and John Day River — to name a few. Honey and I straightened many a bent road on our fantastically inefficient one-day jaunt to John Day, Oregon.

These roads were fresh to me, but not the region. Growing up in the Pacific Northwest, I always itched to leave for some less boring place. Now, wherever I go in the world, I always know I'm coming home to here. Polite people living among stunning natural beauty are not easy to appreciate until you've un-spoiled yourself with grimy Third World exotica. Musical accompaniment this day included the constant murmur and splash of clean, fast water; rush of wind through the trees; hum of tires older than my teenage daughter (!) and the balanced drone of aircraft-quality, vintage German engineering.

•••

Known in her day as the Gentleman's Express, BMW's dreamboat R69S easily nabbed the U.S. coast-to-coast speed record in the mid-Sixties. Smooth, powerful, durable, well-featured and classy, this was the bike for chomping big bites of highway with swift ease.

"Gentleman's Express" or not, a 1969 time capsule is nobody's hyperbike today. This was the last of the Slash Two BMWs, produced the same year Honda shocked the world with the first "superbike," its CB750 with four buttery little pistons and an hydraulic disk brake. Suddenly, BMWs were considered more premium for their prices than for their engineering — even if they weighed in at a hundred pounds less than the big-chested Honda.

Unlike my late-lamented, rubber-band Ducati, since passed along to a steadier lover, you don't chainsaw up the road on an R69S, dodging gnats and hula-hipping the rear with tight throttle grabs. You don't stand her on her nose at a corner entry, nor paw at the air in the lower gears. Honey offers a balanced palette of subtler colorations.

Too mature for slam-dancing, she asks for more of a graceful waltz. Even with a fresh shot of 7w Bel-Ray, her long-travel fork is on the squishy side. The big ass cushion squeaks like an old bed spring when you jounce over potholes or speed humps. A hard hand on the double-shoe front drum slows you at a predictable rate; "controllable" is a sweeter description than "weak," but that control requires a powerful paw. Anyway, Honey's lovely low CG and modest torque mean it works best to simply carry speed through the corners — always with attention to those tires. Step, shuffle, *sli-ide* to your right; step, shuffle, slide to your left. It may be slow dancing, but it's still dancing, by God. And we danced and danced and danced …

•••

I don't do lunch on bike trips, unless there are others along. A late breakfast can carry me all day if my machine is willing, and I just suck down water or Gatorade at gas stations when I'm "on mission." When I hit John Day around eight that night, where I planned to roll out a bag at Clyde Holliday Park, I was righteous hungry. The Ore House on the Main vein accommodated me with a steak barbequed rare and the stout, cheerful waitress easily conned me into a colossal "individual" berry pie afterward.

With the joy of just riding and the surprising degree of comfort in a "yesterday's standard," it's hard to realize

70 minutes after I walked outside with my rucksack. That's one way to warm up on an ice-cold summer morning.

I was a hundred miles down the road before I realized that I'd never tickled her prime buttons. Not even once. For the rest of the day, Honey winked at me by starting first kick, every time. And that was good, because my leg needed the rest. I should never have tossed that old t-shirt my dad gave me, the one that read, "I'm not real smart, but I can lift heavy things."

•••

Caught final directions to the Brownlee Reservoir from a guy gassing his truck in Baker City, Oregon, where my dad lived on a cattle ranch during his high school years. It was just plain "Baker" then. Now it sports about 50,000 people and, per my service station directional patron, around 35 percent unemployment.

"I've been looking for a job myself for seven months," he told me, looking not at all bothered about it. I resisted the urge to tell him the military could always use another good man. He was nearly my age, way too old for our various wars.

Richland, Oregon is close to the Idaho border, close to the reservoir, and billed as the Entry to Hell's Canyon. I went straight on past a sprawling boneyard of obsolete agricultural equipment under a sign reading, "The Power of Yesteryear," and stopped at a fuel station in the hamlet of Halfway, just in time to get beat to the pumps by six glistering HDs burbling in from the other direction. I nodded politely, snapped my shield down and went on back to the highway, unwilling to wait and not wanting to talk.

Their bikes were as new and shiny as the Harleys I'd seen in Detroit, mostly stock with a frosting of shiny gewgaws. One-percenters would call those windshielded baggers — the SUVs of the motorcycle world — "garbage wagons." Of course, one-percenters are jackasses.

The riders, bottle blonde women in XL chaps hugging men wearing Kirkland jeans and lightweight beanie helmets to preserve their follicle plugs, had what the Chinese call a "prosperous look": well padded around their chrome-tanned middles. Doubtful that any of them popped extra for the toolkit; that's what credit cards and cell phones are for.

As the army seal says: "This We'll Defend."

Sneer though you may about the Costco biker set, they do get out and ride. You might be faster, and you're probably cooler (keep telling yourself that; it's important), but I'll bet they post more mileage. "Real" riders work on their own bikes and memorize every racer's name from Mike the Bike Hailwood to that Italian kid, Rossi, who smokes everybody now. These people just go out and ride, find out or remember that it's helluva a lot of fun, then go out and ride some more.

Keeping to secondary roads for nearly two thousand miles on this trip, I saw a ton of Harleys, a fair number of Wings, a handful of Beemers, zero "standards," shockingly few sportbikes. And not one bike as old as Honey, but I kept telling her she's much classier and more beautiful than a bikini-clad Speed Triple or some tit queen Harley. Hey, some people talk to plants.

I made my gas stop at a last-chance station perched on the edge of Hell's Canyon, serving one flavor: 87-octane unleaded, perfect for this year's Mercury outboards but less than outstanding for a late-sixties, high-compression roadburner like Honey. A well-tanned, well-fed, thirty-ish canyon coquette walked out and looked at me oddly until I remembered there's no self-serve in Oregon.

"Uh… mind if I fill it myself?"

"Nope."

"Got any premium hidden around here?"

"Uh, nope."

"Do you sell octane booster?"

"Ee-yep." Which brought my price for boat gas to about five bucks a gallon. Thank G-d for good mileage. Honey had returned a 47.2 mpg average over the first two tanks I measured, mostly in town as Paul and I shook her down. On the Great Road, she was making well better than fifty. Checked the oil, transmission (four speeds forward, as *Gott im Himmel* intended), shaft housing, and rear box. All levels good, and no gear oil blow-by on the back rim. Perhaps it's time to adjust that idle again.

And thence we went down by the riverside. Down by the riverside not to lay down my sword and shield (I may need them again), but surely to leave some things behind.

The road edging the water shows up on the map not in black (and therefore paved) nor in gray (and therefore dirt), but in brown. At its entrance near Oxbow Dam is a large sign, advising in the strongest possible terms that it is a private road, the county and state are not responsible for maintenance, and you are in every way at your own peril should you choose to take it.

We took it.

Winding along the edge of the lake, sometimes well above and often just at the water level, the Brownlee Reservoir road is no superhighway, but it is competently maintained by the power company. It is also narrow, barely graded, high-crowned… and virtually abandoned. We waved at three fishing boats pursuing the elusive bass, passed two parked trucks with empty boat trailers, and saw zero moving vehicles on this road.

Burbling softly through the late morning stillness, I looked to my left and saw sepia and green hills sloping down to and into the hushed waters, so calm that the negative reflection continued all the way to perfectly rendered hilltops halfway across the reservoir's surface. My grandmother's favorite verse from the 23rd Psalm came unbidden to my mind: "He leadeth me beside still waters / He restoreth my soul." I stopped and dismounted, sat on my goat hide jacket at the edge of that well of peace and looked long, and prayed hard, and remembered:

A sergeant from Michigan, on his second tour, who didn't have to be there. He was gunning a Stryker, running up his enlistment so he and his wife could settle back home with their kids and he could take his place as a diesel mechanic in his uncle's Lewis County shop.

A sawed-off butterbar who rode his bicycle all over FOB Sykes. He loved a good joke and could take one, too. We used to jump out at him and salute, see if we could make him crash trying to return the salute. He grinned big, and laughed readily, and I never saw him mad.

An Iraqi major, commanding a line company patrolling from Tall Afar to Muhollibiyah. He used to freak out Americans who didn't know him by insisting on a face kiss. I got out of our up-armored HMMWV and rode standing in his tiny, weaving, grinding jeep with a squad of six IA soldiers. No roadside bombs that day.

A hundred thousand other soldiers I either knew or didn't, who either died or didn't, who believed in our cause or didn't, who were American or weren't, whom I liked or didn't, who swore an oath and went and struggled, and did the best they could while they walked on this earth.

I sat in the Oregon dirt and thought of those guys, and pulled a small, heavy chunk of metal out of my pocket. Once on a castle wall, it zipped into the sandbag next to my head. *Sss-SS-zzss, thwip.*

"What was that?," Steve, our commo sergeant, asked.

"SKS, maybe."

"Oh. We should get down." And we should have, but I wanted to find that bastard and greet him properly. I never spotted him.

Later that evening, after the AIF sniper stopped ops for lack of night vision equipment, I dug his slug out with my Leatherman and looked at it for a long time. It wasn't the only bullet, the first or the last. But it was perfect, virtually undeformed by its muffled collision with bagged silica. I kept it close as a lover, and it whispered to me for months, chasing me like a ghost. It was my rosary, skeleton key, ballistic lodestone, taunting me with a papery laugh even after its author died in his barricaded window, head-shot by a better soldier than me. *Zzzzip.*

I showed it to no one, as ashamed to carry it as if it had been needle tracks on my arm.

Now I stood and held it up to let it know a place of peace before I drowned it. Then I threw it as far as a shredded rotator cuff could manage, out over the reservoir and down to the bottom forever, hushing its sibilant hiss, killing my own death.

For now.

Back underway, we putted across the one-lane Brownlee Dam bridge and climbed slowly up over the canyon rim, through Midvale and on into Cambridge, Idaho. Honey was still toting my rucksack's worth of baggage, but it felt somehow lighter.

•••

Cambridge was enjoying a tourism mini-boom of lady bicyclists doing the Ride Around Idaho, which benefits research into cancerous female troubles. Temperatures were in the nineties, and part-time pedal pushers relaxed in the shade of a handful of bistros and cafes that I don't remember from when I lived near here.

Staying well out of their fashionable way, I downed an iced double mocha. I poured ice water over my hair, soaked down the t-shirt under my jacket and the bug-stopping bandana around my neck. That attracted a few stares, but odd looks from women dolled up in hyper-stressed orange Spandex carry low credibility with me: "WARNING: Contents Under Pressure." A wardrobe failure here, and somebody loses an eye…

Winding through the high mountain valleys of western Idaho felt more and more like another piece of home. Passing between the peaks en route to New Meadows, I murmured briefly through Council and saw its familiar press offices staring empty-eyed over Main Street. About a decade back, they printed a book of fictional local news columns (*Kokanee and Other Tales*) under my *nom de plume* of "Gunnar Cratchit." *Kokanee* sold out its massive press run of 300 paperbound copies. Eventually.

McCall, Idaho is nothing like it was, for good or otherwise. I remember when my dad dropped through there circa 1991, pre-bankruptcy when he could fly his own airplane anywhere on earth, and it took an hour to locate the house his parents had owned, since doubled in size and transmogrified into a clothes boutique. Since then, the same has happened to the entire town.

Once the area's one assigned Idaho State Policeman (Gus; I knew him only too well) could park his Blazer on the downgrade from Brundage Mountain ski hill and issue a booklet of speeding tickets as fast as he could scribble. Now you pass the 30 mph signs at a blistering 18-per, trailing a line of home center trucks, building contractors, new second home owners and chromed-out Hummers. Payette Lake is still there, and still probably the last place in the U.S. that meets municipal water standards without purification, but I didn't go to the water's edge for fear of trespassing over some condophile's postage stamp of Heaven.

Stopping for a cold Coke at a street café, I stumbled back out to find a knot of people clustered around Honey. Their consensus, despite holes in the seat cover and fresh bugs over old dirt: "great looking bike!" And she is. At a distance, Honey strikes a pose as alert as a Rottweiler, strong as a Lab, friendly and eager as a beagle pup. Up close, she's much more special.

Older BMWs were generally issued in black, with no more adornment than white pinstripes on tank and fenders, plus the pretty cloisonné tank badges. And, like a good worsted suit from Savile Row, lack of cheesy pretension points up deeper aspects of quality. Honey's double-cradle frame wraps around a gorgeously sand-cast engine, perfectly rendered right down to its classically proportioned aluminum fins. Her substantial "comfort" seat, air-cooled engine and questing, chrome-ringed headlight put one in mind of mousy Ralph's steed in that kids' classic, The Mouse and the Motorcycle. It's all I can do not to sit on her seat and say, "Brrr-RRRM. BR-*RRMM!,*" and see if she'll start to move. Since it looked like one of the kids had that same idea, I cut through the crowd, cranked her up — on just the one kick, thankyaverymuch — and broke camp from McCall.

Down the Long Valley, then, through Lake Fork and Donnelly over the highway I've driven before through foot-deep snowdrifts, interpolating the right of way by adding the parallel fence lines and dividing by two, to the county seat of Cascade. I can't call it the Town of a Thousand Loggers anymore since the population dropped by 50-odd souls in the last census. Their mill, once the economic heart of the valley, has been razed flat as a clear-cut. Its massive buzzsaw blades are probably backgrounds for folk art now.

But don't think that Cascade is immune to Idaho's tourist boom. If Montana is, as William Kittredge put it, "the last best place," then Idaho has surely been crowned the "next great place" to mint a pile of development money. Cascade Reservoir keeps their boat launch busy with Boise fishermen pursuing athletic, foot-and-a-half-long kokanee (hint: it's a fish, not a beer). Tamarack, the new mega-resort perched on a nearby mountain, holds untold revenue promise. Here then is a toast to trickle-down, and may it really happen for families who hunt to eat, not to display the glass-eyed heads of ruminant corpses.

Feedlots are practically illegal now in this valley that's hosted an annual cattle drive since the 1850s, and the zoning commissions steadily dice up minimum lot sizes to accommodate lifestyles of the rich and famous. Was it Kurt Vonnegut who described us as a nation of realtors? Real estate agents busily buy and sell the town where I once jammed gears on a twenty-year-old Ford pumper for the Cascade Rural Volunteer Fire Department. They're probably still driving the damned thing. It'd be about Honey's age now.

Maybe it still holds water.

I parked in the old *Advocate* lot, got directions from some new gal in some new little office of some new agency, and lumbered across Highway 55 to where a brown-eyed, hand-some man with a walrus mustache stood grinning at me.

"Big Jack! I knew that walk. What're you doing here, man? How've you been?"

"Well, I try to come by every decade or so, whether I need to or not…"

"What kind of bike're you riding this time?"

Mike Stewart is Cascade's editor-publisher, general purpose hell-raiser, and my old boss who taught me to fly fish badly. He stood us to root beers next door to his office with too many free refills ("they know me here"), and we caught up on a lot of time and a couple of wives passed. Mike's still got a gleam in his eye, battle in his heart, and plans to make "big money, BIG money in this valley." I walked out of there already making plans to go back. Life is too short when you have friends, but it sure would be long and bitter without them.

Pocketing another piece of home, I adjusted Honey's idle again and set off down Highway 55 to where it edges the middle fork of the Payette River, one of the West's better roads when uncrowded. Every winter a half-dozen or so cars shoot off inside curves and wind up in the drink. Some are never recovered. That's how good it is.

On the straight stretch south of town, a carload of kids in their mom's shiny new Hyundai, frustrated by my 65 mph pace, blasted through a fractional gap between oncoming county concrete mixers. Their license plate number started with 1A (we used to say "One Asshole"); obviously Boise flatlanders fleeing the mountains after weekending in McCall. I smiled a little, behind my chin bar, and kept tiddling along on my 594cc of antique fury.

Three miles south, the road started to shimmy. I was parked in their trunk inside of three minutes. Just for grins, I passed the little sedan between curves, boogied away and never saw that car again. I swear I heard Honey snort as we went by.

Midway down the Middle Fork is a pit stop called Banks. Get there early, and the roadside café serves cinnamon toast and eggs over easy to whitewater junkies and anyone else who stops by. But it was well past lunchtime, so I turned east up the tributary creek onto absolutely the best motorcycling pathway in existence anywhere: the road bypassing Crouch, through Garden Valley and Lowman. Idaho's Highway 21 fires up the south fork of the Payette River like a corkscrew rocket and leaps over Banner Summit at 7,056 feet, dropping into a high, wide and handsome mountain valley where Stanley is the only town big enough to spot on a map. After Stanley, it pelts through Obsidian, up over

Galena Summit at 8,701 feet, and cascades down through winding sweepers between the Sawtooth Mountains into Ketchum.

Late sun still roasted the ground when I stopped at the Chevron station in Garden Valley. That station is in exactly the right place, just as I remembered from hustling a Yamaha V-Max — a porky muscle bike with a huge engine that handles like a greased anvil and hides an undersized fuel tank beneath its seat — through here several years back. Slicked up in kit-matched leathers, I wasn't packing much heavier than a credit card on that trip. A young guy with long hair, squiring a camp-packed Slash Five BMW, sneered wordlessly over the pumps at me back then. We evidently didn't see eye-to-eye on the "no bad motorcycles" theory.

Bike on centerstand, tankful of hi-test jet fuel, squeegeed the bugs off my face shield, checked the oil: standard drill. Clucked over my Michelins, which were balding quickly (rear) and badly checked (front), but holding air like champions. Well, that's what inner tubes are for — and repair kits. Found a tap and a shortie hose near the restrooms to soak down my t-shirt and bandana again, almost snapping into hallucinations from the icy bite. That's *mountain* water, by God!

Dripping my way back to the pumps, I ran into a man who didn't ask the standard, "What year is that bike?"

"Is that the 'S' model?" Fair question. Honey's German silver fender jewelry, identifying her as the fearsome 42-bhp powerhouse that is "R69S," hasn't survived the years. "I really like those," he remarked in a mild voice. "Yours looks good."

"I can't take any credit," I shucked. "My step-dad's done the care and feeding for over 20 years."

"So it's not restored?"

"No, she's not. Maybe someday, when I feel rich."

"Don't do it! Listen, that bike's in great shape. It's worth a lot more with original paint. They were meant to be ridden, I think.

"I have a couple of old bikes myself."

"Really?" Disinterested, I wanted to move on. Everybody has a story, an opinion, a posterior gastrointestinal excretory pore. "What kind of bikes?"

He was driving a rusty compact pickup, painted white, toting dirty flower pots in the back. His white hair wisped under his hat brim like a captive fog.

"Well," he said, "I actually have about 60 motorcycles. Some of them are BMWs. I also have some Whizzers and old Harleys and things. They mostly all run.

"I have 75 acres up the road, grow flowers and ornamentals for the big homes. Mostly poinsettias, lately."

Sixty motorcycles? Now there's a singular man. Also single, most likely.

"You should stop by sometime." That I should. I gave him Paul's number, in case he ever needs head work done, and bid him farewell. Forgot to write down his name, of course, or get a number. Or an address. Or a business name. I sure wish that weren't so typical of me.

He left the station before I got my helmet on, depriving me of the chance to show off Honey's good-natured one-kick lightoff. Seven miles up the road, I caught up with his cruddy pickup just as he turned off the highway toward a bank of greenhouses on the hillside. Guess I'll just have to ride Route 21 again sometime, and visit that fellow. I waved big, and kept riding.

Something about that road just encourages misbehavior. Despite reminding myself that there was no one around to police up my bleeding scraps if I blew a corner, despite the gathering dusk, and despite my time away from the saddle, we sailed up that closed-in-winter road like water splashing magically uphill. A twist on Honey's factory-stock steering damper cut down on the chassis wiggles induced by the forty-pound pack lashed to her rear rack, and I made the most of the dappled daylight remaining to us. It's not safe and I know it, but I always ride faster into the twilight.

•••

So speed-addled was I when we crested Banner Summit that I kept edging over 80 mph across the high mountain valley of Sawtooth National Recreation Area — imprudent on a bike whose high-speed harmonic balancer went by the wayside long ago due to an endemic tendency to self-destruct every 2,000 miles. Big speed is also tough on the driveline seals. I would find gear oil hemorrhaged onto the back rim that night.

From my last gas stop in Stanley, it was a smooth drop into Ketchum, the town that is the real heart of "Sun Valley." It's a long, contemplative sunset in the summer there if you're pelting southwest toward the western limit of Mountain Time. The sun was arching orange flames over the Sawtooths, and I took full advantage of the purple mountains' majesty.

My brother Peter was waiting for me when I rolled up. I hadn't seen him in almost five years. Around five-foot seven, he can crush bowling balls in his hands. He gave me a rib-shattering bear hug, even though I was dripping with high-altitude bug juice.

"Dude! Where have YOU been?"

"Long story, bro."

"Yeah, I guess so. Are you all right?"

"Pretty much. Getting there, anyway."

Pete's gotten to be a wheel in the Sun Valley area, way ahead of his big brother when it comes to career tracking. But he wouldn't talk business while I was there.

"Your mission here is to rest, relax, and have fun." Which, ably abetted by Pete and his general manager Jim from Brooklyn ("How *YOU* doin'!"), I did. There are no weekdays in Ketchum during the summer — nor, I guess, during the winter. It's a full-throttle party town. For three days straight, we sampled its wares.

On our third night of semi-pro drinking, I found or made a reason to get back on the bike and ride out of there. After we closed down Whiskey Jacques, the loudest place in town, yelling various good nights to people we either knew or didn't, a young man across the street took sudden and vocal exception to our presence. My little brother, to his everlasting credit, turned and walked away. I stumbled along behind him. It was his town.

But the fella wouldn't let it lay, and when he came after us, I turned and took three steps back toward him. I have conceived a strong distaste for people charging up behind me. I pawed for a weapon to stand him off, and came up with a handful of nothing.

What the hell was I *doing*, walking around without my carbine?

Once in a far-off alleyway, a drunken Iraqi policeman yanked out a 9mm Glock, just like one I have at home, one that we U.S. taxpayers bought for him. He was way too close to the soldier I was overwatching, and he came skinny-close to earning a 5.56mm reprimand before he threw up his hands and showed me his ID. Infantry soldiers assigned to that sector laughed at me: "Hey, he's one of the good guys.

"Ibrahim's cool. He's just drunk."

Later, that same cop went rogue for real. He was detained by U.S. forces after shooting up civilians in his own city. He murdered five outright that day, members of a competing tribe. Shot them in the face. Three were women. Maybe Ibrahim was just drunk again.

This meth-addled local was no terrorist, just punked by badly managed testosterone that snapped him into junior high-style, chimpanzee-territorial mode. He probably would have jumped around, waved his arms and gibbered. Not much more. He was just trying to impress his girlfriend, but I haven't the patience to sort faux threats from real.

He twitched a punch toward me. I neutralized the threat with a straight right that laid him out flat.

From half a block up, my brother arrived in two or three seconds. We recovered my specs, left the guy sleeping peacefully, and exfiltrated the AO without the old t-shirt that his girlfriend had shredded off my back. Acceptable losses.

The next day, on attorney's advice, I left Idaho. Abandoning plans to wash and wax the bike, I settled for a quick oil top-up of the shaft, and hasty packing. Who was coming up behind me now?

•••

The journey home turned bleary. My hand ached, but I couldn't pull my glove on over an Ace bandage, so I ignored it. My perfectly fitted Arai helmet suddenly felt too small, and the pounding in my ears seemed to echo off its liner.

I changed Honey's oil that night in La Grande, Oregon. Froze my ass the next morning until stopping by the Pendleton Woolen Mills and scoring a thick wool offcut — for two bucks! — to use as a scarf.

I bought a 2001 Reserve Merlot for my wife at Columbia Crest Winery around Paterson, Washington; crossed myself at the Stonehenge WWI memorial, overlooking the John Day Dam where my granddad had kept the books; crossed the river again to buy gas at Biggs, Oregon.

After being blown around like a leaf by triple semis blasting by at 80 per, I abandoned my original idea of droning straight back on the superslab, and instead wended west on Highway 14 along the north bank of the Columbia Gorge until breaking abruptly north through White Salmon, along State Route 141 and on into the Gifford Pinchot National Forest, where I have been lost before.

Honey and I nosed our way northward through to State Route 12 at Randle without incident, except to cough out her mirror glass on a twelve-mile stretch of bumpy dirt. A real "standard" can be ridden anywhere, I think.

West from Randle to Morton, then north by northwest through McKenna, where we own a rarely visited woodlot, into Yelm and along SR 510 into Washington's capitol. In Olympia, I collected the name of an excellent VA counselor from a friend who was once court-martialed by the Marine Corps while he lay in a coma. He woke up, against all predictions, and pushed their shamed faces to the wall. Now he's a medically retired sergeant, all-around crazy Irishman and beloved friend, married to another beloved friend. We ordered pizza, talked for hours. For at least the third time, Rusti and Sean proved to be better friends than I have earned.

And so on to Seattle, to home. At ten of midnight, I dug a carefully interred house key out of my bug-smeared jacket, quietly opened the door, and walked straight into the arms of my wife.

"I missed you," she said into my shoulder, holding tightly, but I could not speak. Warm is the woman who welcomes you home.

None of this may make a lot of sense now, thumb-typed with a padded aluminum splint bandaged onto my broken throttle hand, through the fog of my elastic memory, coruscated through crisscrosses of grief, panic, warmth, nostalgia, paranoia and love.

I'm home again, back from long blue roads, from wars abroad; back to the *jihads* of internal struggle and marital strife and off-site parenting. I have a business to build, a household to husband, a heart to heal. I have a cat who rides on my left shoulder and growls into my ear when I put a foot wrong. Everything familiar is here, but I see it all new, through wondering eyes, as though I were a Japanese tourist fending off this shocking reality with a battery of loaded Nikons.

I will carry no weapon, because I am not afraid — but I miss my rifle every day.

Being not-dead makes decisions and actions imperative. It's not me who caused the war to kill my brothers. It's not me who hides behind yellow car magnets, or picket signs; not me who asserts that we may not discuss war until it's over and the dead are counted and stacked — or that moral justice demands irrational, emotional reaction. Those protestations, those loud assertions are a luxury earned for (not by) the privileged many; earned lately by 2,000 men and women who authentically learned what it is to leave it all on the field.

I took my chances, spun the wheel, prayed every day to bring my guys back alive. They came back scuffed but whole, and I'm back, too. After a long swim under burning waters, I surfaced beyond the flaming slick to gulp cool, northwest air into my urgent lungs.

It's time to be off now. Time to get started, time to get unstuck. My war fighting days, my bar fighting days are behind me. I need to stop looking back there, head into the wind and make progress forward. I find myself once again a live man, at large in the broad world.

And once again, there's a motorcycle parked in my garage. Could be time to get that idle set just right.

August 2007 Motorcyclist
(abridged version)

WHAT KILLS US

This column is addressed to combat veterans. If you're not in that group, turn the page now. Nothing here will be explained to your satisfaction.

Listen up, people. You need to stop using my favorite sport to decimate my only respectable peer group.

Picture of a soldier ready to die, as outlined on the U.S. Army Combined Arms Center safety blog: male, grade E-4 or E-5, 20 to 24 years old. Redeployed for less than six months, SGT Snuffy crashes his high-speed-low-drag sportbike and sounds off "dead" at his next formation.

It's so safe here in the Land of the Free that it feels wrong all the time, and some of us go looking for risk just to remember what it feels like to punch the Reaper in the beak. As my former gunner said the other night, "It's like, what're ya gonna do — kill me?" He rides a 2009 GSXR 750 with a pipe and a Power Commander.

We already walked through the world's worst neighborhoods with bullseyes painted on our chests and drove every single highway to Hell in dog-slow trucks with hillbilly armor. We look twice at things most Americans never even notice. We check the pattern. We watch for movement.

The only enemy capable of putting us down is… us.

There was a different guy in my detachment. We'll call him "Hi-Speed." Hi-Speed was impatient with our training. He thought it was weak.

The rest of us just held Hi-Speed back. Hell, all of USASOC held him back, especially when it issued us M16A2 "muskets" instead of carbines. Then one day at Ft. Bragg, our spankin' new M4s showed up, complete with ACOGs. Hi-Speed "got wood" (yeah, I'm quoting him), but Hi-Speed was ate up like a soup sandwich.

He shot our one and only bolo. Turned out it wasn't about the Cool Guy rifle after all. It was about training. It was about keeping your shot group tight.

If you redeploy, throw your SRB down on a hyperbike and set out to see how fast you can cane it down the road, you're likely to go down like a sack of hammers and crashing is messed up. Crashing is a No-Go.

Big Boy Rules apply. Walk into a motorcycle dealership with a fistful of folding green freedom and they won't talk you down from that Hayabusa or Streetfighter — not in this economy. Their job is to sell bikes, not take care of the troops. Yet those bikes deserve the same respect, training and professional awareness as a weapon — and you never got issued weapons without serious training.

The most at-risk riders in the military community are risk-tolerant, adrenaline-juicing combat professionals — airborne, jarheads, PJs and door kickers of every persuasion. You know who you are. Guys with wings and tabs and combat badges. Cocky guys who know some stuff.

CQB and CLS training doesn't make you a better rider, and being a vet might just make you a worse one. Yeah, I went there. You can be the best Mk 19 gunner who ever walked, but it won't keep your cheek off the pavement if you outride your motorcycle skill set.

You're either the best or you're not. Dying on bikes more easily than squishy civilians is not evidence of being "the best."

The Joint Service Safety Council identified motorcycle safety and training as the number one non-combat safety concern across all services. Why? Because the Insurance Institute for Highway Safety estimates annual U.S. rider fatalities at around 7.5 per 10,000 — but for the Marine Corps, that rate runs almost 10 in 10,000. In 2008, we lost more Marines to motorcycle accidents than to *hajji* action.

Unacceptable.

•••

An old cadence runs like this: *If I die in a combat zone, box me up and ship me home. Pin my medals upon my chest. Tell my mama I did my best!*

There are no medals for sliding under an SUV and crushing your chest, none for smacking a Jersey barrier and bruising the one and only brain you'll ever get issued. Pending a line of duty investigation, you could even be denied your medical benefits or death gratuity if you weren't properly trained and equipped. Will they tell your mama you did your best, or just quietly hand her a hospital bill alongside the folded flag?

Most commands have long prohibited riding on- or off-post without passing an approved motorcycle safety course. Rider courses are FREE for active duty, so go sign up if you're still in. Bring a protective jacket, retro-reflective vest, quality helmet, solid boots and riding gloves or they'll send you back to try again later.

Already know it all? Try a higher-level course, tough guy. Some army posts and all naval bases now require MSF's Military Sportbike RiderCourse if you want to ride a sporting machine. And you do want to ride a sportbike, even if you don't know that yet. As Lawrence of Arabia put it, "A skittish motor-bike with a touch of blood in it is better than all the riding animals on earth."

The army even springs for virtual reality immersion courses. Emplaced at Camp As Sayliyah, Qatar, the Honda Safe Motorcyclist Awareness and Recognition Trainer (SMARTrainer), a kind of flight simulator for bikes, helps prepare redeploying soldiers for the realities of Stateside riding in mixed environments.

CONUS bases host motorcycle safety rallies like Ft. Hood's Phantom Thunder and Ft. Gillem's First Army Commander Safety Ride. The army also cribbed a rider mentoring program from the air force.

Former 500cc world champion and superbike guru Kevin Schwantz has become a Pentagon spokesman for rider training, and 2006 MotoGP champ Nicky Hayden films military safety spots funded by the American Motorcycle Industry Council. The services are spending money, forging alliances and working hard to drive down off-duty accidents, so do your part.

What about prior service road casualties? Nobody tracks the number of skitchy vets who pop smoke on bikes. Freshly released from General Order Number One with money to burn, adjustment issues and no chain of command to shove the cork back in the bottle, we don't need no stinkin' safety course. Hell, we can ride better drunk than civilians could ride on their best freakin' day. We got… we got *situational awareness*! And fine, fast bikes.

To crib from Lance Armstrong, it's not about the bike. What kind of rider are you? What kind of man are you?

Something different than you were before you got shot at, blown up, mortared, fragged. Traumatic brain injuries and PTSD etch permanent physical changes into your thinking apparatus. If you have trouble remembering things, lose your way sometimes or your temper a lot, fight with strangers or stay on edge all the time, don't try to work it out at 130 mph on the causeway. Go see someone at the VA and get in touch with your inner amygdala. The counselors there know a few things that you need to learn. And practice.

While you're at it, take a rider training course. Practice that, too. Ride more, suck less.

•••

I'm no holier than thou. Every stupid thing you could do on a motorcycle, I've probably done twice. I've ridden like a jackass on public roads, failed to PMCS my equipment, gone "just around the block" for a few hours with no pro gear because it was hot out. Like *hot* is some big deal…

I've ridden twisted, too. Fast and hard. I didn't care what happened, and I *liked* not caring. I wanted to ride so blindingly fast into the night that it would all drop away behind me and I would be clean again, and free. I couldn't hurt anyone but myself so it was okay…

Don't do that. It's not the way home. Someone I care for very much asked me not to do it anymore. She reminded me that I would hurt my people that way and maybe someone else's people, too. For that reminder, I bless her every day.

Someone cares for you, too — maybe someone you haven't met yet. Don't blow that chance. You have a duty to the future.

Find a racetrack or a superbike school, and do your need for speed right. Go ride up the canyon with your buddies without setting the interstate lap record. Get a dirt bike and hit the desert races, or screw on supermoto rims and scare yourself silly skittering around paved courses. Don't use the public road to show everybody what a bad motor scooter you can be.

We already know what a badass you are. Thank you for being that when you were called — we couldn't have had anyone better. Thank you for not being that around my family, and for not using my favorite sport to take yourself out of the gene pool.

When the best of Americans smear themselves into wet, red stripes it doesn't just embarrass us. It defeats us, and I *hate* losing. I served with winners and earned the right to ride with you. So vets, tighten up your shot group.

Going out in a bright white bang, still young enough to make a good looking corpse, may sound more honorable than slow death in suburbia, surrounded by peace-fattened civilians, but you know that "slow death" you're worried about? It's called "life."

You earned some.

September 2009, Motorcyclist

FLYING ACE

This piece, pitched successfully and then written for Motor-cyclist, *languished for months before Editor Catterson finally decreed that an ACE Cycle Car wasn't a proper motorcycle. It was hard to argue the point, but the little road beastie was too delightful to entirely discard. Happily, I wasn't the only one who felt this way.*

Completing the orbit of British open-air motoring from the cloudy Pacific NW back to its rain-soaked roots in Old Blighty, Britain's Morgan Motor Co. bought the rights to Pete Larsen's ACE and began producing the tiny road scorchers under a spinoff company named Morgan 3 Wheeler, Ltd.

It's since been reviewed by everyone from Top Gear *to* Road & Track. *Jay Leno (who once bought a race-prepped Ford Falcon out from under me, but that's a different and less interesting story) owns an M3W.*

The spec story I expected to run never did, but the little car that no one expected to make it is a worldwide phenomenon now. Tally ho!

Helmets on, we wriggled into the ground-hugging projectile and prepared for launch. Pete thumbed the stainless steel starter button and 103 inches of high compression twin, strapped Sopwith Camel-style to the sloped aero nose, crack-boomed into Columbia City's pre-dawn. Lowering his leather-trimmed goggles, Pete made a quick head check, fed in 2,000 rpm to keep the oil moving, then let out the clutch.

The ACE Cycle-Car leapt into the darkness.

By 0600, we had boomed over the I-90 bridge and were circumnavigating Mercer Island, cackling out loud while railing corners at double the posted limits without beginning to strain the little missile's composure. It was 40 degrees out when we squeaked round a tight corner and skittered across a slick of wet leaves. Pete feathered the throttle, salted in a dash of countersteer and dodged a stray purebred as we pelted past a sign reading CHILDREN AT PLAY.

"Truer words were never spoken," I yelled over the wind, grinning hard enough to freeze my lips onto my teeth.

What exactly is an ACE Cycle-Car?

Not a motorcycle, certainly — although it registers as one, small license plate and all. A three-wheeler allows you to fly solo down the diamond lanes, and even up to the front of the ferry line in Washington State.

Surely it's not an automobile, not in this land of DVD player-equipped minivans and SUVs encompassing more cubic pork than a Costco butcher counter.

A flivver perhaps, in the classic sense — a throwback to motoring's ancient origins, when people dressed the part and hared about in cars for the sheer lip-chapping, life-squeezing joy of it all. It's what technology is for: to make life happen better, not just faster.

The progenitor of this happy madness, Pete Larsen, is unhelpful with definitions. His dreams are best described in fiberglass and aluminum, subtly accented with pinstripes and unsubtly accompanied by burbling fishtail exhausts.

"It is what it is," Larsen said. "It had to feel right, look right. This is my motorcycle, but it's also my car. I could drive this car every day for the rest of my life, take it places or let it take me places.

"You've got nothing to compare it to."

•••

The ACE is a toy, but a toy with an exponent; a quite amazing toy with racecar fabrication, antique looks, American power, Japanese final drive and the concentrated DNA of a thousand English madmen. If the difference between men and boys is the price of their toys, the ACE is the brightest red Radio Flyer wagon with oak side slats that ever showed up under a Christmas tree.

ACE is also the singular vision of Pete Larsen, 18 years the proprietor of Liberty Sidecars. Liberty produces bespoke sidehacks, exclusively for big twin Harley-Davidsons, boasting a vintage 1930s look overlaying current technology. The Liberty cars are pretty things, quaint and richly finished. They keep the crank turning at Larsen's shop, and doubtless enhance the lives of their owners. But the ACE is to a Liberty hack as a mink is to a tree sloth: quicker, lower, sleeker and far more aggressive…

Larsen turns every bolt himself. He keeps a large, spotless, thoroughly fenestrated shop on Rainier Avenue with a staff consisting of himself, a part-time welder and occasional bookkeeping work from his wife. Like Caractacus Potts in his woodshed, Larsen has banged, cut, forged, synthesized and emerged with something perhaps not unprecedented, but entirely unique.

There are other three-wheeled cars out there, modest successes including Britain's Triking Cyclecar — and any number of well-funded failures. There are sleek hybrid prototypes like the tilt-a-wheel Persu and the Aptera, which looks like something George Jetson's boss might drive. The ACE alone synthesizes effortless steampunk style with top-shelf technology in an unprecedented fashion — and it exists. You can drive one today.

"It became an obsession," Larsen said of the notion to build an updated Morgan three-wheeler, a notion that first took unyielding hold after he upgraded to his current, larger manufactory a few years back. Judging by the high finish level on his product, you wouldn't want to be on the wrong end of one of Pete Larsen's obsessions.

He's gobbled up premium components from anywhere and everywhere to produce a toy with Fabergé polish and the guts and pedigree to run hard on tight roads. What he couldn't find, he built or commissioned. His files contain over 200 precision drawings, each one hand-drafted by Larsen.

The results are dazzling.

Larsen's attention to detail evokes the fanaticism of Bimota and Fritz Egli. I pored over the car for hours in an unapologetic search for the cheesy hallmarks of kit car mentality, but found not a single shortcut or cop-out throughout the vehicle.

Chassis and suspension are laser-coped tubing, all TIG welded. Every fastener is properly finished and "dress right, dress." You can see the chrome reflected in the paint almost as clearly as the paint reflected in the chrome.

Three hydraulic reservoirs for front brakes, rear brakes and clutch are tidy CNC aluminum bits because "I just couldn't stand to put black plastic under there" — not that anyone can see them unless you pop the bonnet. The boot is trimmed with a fitted shroud that sub-fenders the rear drive, covers the battery and incorporates a tidy bucket ideally suited to jugged Chianti, crusty pumpernickel and a wild blue Stilton that travels well.

The ACE is built the way you might build your own special project — if your education combined the exactitude of mechanical engineering with the flowing integrations of landscape architecture; if you had access to a wealth of carefully nurtured motorcycle industry relationships; if you were immune to investor pressures for instant return on investment.

And if you had a close working relationship with serendipity, knew exactly who you were and maintained a careful respect for the indescribable rightness of proper things.

Larsen describes his ACE as "an enthusiast project — you either get it or you don't. I want to see my cars on the road.

"I don't see this as an investment opportunity."

Nor much of an employment opportunity, it seems. Larsen is a lone *artiste* who keeps his own two hands around every step of the production process. Seven mornings every week, Larsen shows up before sunrise to start his shop day. He spends most of his work time alone, selling the occasional hack, building three-wheelers and solving problems. He's not in it to build a company, but to build ACE Cycle-Cars.

Larsen's evocative styling riffs on Brough Superior, deHavilland's Gypsy Moth and the ACE's conceptual sire, a Morgan Super Sports Aero parked quietly at the end of a row of its smartly polished legacies.

The seminal "Moggie" appears cute but cobby, a sporty 1930s update on its econo-bucket origins. The exposed valve springs of its ohv Matchless engine, flimsy mudguards and pigeon-toed, sliding pillar front suspension are reminiscent of the once-saucy auntie now comfortably settled into dowdiness. The ACE sitting adjacent is her hawt niece, sexier in a period flapper dress than any number of today's tattooed, belly-ringed skanks.

Beauty is skin deep, but engineering goes to the bone. The 103-inch Screamin' Eagle crate motor chuffs along contentedly and snarls when you poke it. At 950 lbs. with ten gallons of premium in the tail, this romping raindrop weighs less than a Heritage Softail Springer with sidecar, and is orders of magnitude more agile and aerodynamic.

A Borg-Warner T-5 transmission, graced with a short-throw linkage of Larsen's design, shifts precisely and pulls this funky little bullet firmly out of the kit bike category with solid synchromesh feel and a real reverse gear. The hydraulically actuated dry clutch rings at idle with a *pur sang* Ducati rattle.

Damped by custom-built Works Performance shocks, the house-built front suspension cambers eagerly in toward corner apexes, channeling cornering forces much in the manner of motorcycles. The rear wheel, mounted to a swingarm sourced from a GL1800 trike conversion shop, maps the road surface closely with its single 195/55-16 all season radial.

The rumpety bass line articulates through Kerker fishtail exhausts, handsomely heat-shielded.

Where he can't source perfectly optimized parts, Larsen welds them up, machines them down, or draws them and sends out for CAD work. His power coupling, the key secret to keeping drivetrain components sound behind the thudding twin-cam, is a taste of engineering elegance too proprietary to discuss. For a little under fifty grand, you can have your own special coupling delivered — and it'll come with a really cool landspeeder wrapped around it.

Considering the challenge to lash it up properly, why the Harley mill? It's a precise *homage* to the original air-cooled, bike-derived v-twin Morgans, of course, but it runs deeper than that. Harley crate engines — including the considerably peppier Screamin' Eagle versions — are available off the shelf with full factory warranties. Larsen's long history in the sidecar business meant that H-D power fell right in his comfort zone.

This also may be the best application in recent memory for Milwaukee's recent bottlings. It pulls the passenger pod along with smooth alacrity, sounds mellow through the sidepipes, and has always exhibited car-like flywheel characteristics. It also looks like the top cylinders of a radial engine when you sight down the rounded snout of this latter day Stearman.

"If we were going to make this in America, it had to have a Harley engine," Larsen said. "People respond to it — it has the look, the sound.

"It just feels right."

●●●

People do respond, but not just to the chick-baiting soundtrack. Hipper-than-thou Seattle bicyclists, predisposed to sneer at poseurs on butt jewelry, smiled with surprised delight and waved furiously at the wholly unexpected veloci-tub zipping past. The ACE may be seriously over-engineered, but it's puppy cute, too.

Down by the lake in Seward Park, I took the wheel. "Taking the wheel" carries a certain Bugs Bunny resonance with the ACE's NASCAR-style detachable helm. Unsurprisingly, the wheel is fabricated in-house. Larsen couldn't find the perfect one, and perfection is his benchmark.

Stuffing my full-figured body into the Kate Moss-sized passenger seat had been distracting — statistically few men desire a rigid driveshaft knocking up their back door — but the driver's cockpit is proportioned more in the L to XL range (XXXL pilots should give it up, buy a Gold Wing trike conversion and donate the swingarm to make an ACE for someone more lithe). This rig features sportbike seating — i.e. one full-sized operator and a *real* skinny copilot — but there's room to maneuver on the left. While I have trouble moving my size 12 Börns around the footbox of an MG Midget, Larsen's ACE gives adequate room to tap dance on its Tilton Racing pedal set.

In common with hyperbikes or a Pitts S2S stunt biplane, the ACE demands commitment. In that way, she resembles a motorcycle more than, for instance, scooters do. Strapping on a helmet, clicking into a three-point racing harness and snapping the wheel on after you bespeaks imminent serious driving.

And drive she will. Snappy acceleration scampers to a 120 mph top speed that should pull any Harley running the same mill (for enhanced git, an optional 120bhp engine from JIMS will raise the ante — and your pulse). She corners flat and hard with a nicely neutral balance, but you need to stay on your game in this beast. Drivers only need apply.

While the track is wide and stable, the ACE's vanishingly short wheelbase means that spins develop quicker than ground looping a Cessna 190. Try to steer this critter with one thumb while texting with the other hand, and it will turn from puppy to pit bull and bite you in the A.D.D. No video game with a steering wheel, any drive in the ACE quickly becomes a full-immersion episode that taxes your skill set as pleasurably as a shifter cart disguised under a license plate and vintage styling. Like vintage Porsches and English motorcycles (and American girls), the ACE makes constant demands on your attention. Eternal vigilance is the price of freedom…

RPM should stay in the two to four thousand RPM sweet zone. She'll pull from lower, but Larsen says the power plant oils better over 2K and I wasn't about to abuse an engine still on its break-in miles.

Those unwilling to double-clutch and match RPM to road speed should buy tickets on a different ride. You may crush downshifts through the synchros if you insist, but such clumsy box wrangling can crow-hop the tail. There is no dead pedal, because this is not a touring car. If your clutch foot goes idle long enough to need a resting plate, you've mistakenly gotten onto the wrong road.

You sit right there in the cheek-burning wind where you belong, and if you require entertainment beyond a winding road skimming by close enough to strike a match on, you're not paying sufficient attention.

There is no heater, no radio, no doors, no windows, no roof — nor are they options. The dashing Brooklands screens — vestigial salutes to Fangio — mean that you will not merely experience the weather; you will wear it. And if none of this makes any sense on a car produced in the Pacific NW where it rains 150 days a year, please remember that the Morgan and virtually every other stripped roadster you can think of originally emerged from the drippy isle of England. Such audacity of hope also explains why Seattlites own more sunglasses than you do.

Still, this is one of the few cars built since World War II with fewer "luxury" options (and one less wheel) than a Lotus Seven. It's also the only car in America built to such a glossy production standard, from such a singular vision, by one man working alone.

In the end, it's a "special" in the old-time idiom. If the ACE were a rifle, it would be an Ed Yost Schuetzen; if a motorbike, an Egli Vincent. The ACE was born of cleverness married to fanaticism by a reverend named Art.

So call it a toy, if you wish: a car, more or less — more to a driver, and less to a family of four. A motorcycle, legally. A retro ride for the nostalgic, and a Porsche-zapping autocrosser for the committed.

Pete Larsen doesn't care what you call his creation. You either get it or you don't.

Either way, he'll be back at his shop again tomorrow before sunup, as he is seven days a week. You'd expect no less from the ace of ACEs.

But before he sets into his chores, Pete will roll out a crab-eyed sports machine with an invisible rear wheel, tug weathered goggles down over his gimlet squint, push the go-button… and smile like the Red Baron.

jaxworx.com

STALIN'S REVENGE

Leather-bear bikers go to Sturgis and Daytona in custom Ford pickup trucks. Sport riders have the Golden State, in all its year-round riding glory. For one-off exhibition bikes, there's the fabulous Cologne show.

And what of we beflanneled rain wranglers, splooshing through the Pacific Northwest? We have a jeep, crossed with a riding tractor, served on the rocks with a twist of Communism.

As many do, I know a guy.

Ivan is a mechanic from Russia. He keeps a shop in Kenmore, a greasy tatterdemalion of parts bins, overflowing tool drawers and half-corpses of intended and unintended donor machines where he'll fix anything with wheels. Like sausage-grinding, his work is no spectator sport for the squeamish.

"In Russia," Ivan tells me, dropping his mask and firing up the torch for an acetylene death match with an '84 Caddy, "everything is shit, shit... *nothing* but shit!

"We learn to make shit good."

Which brings us to our subject, the Ural. Ural is famous for three things: obsolete electrics, massive build and low performance — but that's the Ural electric guitar.

Like Yamaha, Ural's name appears on musical instruments. Like Kawasaki, there are Ural generators and industrial equipment; like Honda and Suzuki, the global Ural hegemony (!) has produced cars and trucks as well. All of these products appear carelessly tuned to a vast sucking sound.

The motorcycle bears a richer story, starting with its curious provenance. Competing stories exist. Enthusiast mythmakers recount a tale of five BMW R71s purchased through Sweden (an equal-opportunity collaborator) and subsequently reverse-engineered by Soviet *intelligentsia*.

The prosaic version is that BMW re-tooled for its new R75 and passed off its obsolete R71 production line to the Sovs as part of the Molotov/Ribbentrop Pact, a non-aggression treaty signed in 1939 that resulted in various other technology transfers, including equipment to build the Opel Kadett K-38 car.

The R75 successor model represented the state of mid-century engineering art with a locking differential, hydraulic brakes and a dual-range final drive. When the *Wehrmacht* drove across the Soviet frontier just two years after Hitler's wink and a nod to Stalin, they were saddled up on these refined chariots with meticulously machined MP-42 *Maschinengewehren* traverse-mounted to the noses of their sidecars.

Prior to the *blitzkrieg*, the Soviets (née Russians) had hastily tooled up a Moscow production facility and cranked out several hundred straight copies of the predecessor R71 bearing non-driven sidecars, cable brakes and a single final drive ratio. Designated M-72, they were dead simple and field-repairable by farm boys.

Cossacks brandishing stamped-steel PPSh submachine guns clanked out to meet the foe on their atavistic steeds, determined to prevent the Fatherland penetrating Mother

Russia. War with Nazi Germany cost the Soviets some 23 million casualties — nearly 14 percent of their population.

By the time *Operatsiya Bagration* pushed the Germans out for good in 1944, the Soviets' motorcycle production had been moved from the ZIS auto manufactory in Moskow to a safe location in an Irbitzk brewery near the base of the Ural mountains, and *Irbitskiy Mototsikletniy Zavod* (IMZ) had delivered 9,799 military hacks to Russian recon troops.

The IMZ/Ural plant continued to supply army *materièl* until the late 1950s, when Ukraine's Kiev Motorcycle Plant (KMZ) took over Red Army supply and IMZ switched to civilian output. As in Britain, postwar economics made sidecar rigs attractive alternatives to cars and trucks — although how this could possibly be true in western Siberia, where the Ural plant is located, is something you'd have to ask a qualified Russian.

In 1964 the Soviet army received updated rigs from Kiev with 750cc, overhead-valve engines and driven sidecar wheels and could finally claim they'd nearly matched the engineering mark set by the Germans a quarter-century before (still no selectable-range final drive, though). Those Ukrainian-built bikes, called Dnepr, are out of production and included here primarily to confuse you, good reader.

Further muddying the waters, in 1957 the M-72 specs and molds were sold to China. Thousands of 750cc, 22-bhp "Dneprs" were built by Chang Jiang for military and civilian applications. Seeing dozens of them in and around Beijing, each one reverently sidewalk-parked alongside streets teeming with scooters, donkey carts, bicycles, imposing Mercedes and tiny vans, I wondered how many Chinese privates were beaten bloody when they couldn't get their vehicles moving.

Between the Russians, the Ukrainians and the Chinese, some 3.2 million of these commie Clydesdales — the AK47 of adventure touring — have been delivered worldwide. Bizarrely, that may just make the R71 derivative BMW's most successful model.

•••

So what of these modern-day Urals? When Tom Lynott started importing them through Washington as a kind of moto-novelty in 1994, they were so unreliable that he simply rebuilt them at the distributorship. The bikes broke anyway, but accrued a merry following.

According to Madina Merzhoyeva, an employee from the wayback Ural America days who now serves as Vice President of Sales & Marketing to current corporate iteration Irbit MotorWorks of America, "Those bikes were pretty much a project for the garage."

Now under private ownership, IMZ still forges bikes in their repurposed brewery, but leaner times mandate crisper efficiencies and new focus. No longer a weapons platform or light farm truck, the Ural combination is marketed primarily to Western markets as a kind of full-scale Dinky Toy — simple, decorative and built of solid steel. The customer cohort is no longer cranky old *komendatura* with billion-ruble budgets, but newly-minted grandfathers who buy a bike for cash. Compared to a Harley-Davidson Ultra, Urals are cheap by the pound. Annual deliveries now hover in the hundreds, not the hundreds of thousands.

To raise the quality bar for new markets, by 2007 Ural had become a "world bike." While a three-foot tool roll and roadside wrenchability still lead the features list, the factory incorporated a long roster of foreign-sourced bits to cut down on the number of times you have to break out that roll. Per Merzhoyeva, 14 countries now contribute components.

From Japan, 770 watts of Nippon Denso bright-think replace the crumbly Russian alternator and Keihin supplies the carbs. Ignition by Ducati and a floating Brembo up front grant Italianate suaveness if you squint until the tears come. Solidifying the Axis triumvirate, gears are now cut by KTM's Austrian supplier Herzog. In a Cold War rapprochement, the wiring harness is U.S.-designed and Chinese-built.

Power is also expected now, and the Ural has... some. Chrome cylinder liners and 8.6:1 compression pound out 40 raging bhp on 91 octane fuel. Sporting only two fewer ponies than a 1954 Triumph Tiger Cub 110, the Patrol model's recommended top speed is 62 mph — actually pretty good for a military vehicle. I drove M151 army "Mutts" in the mid-80s, and those things were spooky over 40 mph.

Which underscores the obvious: This *is* your grandfather's Oldsmobile. Urals are clunky, low-tech, retro... and delightful. Exterior styling, frame and bodywork belie its modernized innards.

The spare tire mounted over the Ural's boot shows Model A Ford charm, and its leading link front suspension is more steampunk than reruns of *Wild Wild West*. It's the only production vehicle simultaneously as agricultural as a Massey-Ferguson and frivolous as a parade float, guaranteeing more social intercourse than 30 grand worth of turbo

Haya-blinga. Squids, soccer moms and O.C. chopper wannabes all grin at Stalin's Revenge.

Slow down to enjoy the scenery on a sportbike, and some jackass hustling his four-by to the pose lot will blast you right off the road. Do it on a cruiser, and some jackass on a sportbike will do the same thing — but feel free to just amble along on a Ural. People *will* smile and wave.

Ural rigs are delivered in three configurations. The Tourist, with non-driven sidecar wheel, is the basic goodness. Patrol models — default color Subaru Forester green — are fortified with sidecar drive. The Gear-Up and Sahara are camo-painted, post-apocalyptic survivalist vehicles based on the Patrol.

We shall not speak of the carless Ural Wolf, chopperized spawn described by factory literature as "a wild child created from an unconventional union between the Ural factory and the Russian Night Wolves biker club," as it makes your faithful correspondent want to stick forks in his eyes. Unconventional union, indeed.

Compared to a 1967 Vanagon, Ural's tech sheet is awe-inspiring. There's a real disk brake on the front wheel (rear, car and spare wheels have matching drums), a boot suitable for unlimited picnicking, and a selectable reverse gear.

Forty horsepower may not be much for roll-on poke, but when backing half a ton of loaded hack uphill it beats hell out of a Gold Wing's starter motor. Ural is likely the world's fastest motorcycle in reverse.

Reverse isn't the only lever mounted alongside the exposed driveshaft and its truck-like u-joint. On Ural's Patrol, Gear-Up and Sahara models, a lever near the rear drive engages a driveshaft to the sidecar wheel for solid-axle,

2WD traction that converts it into a sort of Jeep with a zero-slip rear end. It should be rigorously avoided on pavement unless you've dispensed with the notion of intentional steering, but in a notorious Craigslist swap, a Ural Patrol is said to have replaced Alaska's gubernatorial jet.

The Ural is a go-kart, a poseur's pet, a jeep, a startlingly effective chick magnet... even makes perfect French fries! This critter defines its own niche as uniquely as a tole-painted half-track.

More specs: three nineteen-inch alloy-hubbed steel rims (plus a spare); four speeds forward (plus reverse); five Sachs shock absorbers; six inches of ground clearance. Valve seats are hardened for crappy unleaded fuel (91 octane), and thanks to some early prototyping by Seattle Guzzi dealer Moto International, electric start complements the old reliable kick lever.

A comprehensible fuse block — no CAN-BUS nonsense here — mounts handily under the car's cowl. Romantic absurdity once lurked in an aircraft-style master electrical switch under the saddle, but the upgraded wiring harness no longer admits of constant small losses while parked. Also missing from the crank-up routine is turning on the gas, as Urals now feature vacuum petcocks.

"Now people don't fix them," said Merzhoyeva. "They ride them."

Still, the motorcycles remain rough, ready and cobblestone-simple.

Some bikes are made to be worked on at the dealership with specialty tools, others you can tackle in your garage. A Ural is meant to be repaired in a bar pit, using only its onboard toolkit, a cornucopia of canvas-wrapped chrome including every wrench you need to get below the base gaskets plus full-scale tire irons, touch-up paint, tire pump and even work gloves.

Despite recently extended service intervals, Urals demand commitment. A factory maintenance manual (happily available in English) is strongly recommended, but chores are straightforward and the tinkering is pleasant work. If you can cold-start your own lawn mower, you'll be fine — but if you report to your dealership for tire pressure checks, try a different bike.

A Gear-Up package won't impress the kid jonesing to screw blue neon pose lights and a Hot Bodies undertail onto his R6, but will bring a smile to anyone who remembers *Rat Patrol* on afternoon TV. Decked out with shovel, spotlights, red-starred ammo box, camouflage tonneau and a jerry can, the Gear-Up appears as grittily self-sufficient as a Land Rover Carawagon. Mount a winch, lifting shackles and a crew-served weapon and you could head straight for the front lines.

Of course, you could go the other way and shun drab camo for the carousel colorations available to the Tourist buyer (this year's options are bright red, glossy black or maroon) or the tuxedo-sharp Retro in pinstriped black.

The Tourist I rode was dolled up by factory pin striper Svetlana Zyryanova in *gzhel*, a fluidly hallucinogenic Russian folk art reminiscent of scrimshaw crossed with Delft ceramics. Hard-bitten Cossack Corps lineage notwithstanding, it's the frilliest bike I've ever ridden.

Ran nicely, too, subject to one small glitch. The bike lit right off with the choke plungers drawn out, but only after some quick nutdriver action to reinstall an intake manifold that fell off the left side carburetor at 53 miles of recorded travel. Like a trusty old Shovelhead, obsessive attention to fasteners may reduce such inconvenient back-outs. Also like an old H-D, nearly every bolt on the rig can be duplicated at any decent hardware store — or found in that rusty coffee can on your garage shelf.

And then I was off into the world, bobbing and weaving and waving at girls, as enthralled with the moment as Mr. Toad barrel-assing through the Wild Wood in a pink Cadillac convertible.

•••

Town or countryside, poking around on Urals is a full-immersion experience, and not just due to the sundry social distractions lumped under the heading of "UDF" (Ural Delay Factor). Herding a hack is something like riding a motorcycle but steering a light truck — right up until the third wheel flies and you're countersteering all over again.

Sidecar inertia makes the rig pull right on acceleration and dart into oncoming traffic under braking loads. "Pull away, come together" is a useful mnemonic, but good luck remembering it in a picosecond. Like any flavor of motorcycling, it's best to practice correctly until muscle memory becomes reliable. Pretty soon, you find yourself automatically fudging the bars to the right every time you declutch for an upshift.

On the road, our Ural toddled along cheerfully, cheating slightly to one side or the other whenever the radius of the road crown shifted — ever wonder why hacked bikes lean left on the level? — occasionally frisking a bit on right turns, and asking little more of its rider than hanging off in turns like a Columbia Gorge windsurfer. I sustained semi-permanent sidecar marks on my butt from performing right-handers with the car unladen.

The new gearbox, orders of magnitude improved over a few years back, shifts about as well as a 1978 Kawasaki Z-1 that was only drag-raced by a little old lady on Sundays. Neutral is easily found — frequently well north of second gear — but the neutral indicator is elusive.

The massive front suspension felt immune to side loads, allowing me to spin along with the sidecar flying at its balance point of around 40 degrees, wheel cocked up in the air like the hind leg of an insouciant hound. Easier than wheelying and you can do it at a sedate 20 mph all the way down your block, cheerfully saluting perplexed neighbors with an unobstructed view of your undercarriage.

Riding down in the sidecar is a separate reality. People and dogs often giggle about it, but then some people pay to be flogged with knotted cords. I generally prefer to keep my whip hand on the throttle, but sometimes it's your turn in the barrel…

Tipping the windshield forward raises the chrome grab rail out of your way. Once ensconced, the rail drops across your lap like the safety bar at Six Flags over Siberia and off you scoot, chair monkey for a day. Legroom is generous and weather protection excellent, but you pell-mell along with the fatalistic resignation of a mosquito in a twister. Throwing your mitts into the air and squealing like an eight year-old girl does enhance the affair, but when I did that, ride wrangler Sergei admonished me firmly in Russian: "Keep your hands and arms inside the car at all times."

The more riding experience you have, the more readaptation is required for the business end of a hack. Pushing the front end is perfectly acceptable, and with a little practice you can slide the tail with fine control even at walking speeds. One sidecar show-off trick is to spin it into a curbside parking spot and wind up facing the street, then nonchalantly hop off and walk away whistling. Properly done, a Ural will rotate inside its own length.

•••

Tales of the cultic legions of Ural assume the patina of legend: a couple with two Great Danes who bought a pair of Tourist rigs to leave no dog behind; a P.U.D. worker who threw a chainsaw and come-along into his Patrol and went out to clear roads in a blizzard when the county trucks couldn't move.

What won't the Ural faithful try? Not much. In the lobby of IMZ sits a streamlined Ural on which Fredda Cole earned a fistful of land speed records in 2001.

I always thought sidecars were for lazy old fat guys. Turns out I needn't have waited that long. It's more physically draining to push a hack to modest speeds than to ride a streetbike fast, and it requires equal concentration. No matter your riding experience, the first time a sidecar shows its badger-like teeth it will command your utmost attention. There's nothing like floating into the oncoming lane of a busy arterial intersection to jack your pupils right open.

And that's entertainment. Feeling jaded by $10,000.00, 100-horse literbikes? Try a $13,000, 40-horse, 2WD bikeo-saurus. Riding a Ural — to the store, to the mountaintop, to the symphony with your sweetie, to the middle of nowhere with your dog wearing goggles — may not convert you to a babbling sidecar proselyte, but it will permanently expand the way you look at motorcycles.

Crank 'er up with the button, or use the kick lever if you feel nostalgic (and why wouldn't you?). The Ural sits panting like a puppy with a ball, slyly inviting you to go play outside.

Listen to those valves tick. Are they counting away your dead-end life, or calling you to go seek your misfortune? Excuse me a moment...

I need to go find out for myself.

May 2009, Motorcyclist

GREEN FLASH

There are a number of better endings to this piece than the one published herein. To hear those, you'll have to ask Pretty Wife yourself.

It was just a three-hour business drone from Seattle to Portland. Then Tacoma commuter traffic crunched over my patience and left it bleeding by the Jersey barriers of Interstate Five. I broke right and peeled off west out Highway 16 toward water, peace and two-lane solutions.

Out past Gig Harbor sits a seafood 'n' ice cream pizza emporium. Nobody in his right mind passes up a fried Hoodsport oyster burger washed down with fork-thick chocolate malt and I don't, either.

Waddling back out to my new R1200S (aka "Black Betty") after lunch, I waved at the ST1300 rider I had waved at on the way in, but he was still nattering into his cell phone. My cell phone, which doesn't work on good roads or sunny days, was tucked into my tank bag.

BMW makes hella expensive bike luggage and their zipper pulls are crap, but they're stubbornly waterproof, fit close and look sharp as a Nazi officer's coat. Thanks to the joys of employee discounting, my Betty sported a tail bag to match. And rocker cover guards, six-inch wide rear rim, Swedish shocks, smoked screen, *monoposto* cover and a booming carbon-ti stinger in place of the stock baboon's arsehole. As Truman says, "shop to ride, ride to shop."

Black Betty's final touch is black speed wheels, which the inscrutable Bavarians refuse to sell on their *schwarzer* "S" bikes. Betty's stock silver wheels were swapped onto a candy cane 12S and delivered south to ferry a spiky girl around San Francisco.

Onward, then, west along where SR 302 curves two sweet lanes around Case Inlet's northern reach, past the road leading to Penrose Point State Park. Twenty years ago in that park, I stood and bawled into the stony salt beach for my one true Catholic girl, cloistered into the nearby women's penitentiary at Purdy where she still haunts a cell today. I didn't stop this time. The freshly paved road was too curvaceously inviting for parricidal reminiscences.

So there I was, burbling lively along on a spankin' new bike, bound for my first reading of new material at a major bookstore and the first long ride with my self-selected "number one groupie." Great roads rushed up to meet me like old friends returned, bathed in northwest sun (another old friend returned from seasons away). Chilly salt air bit my nose and a Gerbing electric liner gently toasted my chest. Freshly debrided Metzeler Sportecs stuck to the road like bandages on a wet scab.

Life is pretty good, I thought. Wandering south on a congenial errand, a couple hours overdue with a pretty girl waiting... *doh!*

IDIOT BOY!

I pulled over and left a *mea culpa* on Pretty Girl's voice mail, then beat it down State Route 3, past Hartstene Island's beachcombing shacks and the Squaxin Island rez and across the base of the rain forest peninsula through Shelton. From Isabella Lake I took the 101 into Olympia the back way. Mandatory slabbing to Portland wasn't excuse enough to divert out on Cooper Point and drain beers with friends, so I droned south, cheerfully waving at big women on Harleys.

•••

On Broadway in downtown Portland, the Marriott's doorkid was explaining their valet motorcycle parking ("a couple of our guys have endorsements"), when someone seized me from behind and I nearly leapt out of my leathers. I hate getting jumped from behind, but the Lord loves a grinning woman and so do I.

Pretty Girl had been pounding on her laptop in Peet's coffee shop when she detected the subtle whisper of Betty's Akrapovic exhaust fracturing windows up and down the street. The BMW catalog calls it a "sport silencer," which is half-true. I am not a nice man, but I know what makes me happy: black bikes, blacktop, black leathers. And Pretty Girl, who isn't big enough to be a Harley girl yet.

A weekend in Oregon with a delightful woman, a reading, then a spring ride to the coast. How bad could that be?

En route to my reading the next day, Pretty Girl took a call from Seattle's Moto International shop. She snapped her phone shut, looking defeated. Seems her beloved Moto Guzzi Mille GT hadn't just spun a crank bearing. "Sal" would require a new camshaft, too. She wordlessly pointed at a Pearl District dessert shop. Playing my first responder role, I swept her inside for dark chocolate and espresso, patted her hand and congratulated her on her foresight in procuring a backup bike.

A few quality ringers, including my undeservedly loyal mother, attended my reading at Powell's City of Books the next evening. It went well and we celebrated afterward at Kelly's Olympian, the third-oldest bar in Portland. The Oly features a menagerie of shiny old motorcycles, a tap line of micro-brewed inspiration and kick-ass onion rings.

•••

The second morning, we checked out and blasted down Canyon Boulevard. Pretty Girl felt slightly less bereft of her Guzzi once she pulled her very first wheelie on her Tweety-yellow 2002 BMW F650GS. Such a sparkly stoplight smile I never saw before.

Two miles later, a 20-something dude pulled up and ogled Black Betty's Öhlins-enabled legs. "Can that bike wheelie?"

"With all this luggage on?," I said. "You're nuts!" He shrugged and grinned.

It's common knowledge that shafties don't wheelie. Figuring to show my date a for-real wheelstand, I quit stroking Betty's throttle bodies and gave them a heavy grope.

The rangy black bitch was bellowing and stretching toward heaven when I fat-toed her into neutral. She crashed down faster than the walls of Jericho at a bugle recital. *Uff da!* The brochure never mentioned a fully interactive crotch-tank interface. Well, it probably wouldn't hurt unless I tried to walk, or breathe, or something. So impressive to the new girlfriend...

Out of McMinnville we headed north toward Yamhill, then meandered west along Panther Creek, past grassy Meadow Lake reservoir on a road that jukes bluesy through the Coast Range, keeping time to the syncopated curves of the Nestucca River. Fissured and crumbled, graveled and frost-heaved, that road jerks and slashes through the trees like a wino with a chainsaw. I reined Black Betty in, trying to be sociable.

After 20 minutes, Pretty Girl putted up at a stop and told me to quit dawdling and "go have some fun." The heavens opened, and choral music issued forth. Who raises such women — and why didn't I meet one years ago? When I realized I could also write this trip off my taxes, I suddenly understood the angelic choir. Obviously, I had died and been delivered to the wrong address.

Not once did Betty put a wide black wheel wrong. The 2007 R1200S is sure-footed like a mountain-bred mustang. Two big slugs squeezing 12.5:1 compression, four spark plugs, cam in head, about fifty pounds porkier than my old Duc but packing fifty extra horsepower and room to store my legs. Greatest old man's touring bike *evah*.

We were touching 90 on a short straight when the road zagged left and turned to muddy gravel. *Oy vey!* What a terrible dirt bike! Eight minutes later, Pretty Girl zipped past with a big wave, backed it into the next corner all crossed up and dragging her Givi saddlebag, then disappeared up the road while I tippy-toed effetely around potholes with trembling clip-ons.

Once back on hardtop, we barrel-assed into Beaver and soared north on the open coast road. Paying her back a little, I waved and let Betty out to gallop the long sweepers. Pausing for a short discussion about endurance, we backtracked to a scenic loop I've been bypassing for years. From an overlook 200 feet above the booming surf, we envied the parasailers frolicking on afternoon thermals.

"Hold me for a minute?," she said. "I'm a little cold."

Pretty Girl's Gerbing had died without a whimper somewhere along the forest road, leaving her with two unheated layers, under a mesh jacket, in early spring, on the clammy Oregon coast. With my Heat-Troller cranked up to "magma" and my heated grips on "fricassee," I was chilly myself. We swapped Heat-Trollers, but her jacket was fried. Adding layers helped little.

As the sun fell, the temperature dropped from the low 60s into the 50s, then into the high 40s. Sunshine turned to mist and graduated to squalls.

"Want to ride Betty?," I said. "She's got heated grips."

"Don't want to ride an unfamiliar bike when I'm not on my game. My ruler's a couple inches short right now."

What man would admit to that?

I had nothin'. They say the true test for a couple is putting up a tent together in the rain. We were sodden with all the frustration, cold and fatigue — just no tent. This had become a forced march, not a dance. We trudged on, private thoughts giving way to mindless endurance.

At Fresh Seafood NW in Tillamook, rubber-booted fishermen toted in dripping string bags of cold-water oysters and Dungeness crabs from rusty Chevy pickups. When we pulled in, the stouthearted proprietress took one look at Pretty Girl and un-closed her lunch counter. Bustling purposefully, Kari scooped us a bucket of meaty white chowder, boiled up fresh coffee and told us to ignore closing time. Hands wrapped onto steaming cups, we slurped hot, salty fluids until we felt approximately human. Then, sighing, we clumped back out into the cold, alone beside each other in the gravel parking lot.

"I'm really having a good time."… *compared to a Vice-Grip pedicure.*

"Are you sure?" *Are you off your meds?*

Her face was windburnt and her hair was snarled, but her smile was true clear up to the eyes.

I'm not a good babysitter. I don't do group rides and my buddies are not riding buddies. My first modification to a new bike is to unbolt the passenger pegs, put them in a box, and lose the box. The motorcycle is for me. But here was this girl, pretty and brave, riding her own and gutting it out. A puzzler.

At stop after stop, I plied Pretty Girl with every possible form of warmth, waiting for the first little whine to breach her dam of resolve. All I heard was, "I'm OK.

"Just hold me for a minute."

On we slogged as the road unreeled, slow and cold. Shadows inveigled our highway down into their dead embrace. Ghosts darted from corners. But we were on our bikes, going through it together.

We had two hours separating us from a bed in Gearhart when we pulled off at Wheeler to watch the sunset. Our chances looked worse with every stop, but hypothermia is not indefinitely negotiable. I curled my arm around her shoulders, faced west and held on until she stopped bucking with shivers.

"My grandfather told me," Pretty Girl said, teeth chattering, "if you watch the sunset just when it disappears below the horizon, you can see an afterglow.

"It's called the 'Green Flash'."

"Sounds like a comic book hero," I said, being sensitive like that.

"Grandpa was my hero." *Oh. Nice one, Lewis.* "Sometimes you remind me of him." *Oh...*

I pulled Pretty Girl inside my jacket and we watched the flaming slick of sun drizzle over the edge of the world. Seabirds cruised low over the salt marsh, and bulrushes rustled across the estuary where the Nehalem River tiptoes in to slip between the sheets of the sea.

I looked into my riding partner's face. Her blue eyes flashed green just as the last orange fire flared out of the sky and branded the image of her smile into my mind.

Standing with her in the dark, I started believing we could make it.

• • •

Cold and dark it was when we finally fumbled our way to my Mom's "beach cabin," a former real estate office situated on a quiet Gearhart street that has gentrified alarmingly in every direction.

We proudly parked our bikes in the only remaining all-grass driveway on the block, turned on the water, wrestled the door locks open and were only mildly perturbed when we couldn't get the lights to come on or the furnace fan to run. I did manage to get the burners on the gas range going.

"It's okay," said Pretty Girl. "We'll go get some pie and heat it up, and it'll make everything smell like home, and get us nice and warm." She may have noticed the ol' cabin was a touch musty.

Piling two-up onto the mini-Beemer because it still had rear pegs and a pillion, we repaired to the Seaside Safeway for frozen cherry pie and some light bulbs to replace the ones that mysteriously popped every time a switch was thrown, with a fistful of candles and a box of stick matches for backup. When we got back, we discovered the gas oven wouldn't fire up, either. That pie would need to go into a freezer, but I was afraid to crack open the crypt-silent fridge.

Sigh.

Pretty Girl shook out some sheets, and they exploded with bird dust and seeds. Silently, she drifted into the front room and sat down on my aunt's old leather sofa with a blank look.

1930s USN-surplus cots awaited us, sort of like a wooden rack featuring a hammock crossed with a straitjacket. Any bed beats no bed after a good, long, cold day. Pretty Girl crawled gratefully into the nearest one, and stiffened up. "It's... *wet.*"

I lunged for the spare sheets. They were damp, too.

Please, G-d, don't let her cry. I'd been telling Pretty Girl about the good old family cabin practically since we had met — how we used to pick blackberries in the summer, pull dinners of mussels off the rocks, play in the tide pools, and catch crabs by hand in the brackish river. She knew how important that place was to me.

"It's... always like this?," I told her, trying to remember if it was.

"Hey," she said, reaching out a hand. "Why don't you get in here and warm me up?"

Well, a few more bars of angel music wouldn't hurt anyone.

The sheets were dry and warm when we woke up, lending credibility to hypothermia guidance dimly remembered from my 70s-edition Boy Scout Manual. I turned on all four range burners and opened both doors to let the cabin hiss out vapor like a Mt. Saint Helens steam fissure, while

Pretty Girl rummaged through her gear and came up with a multi-meter.

"You carry a volt/ohm meter everywhere you ride?"

She looked at me like I'd just jammed my thumb in my nose. "Hel-LO! Guzzi owner?" *Oh. Yeah.*

At the box, I figured out that we had one leg of power out. The power company emergency line had a crew dispatched within a few hours to put it straight, and we enjoyed one halfway warm and better-lit night before heading south along the coast, toward closer approximations of home. I yanked off the road reflexively when we got to the Tillamook crab shack.

"Nice to see you!," Kari said, setting up a fresh pot.

Gurgling full of warm seafood, we struck south down the 101 past Beaver through Hebo, Cloverdale and Neskowin, over the summit past Otis to Neotsu and on through Lincoln City before turning east on SR 229. That road gambols south over the Euchre Mountain through Siletz before banging broadside into the 20.

Between Chitwood and Blodgett, Highway 20 is a veritable research library of smooth sweepers. It's abysmally mired in Airstreams and Winnebagos every weekend, but this was a Monday. The biggest blockade we saw was a horde of touring bikes led by a BMW R1150RT, painted a light enough shade that I tested the limits of ABS before realizing it wasn't piloted by a cop. We promptly returned to the kind of frisky behavior that resulted in my 190/50 getting cleanly scrubbed right out to the sidewalls. Pretty Girl and her Tweety weren't wasting any time, or lane space, either.

"You know you're on knobbies, right?," I asked at a sunglasses stop in Philomath, after our road's interest had broadened from the wiry technical toward the fatly scenic.

"It's a light bike," Pretty Girl said, grinning. I used to be amazed by people whose smiles could light up a room. Now I know one who can illuminate a whole highway.

She looked at me for a minute. "When we get to the junction —"

"I'll head north up the 99 from here," I said. I had work to do. In Seattle as in many places, the week starts Tuesday at motorcycle shops.

"Yeah… if it's okay with you, I'm just going to pretend you're on an errand, and you'll be back in a little while."

It was pretty close to true, and she was pretty close to me, so I reached out and hugged that pretty girl, as Arlo Guthrie might say, "once more… with *feelin'*."

Then she grinned, and flipped her visor down, and gassed that little Beemer up the highway. I rode in formation with her until the overpass at Corvallis, where I peeled off the exit and turned left, and she continued on to hit I-5 south at Albany.

On the overpass, I looked out to my right and saw my erstwhile travel partner burning east on her brave little bike. Golden fingers of sunset played warm over her jacket and ricocheted lightning off her helmet, and she shone like a brand new key.

October 2007, Motorcyclist

CHORD DIGRESSIONS

*Unplugged beats unplayed, no matter
what road you're following.*

There aren't many substitutes for motorcycles, but eleven
inches of sopping snow militates for alternative recreation.
Neither of my BMW S-bikes invite the use of chain straps
or short stainless steel fasteners threaded into their tread
lugs with a screw gun.

Thus it was the holiday season found me noodling around
on my old guitar, an original Silvertone some fifty years old,
filched from my mother the very first day I was tall enough
to reach over its dreadnought body. After leaving it wretch-
edly unplayed and standing in various corners for nearly
two decades to dry out between sprayings from my ex-wife's
cats, I finally broke it out a couple of years ago to re-string
— and promptly busted the tuning head on both sides.

The only guitar I'd ever played, and I'd killed it. Sonboy
offered the loan of his instrument, but I turned him down.
Unworthy even of a beginner model from Sears, I wasn't
about to beat on his Ibanez Artwood.

Pretty Wife (pre-marital edition) encouraged me to buy
another. Entry-level acoustics cost the price of a decent pair
of riding gloves, but I couldn't see it. When you've only ever
gone through one door, all the other doors look like walls.

Besides, I have this other axe, a different kind handed
down from Gramps. It's the double-bitted type that you use
on firewood. Despite regular applications of boiled linseed

oil, it's on its fourth handle. Regular spankings from a mill bastard file reduced one head to a vestigial stub, but the other side still splits old growth fir as well as it did before logging restrictions. While no church ever made me believe in resurrection, good old gear has no trouble carrying the argument.

Anyway it's a poor craftsman who blames his tools, so I headed down the street to visit our friendly neighborhood luthier at Guitarville. Two days later, the old girl had her head repaired, her neck adjusted and a fresh set of strings, all for $86.45. Despite all the dents and scuffs, she played like a new puppy. Maybe the VA should budget for a few experienced luthiers, as surely I'm not the only old soldier who could stand to have his broken head screwed back together.

Re-calibration of fingers after a few years off — like getting your land legs under you after a long sea voyage, or reentering the traffic stream with rusty motorcycle skills — takes some getting used to. Best to practice a bit before embarrassing oneself, but somewhere along the way my new mother-in-law caught me picking at my hand-me-down soundbox.

She raised a sharp red eyebrow but was polite enough not to say anything. By then I didn't care, anyway. In riding or noisemaking, it's easier to beg forgiveness than ask permission.

I just wanted to play. Like my old Slash Two, the old acoustic demands neither formidable skills nor X Games attitude to have a good time. Just sit down, pay close attention and before you know it, you find yourself singing right along. And this is how kind my little family is: no one in the household has yet suggested I wear a full-face helmet and a Respro Foggy when I practice guitar.

Stuck on first position, I don't play anything very challenging. Wide as a BMW twin, the classical neck prohibits barre chords. Gut string notes are plunky and quiet, more suitable for gentling down a fussy daughter with bedtime renditions of "Puff the Magic Dragon" than for "Rockin' in the Free World." When frat rats play air guitar, they are decidedly *not* simulating Sears Silvertone licks, any more than little boys making *rrrrrRRRRMMM* sounds are imitating the gentle burble of an old Beemer on a forest road.

Then along came Chanukah. Santa dropped in — curiously during the hours of daylight, badly road-soiled with his traveling suit gone completely brown and the cuffs worn off to shorts — bearing a bevy of boxes, two of which disgorged a hard-cased electric guitar and a sweet Fender practice amp.

I had no idea that my mother-in-law played guitar, much less a Schecter Omen-6. Turns out she closed that chapter a couple of years ago, hanging up her axe only when arthritic fingers finally stopped her rockin' the house.

Awestruck, I didn't pick it up at first but walked slowly around it, sniffing warily the way you might do if you were a Hondamatic rider about to swing a leg over your first Tuono R. It looked aggressive, capable and intimidating as hell — good enough that I would own every error and furthermore commit mistakes I hadn't even thought of yet.

But just as girls are meant to be kissed and bikes are meant to be ridden — even and perhaps especially the very good ones — instruments are meant to be played. If I wait until I have the skills for it, I'll never gain them. That's how that game works, so I sat down and started to play.

And sucked.

The narrow fret board had my fingertips bumbling into each other like officer candidates on a land nav course. Strings buzzed and distortion crinkled the sound as I flailed and drowned in the deep end of the pool. It was desperately embarrassing, obviously futile.

Eventually, slowly, it started to come together. My fingers recalibrated from the familiar old six-string, just as my throttle hand automatically recalibrates after jumping off my placid Sixties twin to seize hold of the 100-horse light switch of my latter-day boxer.

As with that bike-chotomy, the old guitar offers everything I need for a pleasant afternoon and bears irreplaceable memories to boot — but 15 watts of boost let me do things I never imagined doing on the Silvertone. Every time I unlatch the Omen's case I mess with it for at least two hours, discovering all manner of fresh musical barbarities.

Not just funky wildness and high volume, either. Its narrow neck finally made barre chords a legitimate prospect. Forty-four years old, I played my first proper F chord.

Plunking along a country road on my old bike is profoundly satisfying. I look down at the cylinders warming my feet and appreciate that they're beautifully made in a classic style, durable and effective within their limits. At 60 mph, the beggar's riding position feels natural all day long.

But without gooey modern tires, I won't ride to the edge of the tread. Öhlins shocks, wide wheels, fifty pounds less weight and serious power mean that even I can do things on my '07 S-bike that street motorcyclists literally didn't imagine when the R69S was designed.

The gifts of technology don't make me a better guitar player or a smoother rider, but they expand the envelope. My friendly old bike, with its sand-cast cases and gentleman's kick lever, is satisfying and reliable as Grandpa's axe. The new one, its alloys unapologetically shrouded in deep black plastic, is closer akin to my neighbor's log splitter.

Re-entry into a skilled avocation is always a daunting prospect, especially if you're not as good as you think you were back when — and *nobody's* as good as I remember, at least on bikes (I always sucked on guitar).

But as neither a professional motorcycle racer nor a gigging musician, I have the luxury of time for improvement. Maybe I'll work in some guitar lessons this summer, between track days and an MSF or Team Oregon advanced rider course. You can learn from anyone if you pay attention. You may find that lessons on what brings joy are as important as any other, and a lot more overdue.

Besides, hearing "that's too *loud!*" from my teenage stepson is very nearly as gratifying as provoking him to cluck that I ride too fast.

Maybe I'll work something else in this summer, and take Sonboy along on a moto camping weekend. If I borrow his padded gig bag and strap my crusty Silvertone to a chrome rack behind the pillion of that old bike, we can even play some homemade music around the campfire.

Everyone ought to wick it up sometimes, but it's good to unplug once in awhile.

December 2009, Motorcyclist

SEE AMERICANS FIRST

*Somebody told me that the best thing a vet could do was get
out of the house and go do something, preferably on a motorcycle.
Then, out of the blue, Mike called.*

Every day I look to see what I can do, but I'm not good at
that.

Crunching past the AAFES concessionaire on LSA
Anaconda in summer 2005, I stopped into an air-condi-
tioned hooch to thumb through glossy brochures of Jimmy
pickups, Mustangs and... *what's this?* A silver Harley-
Davidson Road King, posed along a desolate Utah highway,
framed by searing blue sky and a mesa backdrop. The white-
walls and leather bags of fuel-injected freedom.

Our own damned desert, and something to run across it.

I never bought that bike, but I held onto the brochure.
It's filed in a duffel bag, folded into a faded MOLLE pouch
between my lensatic moral compass and my Hollywood
knife.

I found other bikes to ride, but never settled on what to
do.

•••

Camp Patriot founder Micah Clark is no hand-wringing
writer type. A former FMF corpsman, SWAT cop and
gentleman of adventure, Micah returned from an overseas
contractor gig and settled into the 30-day fly fishing trip
he'd promised himself, back in the 'Stan. Right there in a
Montana trout stream, Micah received his mission.

Drawing line for a cast, he flashed on other vets returning from combat zones. "Those guys should be out here," he thought.

Camp Patriot is not a place but a plan, a purpose, an ideal. Camp Patriot produces hunting and fishing trips, Mt. Rainier summits, and even flew geriatric Army Air Force veterans in a WWII bomber, courtesy of the Collings Foundation.

"Everybody wants to do something for the young guys," he said. "We serve vets from World War II forward.

"If we can create a paradigm shift in their lives, show them what they're still capable of in the outdoors, that's what we're about."

Camp Patriot's motto is "giving back to those who have given." With 50,000 members in the Purple Heart Association alone and Camp Patriot (www.camppatriot. org) serving about 1,000 vets per year, Micah says, "Unfortunately, we're not going to run out of customers anytime soon."

With the VA taking on an estimated 10,000 veterans per month, chances are against it.

Mike Bender is another get-it-done guy. Tall, shaven-headed, fit and funny, Mike is a former Marine who deployed to Kosovo before founding Adventure Motorcycle LLC based in Hall, Montana. Once established as a motorcycle adventure guide, Mike decided he'd take disabled veterans on a bike trip. If that worked out, he'd do a few more. Mike resolved to pay the whole tab, mix in great roads and camaraderie, and have that stand as his bit.

"I wanted to do something with my passion for motorcycles," Mike said, " and I wanted to do something for vets."

Both Mike and Micah got frustrated with traditional veterans' resources. Mike couldn't persuade the VA to line up eligible disabled vets for the ride (participants were reached through the medical hold unit at Ft. Lewis, WA), and Micah lamented VFW and American Legion members keeping "one foot on the barstool and the other one in the grave." Showing NCO initiative, they put the ride together anyway.

•••

We would launch from the home of Micah Clark's father, Bill, a WWII Navy vet. At the Clark family's hillside retreat, we awaited our outriders from the Warrior Transition Battalion. Pink and orange fingers had stretched across the Big Sky by the time we heard them booming up the highway from nearby Libby, Montana.

Medically disabled, active duty soldiers Jonathon and Anthony rumbled over the road from western Washington in one day on their bikes, just to ride bikes some more. Either Bender's right and there is redemptive power in motorcycles, or they're just tougher than boot leather. Probably both.

Dismounting his Hyosung Avitar — a Korean arranged marriage between a Harley VRSC and a Suzuki SV650 — Jon stretched, unlimbered the cane strapped across his back and wobbled over to mumble hello from behind a pair of wraparound Wiley X shades. He rarely removes them for anything so trivial as nightfall.

Tony lit up a smoke and sat on his black H-D Street Bob, considering his surroundings. Then he got off, introduced himself quietly, walked to the porch and took another smoke break in the evening calm. Jon burned one, too.

We wouldn't see them again until dinner.

Following Clark family principles, Camp Patriot events are alcohol-free and Christian-flavored, but not pushy that way — there was no proselytizing beyond a dinner blessing. Suppertime conversation started with MOS discussions (the military equivalent of "what's your major?") and moved, like a campfire talk on bivouac, inevitably toward justifying our cripple-dick existences.

Built short and strong with pale eyes and a devilish smile under his watch cap and shades, Jon had been an EOD team chief. Explosive Ordnance Disposal, which sounds vaguely clinical and bureaucratic to the uninitiated, is Hell's own fireworks show. Stateside, it requires cautious professionalism married to extraordinary risk tolerance. In Iraq, it requires Jon.

"I have no sense of self-preservation," he told us, after his migraine subsided enough to eat. "That's why I'm good at EOD."

That's only one reason. Jon can also recite dozens of chemical formulations, hundreds of weapons nomenclatures, and can improvise an explosive device given five minutes, a pocketknife, his teeth and the stuff in your kitchen. "Blow your doors off" means different things to different people.

Despite his capabilities, by his early twenties Jon had suffered multiple, cumulative traumatic brain injuries and "some other stuff." These days, he describes himself as a kid who's about to be retired.

Tony, a vehicle fueler and multimedia specialist, made staff sergeant before developing a tin ear last year. Discovery of a cyst in his ear canal led to brain surgery and the long road to recovery while he awaits outprocessing into medical retirement.

"I just take one day at a time," Tony said, and looked around the table for a long moment. "This is a good one."

After getting blown out a second story window in Kosovo, Mike's "dropping hand" (left side) matches my own. Hashing out a route for the morrow, Mike asked if everyone was cool with it.

"Don't look at me," I told him. "I get lost on the way to the grocery store."

Raising his head from filling out liability waivers, Jon asked for the date and we gave him the digits. Jon wasn't kidding when he asked, "What month?"

It was like a family reunion: "Sick, lame, lazy 'n' crazy, *fall out to the rear!*"

•••

Weighing anchor at 0800 the next morning, we made steam for Glacier National Park. Mike keeps a string of low-mileage bikes, most of them BMWs, ready for delivery to Adventure Motorcycle customers just about anywhere in Montana.

"I can't rent bikes like these," he joked. "They're too expensive! So I bought a bunch instead."

Mike jumped on a bagged F800GS. His wife Melissa drove Camp Patriot's Dodge Ram (donated by Burlington Northern) and traded off with Bill on the V-Strom 650. The Ft. Lewis troopers rolled their own, and I tried to keep up on Mike's spiffy blue R1200RT. Pretty Wife, camera in hand, scampered around my pillion like a rhesus monkey on a rheostat.

If you're taking one day at a time, a good riding day in Montana beats a perfect day most anywhere else. Keeping miles per hour synched to degrees Fahrenheit, we flew up Highway 2 between purple mountains' majesty until we hit Kalispell, grabbed picnic supplies and fueled up for Glacier.

North of Kalispell, the highway is dotted with a truly awe-inspiring assortment of churches and methamphetamine recovery centers. A sign for a game park along the way read, "YOUR CAR IS YOUR CAGE."

Truer words…

Mike proved he could still improvise, adapt and overcome when he got National Parks and Federal Recreational Lands passes issued to our little joint expeditionary unit. The gate ranger looked at us funny when we signed statements affirming "permanent disability that severely limits one or more major life activities."

She saw four guys with all our limbs, each riding a motorcycle, and couldn't know that we all knew the definitions for ankylosis, edema and radiculopathy, or that our brain scans formed diverting treasure maps for lesion hunters.

Maybe that was the point. Thanks to Adventure Motorcycles and Camp Patriot, we got to go out and charge around just like everyone else. Capability over disability leads to possibility.

Over a picnic table in the park, I proposed to swap my H-D summer gloves for Tony's Second Infantry Division hoody. "I don't know," he said. "I'll think about it."

Gloves or not, he's a Harley guy to the bone for good and sufficient reasons. Tony is the second GI to own his Street Bob. The first soldier to own it bought that bike showroom new from Northwest Harley Davidson in Olympia, WA

— then promptly came down on orders to deploy for his second OIF tour. They bought the bike back from him at full retail, then sold it to Tony for $5,000 less.

No wonder the legions of H.O.G. stay loyal. If that behavior doesn't buy goodwill, then goodwill's too damned expensive.

Jon's Hyosung was less pristine, having suffered an intersection tipover at the hands of its mad bomber owner. Jon's key fob, valve stem caps and the handle of his cane are all eight balls.

Riding, he would randomly stand and bounce on the pegs, brandish his stick at oncoming traffic or execute dozens of swerves, cane strapped across his back and one bum leg cocked out in the wind. Snapping lake pictures with his clutch hand, Jon dropped off the pavement edge into roadside grass, but he steered it out with one-handed aplomb and the bulletproof luck of a bomb dismantler who survived to early retirement.

Dodging rocks and waterfalls along the 52 miles of snarling curves lining Going-to-the-Sun Road, it seemed we were the last helmet-wearing nerds in all Montana. Still, goodwill was rampant. Low-handed "cool guy" waves were regularly reciprocated even by rugged individualists on rat rides. Cars ahead actually utilized pullouts, a notion held in low esteem among Washington drivers.

At Logan Pass, 6,646 feet above sea level, we unzipped to let the wind whip through our riding gear and were cool for the first time since breakfast. Innocent of fear, a pair of full-curl Dall rams nosed around the parking lot like junkyard dogs. After watching one of them charley-horse his buddy's thigh, we kept our distance.

When Jon fell out at Logan, we loaded his Hyosung into the truck for the downhill phase. For the light-sensitive, standing on a spire extending 6,000 feet into the Big Sky on a cloudless day is still beautiful. It's just relentlessly painful.

But we had Micah's truck, Mike's ramp and plenty of willing hands. After playing as a group all day, working as a unit came naturally. No bike left behind! Even if it did bleed oil all over the bed…

Back down in the valley that evening, Mike staked us to room and board at Kalispell's Hilton Garden Inn. By the time we gathered for dinner in Blue Canyon Bistro, Jon was vertical again and ready to dismantle one of their infamous Chocolate Bombs.

Before dinner, our waitron favored us with such a juicy description of their bison prime rib that I ordered it instantly. Tony spoke up, too, only to hear that there was just one left. I switched my order to ribs only to hear Mike crack, "Obviously, *you* were never an officer."

Kind words from a fellow NCO!

Ten minutes later, our waitress rematerialized to inform Tony that they'd sold the last prime rib to somebody else and inveigle that for ten bucks more, she could bring him a plate of bison tenderloin. Not one to bitch and moan, Tony quietly poked his nose back into the menu, but Bill and Mike practically arm-wrestled each other for the privilege of upgrading him.

Obviously, they were never officers, either.

•••

What happens on a veterans ride? The same things that happen on any great ride. Experiences are shared, pacts of everlasting fealty are forged and polite smiles transform into rude cracks and belly laughs that make other tables turn and look. In one day's riding, we'd transformed from a group of reserved strangers into a band of synchronized delinquents sharing great stories, terrible jokes and desserts named after weapons. Turns out, that takes more than a few good men. It takes people of good will, and it is always a privilege to pass time among them.

With one more day of riding in store, we headed north the next morning along Hwy 93 through Whitefish, passing among the small and spooky histories of Lupfer, Olney, Stryker, Trego, Tobacco and Eureka to the high bridge vaulting Lake Koocanusa.

Jon was happy as a puppy when we stopped to cool off at an ice cream stand along the way. Predictably, they were out of the flavor Tony ordered. Apparently brain surgery made Tony a cone-half-full kind of guy, because he only smiled and said, "Hey, it's ice cream."

On the far side of Koocanusa, the road lashes like an angry snake. Unmaintained by any regular program, the reservoir road is lined with teetering trees, some hanging so low we could reach up and touch their lichen-limned boughs as we flashed underneath. Graded flat as a kart track, the road whip-curls along the reservoir's edge, slathered with slithy toves of cold patch.

I'm developing a taste for reservoir roads. BMWs seem designed with a margin of safety for unpleasant surprises; it's the flip side of their headroom for joy at the sudden delights with which reservoir roads are rife.

The torquey RT, sporting a stout chassis and vast preload adjustability, ate up the skittery pavement like piranhas on a poodle. With no other bikes in sight and the blue Beemer sliding like a slap-shot slug, Pretty Wife stowed her camera and sat quiescently for the first time that trip.

Lunch was served near Libby Dam at Blackburn's River Bend, a fishing resort with a roadhouse serving up solid grub and longstanding support for Camp Patriot's "Fishing with Heroes" program.

At Blackburn's, Tony negotiated cheerfully with our apple-cheeked blonde waitress. She was the only one surprised when he ordered the one thing on the menu that was out of stock.

Expansive after dessert, Tony went ahead and swapped me his 2ID sweater from the PX for my hot weather gloves from Harley, and we shook on the friendship.

"I can always get another hoody," he said. Cool. I have more motorcycle privileges than PX privileges these days. More importantly, Tony finally got what he wanted. It was his turn.

We crossed the Kootenai River south of the dam and eased onto Montana 37, following it along the river into Libby. Along the way, we stopped to dip our toes in the Kootenai Falls, talk a little more and watch healthy Mormon girls giggle past in the backs of pickup trucks, bound for Glory alongside the rest of we filthy degenerates.

We were almost mission complete. In Libby, the boys would split off to lash it back to Fort Lewis and another formation, another appointment, another checklist, another counseling session. Pretty Wife and I would head on to Kalispell in Mike's one-ton bike hauler, spend half a night in the Hilton, rise at 0400 and meet Mike for a hop to the airport.

What would we all do after that? Hard to say. As Jon put it, "Once you've spent time walking around in 130-degree heat, waiting for some douche bag to blow you up, life's pretty boring after that."

Maybe yes, maybe no. Mike and Micah found things to do, ways to be useful in this slowed-up, peacetime world. I believe Jon and Tony will, too. Dented or not, they're pretty close to unbreakable. Besides, they have motorcycles, time and friends to ride with.

On a good day in Montana, maybe that's all you really need.

January 2010, Motorcyclist

SPRINT ROOTS

This piece ran in a compilation of riders' first bike memories called "The Way We Were."

Our first bike existed primarily to hurt my Dad.

We watched in awe as Dad kicked over our "new" 1967 Harley-Davidson 250 Sprint. And kicked. And kicked. Ethyl dripped from the carb.

"Y'know," said my 260-lb. genitor, "sometimes you just have to get mad at it."

He leapt into the air, crushing down the cruel stub of a kickstarter. The horizontal cylinder blared to life and Dad triumphantly hobbled off on his sprained ankle.

Harley Sprints were popular for dirt tracking, but ours was pregnant with street gear and offended by its spotty maintenance regime. To ensure *multistrada* capability, we ran a ribbed streetie up front and a knobby out back.

One day, Dad hared up our half-mile gravel driveway right after work. The Sprint's engine snarled like a crop duster — then silence. Moments later, the doorbell rang. The creature on our porch resembled Dad on its right side, but its left side was a gooey blend of blood, skin and Hart, Schaffner and Marx suiting.

Blowing blood bubbles from the left side of its face, it said, "I think I sprained my ankle again."

Dad bought a Yamaha and quit riding the Sprint, but I rode it everywhere and learned many lessons, none of which were "trust the tires."

One afternoon I was in the garage, industriously flooding the carb, when Dad came in to offer encouragement.

"Get mad at it, Jack!"

I pinned the throttle, bore down with all 120 of my lbs. and POW! The end cap blew off the muffler, shot across the floor...

...and broke Dad's ankle.

October 2009, MotorcyclistOnline.com

STONED TO THE BONE

One of the dubious privileges of writing for a magazine is the chore of composing photo cutlines (that is, captions). When Motorcyclist *sent the layout for this piece, there were side-by-side images of several riders standing on a stone outcropping near Moab, Utah. I suggested one be cut, and jokingly offered this throwaway cutline: "Seconds after this photo was snapped, everyone pictured tragically plunged to their deaths. The engineer responsible now designs crankshaft bearings for Moto Guzzi." This was a little jab at Pretty Wife's fickle-engined Mille GT, and meant to be an inside joke.*

Art direction being not one of the privileges of writing, that issue went to print with picture intact and cutline unaltered. Joe the art director got the last laugh. We received several letters condemning the distasteful humor, and a couple from literalists expressing horror that we could make light of such a tragedy.

I was in the picture.

Always check magazines.

My antique Savage .32 automatic stows flat across the chest and travels well, with a gracefully nasty profile and no jagged steel to snag on the draw. Two mags should do it, each with a couple of snakeshot rounds up top, backed by eight Winchester Silvertips for enhanced tissue disruption on bigger game… no, wait. Security requirements should be low.

They had set me up for a full-house BMW factory gig, double-secret safety-checked and fully catered from soup to

nuts to deep-chested Bavarian *doppelbock*. Legitimate staff-
ers were booked solid with exciting new bikes, leaving not
a bench warmer in sight to post-pre-review the pre-ridden
F800GS that was already being delivered to buyers all over
the country. Editor Catterson had already gone deep and
bounced off the back of his Rolodex by the time I emailed
him, whining about imaginary back pay from 2006, and
inspiration hit: "Hey, *Mikey*... that dumb bastard'll eat
anything!"

Wheat-tressed Valkyries in six hundred dollar pants,
checking and double-checking, would delicately curlicue
each *scharfes S* and punctiliously dot every *punkt*. Any snake
found on the trail would suck a fangful of Zyklon B, the
last thing its flicking tongue would ever smell in that arid
Mormon rockpile. If pistols were required, I could expect to
be issued a finely oiled Luger holstered onto a sleek, ankle-
length leather overcoat...

Just a copy or two of *Motorcyclist* then, for the hard-core
press credibility that's in it and a soft, glossy solution for any
emergency trailside pit stops. Truly, it's the magazine best
suited to any authentic adventurer's survival kit.

Taking me at my word when I threatened to ride the
event in shredded Levis, piss-yellow ski goggles and tile
setter's kneepads, the Editor set about making connections
as though I weren't some back alley bike *ronin*.

Vaulting past our slavering hound, UPS rodeo clowns
scampered lithely over felled Douglas firs in our front yard
to deposit mysterious packages on the porch. From Western
Powersports came the first off-road pants I've pulled on
since I nearly tore off my lower left leg on a graveled road

in Olympia, some three decades back. Things have changed since then.

Name be damned, Fieldsheer Mercury pants won't make me any more fleet of foot, not with these knees. But serious armor extending from over the kneecap to just about the top of the boot meant my knees might make it through the rock pile without mayhem. The pants zip all the way up the side and are stuffed with zip-out thermal liners lofted from the finest of first-shorn infant peach fuzz. Cozy!

There's more armor over the butt, not enough to make me the world's most callipygian white guy but enough wiggle for a little faux badonka-donk, thank you very much.

What to say about the Fieldsheer Adventure jacket? I'm late to the plastics party. It always struck me as the artificial answer to an unasked question, proper kit for boy-men with pocketsful of iPods and Palm Pilots and Blackberry pop tarts. It burst out of the bag looking like a puffy bench cushion for a metal-flake 70s jet boat, weighing in as heavy as my *alt Schule* Langlitz goatskin.

But lo, attend: how snuggly doth it drape! Pockets every-where, including one perplexing pocket apparently sized for those cigarette three-packs once disseminated by heroin-chic honeys in downtown L.A. hotel lobbies. Spine-protected, weather-cuffed and lined with the same helium-infused infant furze as the Merc pants, it was toasty-soft from the first shrug-on. Once Pretty Wife showed me how to tighten the little snap bands that hold its elbow armor in place, I was all set.

Turns out, neither the jacket nor the pants were pedes-trian Cordura apparel with Scotchlite retro-reflective and Gore-Tex waterproofing (o, simpleton!). They are, if I read the blizzard of tags correctly, "Carbolex," slathered with "Rainguard" and "Phoslite" (the baby fuzz, for its part, is neo-traditionalist 3M Thinsulate). It looked stout, felt fine and whispered the thrilling rustle of new gear.

One box should have produced a fabulous new Shoei Hornet DS cross-dressed, triple-jump, pilot-visored sport helmet, fully suitable for knights-errant of road and desert. Foreswearing a majestic plume, I would elect in favor of technology. Alas, it was not to be.

The Shoei never showed. At the last minute, I borrowed a decade-old, carbon fiber THH hat with screaming yellow graphics from Toucan, a 270-lb. Supermoto racer who promised to crush my head — inside the helmet — if I dinged it up.

Preparation is everything to the professional. Tearing into military surplus boxes overflowing with squandered taxes, I unearthed an NOS pair of "GOGGLES, SUN WIND AND DUST" from the Mine Safety Appliances Co. of Pittsburgh, PA to strap over Toucan's vintage brain can. Next, I clipped a PRM-101 infrared personnel recovery marker to a fresh 9V Eveready and lashed the tiny works to the side of my borrowed lid under a thick layer of combat acetate, sealed down with six turns of duct tape.

If I was gonna test a high-tech package of bucks-up gear, I was determined to test it properly and there was *no* point in trying to find my own way on the strait and rocky gauntlet they had planned for me. It would be up to the search and rescue helo to pull my smoking carcass out of the first abyss to yawn at me like a hooker at dawn… best not to piss anybody off, then. Not right away.

Yanking gear out all over the living room, I crow-hopped into my new pair of Red Sea-parting FLY Milepost boots and tugged on Fieldsheer Aquasport gloves, color-matched to the jacket and obviously suitable for snow machine moose hunting with Troy Palin.

No damn wonder we all think we're ready for the Long Way Around these days. The minute I stood royally attired in that kit, I felt bulletproof for the first time since before I got shot at. Mackin' like that, I clanked out the door in my new armor to chainsaw up a few limbs in the yard.

"Where are you going?," asked Pretty Wife.

"Gotta get some scuffs on these boots," I mumbled. "Credibility's not free, y'know."

"Stand still!," she snapped, snipping off the tags.

With riding gear firmly stuffed into a mammoth rolling case, I spared a fond last glance for my Savage, then stuffed it back under teenage Sonboy's fetid socks where no one has the witless courage to look. My name already blots every TSA watch list, and I knew from bruising experience that their extended queries would be sufficiently probing without the need to explain an eminently portable pistol, no matter how elegant or collectible.

Checklist mostly complete, then. Without the least qualification, I was saddling up for a sere encounter with desert solitaire, plonking along on a borrowed motorcycle, fully kitted out in someone else's clothes. Nothing left to do but pull on my Under Armour and run down to Laughing Buddha to have my blood type, social security number and the letters "ADV" tattooed onto my taint where the flames reach last...

Live to pose, pose to work.

• • •

There would be no way to get the straight story from smooth corporate flacks, chicly attired in BMW Santiago Suits over functional layers, and I wasn't about to talk to any middle-aged "re-entry riders" scrabbling after implanted memories of virility.

No. To get the real skinny, you go straight to the dealership, skirting warily past ownership, management, sales, and anyone wearing trademarked tasteful attire.

Gator, my usual tech connection, wasn't around — probably off beating more probies into his retro-Honda gang, where the beer flows like federal bailout money and you really do meet the nicest people — but Johnny Nipples saw me kicking at the demo GS that was sidestanded out front. Checking to make sure the general manager was hiding in his office and pretending not to goggle at porn clips, Johnny sidled out for a high five on the low down.

"The 650 has the same engine as the 800," he sneered. "Lower seat, weaker brakes, softer wheels. You don't want to jump it.

"Weighs a little less, at least."

"So, basically a neatly gelded adventure Schwinn for whiny little girls and the elderly?"

"Ayep."

"Sign me up."

We watched a Nissan Flagship Battlewagon Armada, hi-viz yellow with dock bumper tires, idle carefully into the no-wake zone and drop anchor. Its silver-tipped pilot slid down the ratlines, programmed his surgically precise features to "gunfighter squint" and sauntered across the parking lot with an arthritic tough-guy strut.

"Must be inconvenient," I muttered, "driving around town in all that Gore-Tex and Cordura."

"He's here to buy a GS," Nipples answered. "They all drive those fuckin' stupid things."

"Got any GSs in stock?"

"Nope."

• • •

I secretly hoped that the press people would stun us with a short, sharp application of the Munich mavens' narrow, nasty new "enduro," 450cc of barely street-legal power with a fulsome top-end snap waiting to drill us into the ground at the clip of a neutering wire, but it was not to be. That bike is for factory riders and X-Games punks with glazed pupils and rubber bones, not middle-fat freelancers sporting expansible trou.

No, we'd be out cow trailing in the care of nanny riders, albeit on Neanderthal stone paths where cows desiccate to jerky in time for afternoon tea. As advertised, we'd be mounted on twin-cylinder, liquid-cooled, fully optioned Clark Kent commuters, ensuring that the first bike to pin me to the rocks would weigh a solid 456 lbs. dry. That's the weight of two (2) Chevy 350 bare blocks with a first-grader jumping up and down on them. Unless, of course, I crashed out on the 800cc "650," in which case my maladjusted first grader would be demoted to a toddler.

What's the worst that could happen?

• • •

"Open up my email and see if you can pull out any phone numbers," I barked into my scratch-fogged flip phone.

"Isn't there anyone there with a sign or something?," Pretty Wife asked reasonably.

"There's like a forty-foot limo out front, but that can't be right."

"You should check. Oh, by the way, your new helmet just came in."

Turned out the stretch Lincoln was in fact occupied by various moto and men's mag journos, insouciantly sprawled across pale blue leather under twinkling starlit ceiling mirrors in the kind of sordid tableaux that constitutes a prom queen's night terrors in full living color.

One of my Bic Round Stics (mark of the working professional) had exploded into my helmet bag during the flight, spattering Toucan's racing hat with smeary, blue-black teardrops. I wiped an ink-sticky palm across my second-hand jeans, stuck it out and shook the hand of the guy closest to the door.

"Jack Lewis, (mumble)cyclist," I growled.

The gig was on.

• • •

BMW doesn't fart around on these junkets. This is well known. But I had no conception of just how pampered an "adventure ride" could really be. Sorrel River Ranch Resort & Spa is a rustic cattle spread on the Colorado River, if your definition of "rustic" encompasses that peculiarly Western novelty of tender cosseting with dulcet luxury overlaid by the thinnest scrim of a rough-hewn aesthetic. It could have been the lodge at Sun Valley, Lake Quinault or Timberline, where the purpose of cowboy hats is protecting $300 foil jobs. I smiled smugly and stopped worrying about gnarly technical bits.

Maybe I shouldn't have.

Fresh off the assembly line, vertical twin GSes were sprinkled liberally around the ranch, including a pair posed against the Colorado River in a gentle wash of color-gelled spotlights. The Colorado itself was conveniently placed adjacent to the hosted bar (just where a pretty river should be), and I was several Dead Horse Ambers to the good by the time we stumbled in to receive a chipper and highly detailed product briefing by several highly informed factory sources. No idea what any of them said, but we were thoughtfully provided with switchblade flash drives stuffed with pertinent data.

A striking German girl (we'll call her "Liesl") then exhorted us all to wear BMW "apparel items" as frequently as possible. Sparkling, deep brown eyes, endless legs and an enchanting Bavarian lilt made Liesl marvelously persua-sive. Epiphanically gob-smacked, the spirit was urging me forward to confess my ill-accoutered sins.

BMW loves us, but we can all do better. You yourself should invest in closetsful of fashionable BMW clothing systems — immediately, please, as your loyal scribe would very much like to go adventuring again in the style to which I've suddenly became accustomed. Zipping open the rondel-embossed organizer placed on the table in front of me, I clicked open my case-hardened, inktanium alloy BMW-logo *Kugelschreiber* and made a note to get right on that.

A few minutes later, Liesl's voice cracked slightly. Fired by lightning journalistic reflexes, twenty experienced arms lunged for iced pitchers. I was first to the pretty girl with a full water glass. Remember, students: kids who sit in the front row get better grades.

It was the last time I'd be first in anything on that trip.

• • •

BMW motor culture is a curious phenomenon, luxury crossed with purposeful seriousness and multiplied by a traditional Protestant work ethic — not the one where Jesus is your drinking buddy, but the one where G-d blesses the gifted and industrious. Accordingly, chow call was 0700; safety briefing 0745; kickstands up and locked by 0815.

I stumbled out to the bike burdened by certain regrets. Liesl had joined me at dinner, smiling, laughing at my slack-jawed jokes and murmuring softly of the sensuous satisfactions offered only by those "BMW apparels." As the only two there who knew absolutely that we couldn't ride off-road worth a crap, we giggled over cabernet sauvignon until well past the dessert course (note to self: espresso ice cream has real espresso in it).

"Enough!," I resolved, mopping up the last drips of pear pudding with a practiced swipe of my supple lower lip. "I must prepare!"

I stumbled out to purge my sins under the coal-black purity of a Utah night but Liesl followed at my elbow all the way back to my room, lighting our path with the magical sparkle of her luminous indigo eyes (a BMW factory option, as it turns out). Ambling slowly toward adjacent rooms under the star-crystaled Utah sky, Liesl pretended not to know about the Milky Way just to make me feel like an expert in something.

Defying the soft charms of her insistence, I kept a white knuckle grip on my fig leaf of journalistic integrity and took from Liesl only test pairs of GS gloves (lighter than my prepacked Aquasports) and Boxer goggles. You have to draw the line somewhere.

By morning, the only thing I could remember to regret were all those Dead Horses beating me. Liesl sensibly opted to drive the truck.

• • •

We rode motorcycles, too.

At the morning briefing, we happy few were split into two groups: the Blue Group and the Kick Jack's Ass group. My false-flag operation as an experienced representative of *Motorcyclist* magazine having borne fruit, I was duly sentenced to the latter group.

Does it need pointing out that these guys can really ride? I was over my head before we left the parking lot, but the quickest way to improve is to play above your ranking…

Incremental practice is the safer road to improvement, but it was too late for that. When last I messed around with off-road riding, I was 16 years old and it nearly took my leg. I pushed that out of my mind as we shut off our ABS (one-button actuation, no key cycling required) and tore into the first dirt section, 13 miles of loose rocks and sand with 22 water crossings. No brain, no pain.

I discovered I freakin' love water crossings, and not only because of the happy otter splash. There's an ego-securing mystery to it when you can't see what's under the surface. If you never saw what knocked you down, it clearly wasn't your fault. Taking my neighbor Tony's pre-trip advice ("Gas on, brains off; you can't get hurt in the air"), I blasted through dozens of creek beds, giggling deliriously as the bike stolidly refused to throw me into the rocks.

As a bonus, the FLY Mileposts only took on toe water once when it poured over the tops — and my feet were dry by lunch without changing socks. There might be something to this technical clothing fad, after all.

Zipping through corners felt sweet, too. The middie GS may not be magic, but I found it a real *au pair* for the dirt, nursing me through a thousand foolish errors with my hide (if not dignity) intact.

Following the faster guys underscored where dirt riding differs starkly from street riding. "Trust your tires" is right out, for instance. But it also reminded me of one great similarity: corner exits are the fun part, but if you blow your corner entry bad enough, you flop through the turn in a bar-sawing, crash-dreading, full body flinch. I got tired in a hurry following those guys (did I mention they were fast?), and after blowing a dozen corner entries in a row finally remembered that they were easing along at a comfy, all-day pace while I was dialed out to eleven-tenths with redlined eyeballs bouncing on my cheek bones.

That first section was tight and rocky stand-up riding with stone cliffs offering stony shoulder berm shots to the unlucky and an unhealthy smattering of crevasses and cliff faces for the truly screwed. *Slow down before you bail, wing nut!* I set myself a second gear limit. Call me a pussy, Bucky, but the bastard does 70 mph in second gear and peels away tire knobs like old, dry scabs. It's like some mutant super-bike for the dirt.

I'd been dreading "Baby Head Hill" since the ride briefing made me sick to my breakfast. Slick and narrow, with one decent line between the ruts and a thousand rolling red spheres the size of toddler skulls, it looked ominous enough on the overhead even before our safety briefers warned us, "It's *way* steeper than it looks in this picture."

We had a few rock-picking slow sections to practice along the way, and I decided the engine was my friend. It may wind out to street bike power — we sure as shit didn't have 85-horsepower dirt bikes when *I* was a kid — but it also pokes along at the bottom of first gear as contentedly as a donkey browsing clover. As for the chassis, it seemed in no hurry to throw me onto my beak. I had to appreciate that...

Still, after one twisting, narrow climb that topped at yet another stunning vista across rusted rainbow canyons, I stopped and pretended to admire the view while I caught my breath and wondered how in G-d's name I'd make it up Baby Head.

My left shoulder compensates for my torn right rotator cuff. It was fried hard. My knees weren't in pain yet but had stopped approximating any kind of shock-bearing utility, and a short stack of herniated lumbar disks were telegraphing threats of lurid vengeance all the way to my feet. The bike was purring like a kitten, tight as a virgin mosquito, but the rider module was smoked. Our ride leader pulled up next to me.

"So, how'd ya like Baby Head Hill?"

There you have it. Some journalists are fast, I am unworthy, and the bike is magic.

Not immortal, though. We weren't three miles in before Ron Larsen's 800 spit off an improperly torqued brake caliper and broke his sub-fender off the left side. Served him right for picking a gray bike. Everyone knows yellow is faster. All his brake bits were found after brief searching, and it turned out to be a trailside repair — but not with the underseat toolkit. The calipers are rider-proofed with *male* Torx bolts.

"It's like a Torx outie," Ron said, scratching his head. "What the heck?"

Seizing my multitool, he snubbed down his caliper bolts. The Leatherman Wave is the American Express of off-the-reservation travel. Don't leave home without it, Hero. Even my brilliant Fieldsheer Adventure jacket doesn't have enough pockets for a rollaway full of tools.

We gave brief consideration to tearing off the unbroken side of the subfender, but since it provides the routing points for all front brake lines the consensus was to let it flap.

Those two front disks are all you need and then some. Even on the street, they're a powerful two-finger stop. Shut down the ABS and you can howl it to a stoppie even on knobby tires.

Second wind for your Faithful Correspondent came when the trail system opened up and I transitioned from herding a two-cylinder trials bus to Mad Max desert blasting. Crow hopping from rock to rock at 80 mph is *fun*, Bubba, an alluring scent of bad fun that'll land you in the trauma ward in a hurry, but this bike is the St. Pauli Girl of motorcycling. No matter how coarsely you slap her broad Bavarian bum, she just smiles and serves up another round.

Cutting way too deep into one corner, I tapped the back brake and got bent badly out of shape, sawing at the bars and kicking lowside rocks out of the way until the only thing left to do was pour the coal to it and pray...

The Yellow Peril's back end snapped around, drooling wanton as the twitching hips of an ovulating stripper...

Snarling and biting at the snaffle bit of my discretion, she clawed furiously out of the turn, perforated the sacred Native American ground with little black scores of toasted knobby, flat-out-belly-to-the-ground and I. Slowed. Down.

I've seen fractures, experienced them, treated them, precipitated them, and run on them. It was time to let the dust clouds stretch out ahead, and maybe live to ride another junket.

Breathe, Lewis. This is just for fun.

Just before our break, on a fast, right-hand, uphill sweeper along a perfectly packed dirt road, nirvana politely introduced itself. Within 150 steep yards, the terrain transitioned from rocky desert to semi-arid alpine territory and we plunged broadside into a whispering boulevard of quaking aspens, quietly chiming their breeze-stirred leaves, yellow as the front fender of my bike. If there is a better way to squander some hours of life than this, I have not found it.

I had remembered my jacket liner in the chilly morning but forgot to ask for a tank bag to stow it in (OK, I didn't forget — the thing pokes up as inelegantly as a podium built by remedial vo-tech students, but it sure looked useful in retrospect and I wished I'd requested it. BMW's excellent Vario expandable hard saddle bags are also available). By the first planned break, I was as knackered, sweaty and out of place as a show pony pulling plow. Over a nearby peak, rain clouds gathered.

"We're going up there," our guides grinned. *Oh, thank, G-d.* I've been hotter in gear before, but rarely as a form of recreation. It wasn't until after I got back home that I discovered my Fieldsheer has a big tail pocket to stow its own liner. Hey, I don't read instructions! Asking directions is for pansies, too. We tough guys just follow the BMW wrangler…

A word about Beemer-style breaks: we're not talking piss-warm Gatorade from the fanny pack (although I found a nice fanny pack in the basket delivered to my room). BMW's event management is as rigorously detailed as Mom's arrangements for my seventh birthday party. Umbrella girls lined up under a sun fly practiced princess waves over the bounty spread before us: iced energy drinks, 40 brands of upscale protein bars and fistfuls of handy pain-killer packs. Go off in search of a tree to water your horse, and they chased you down with a bathroom trailer featuring hot and cold running everything. Like a homeless guy at the King's Table buffet, I furtively tucked a couple of spare lens wipes into my jacket…

•••

Rested, ready and back on the road, I assessed the character of our adventure versus the suitability of the bike. How would an F800GS do in the middle of an African savannah without magic maintenance fairies, goggle nurses and Class A restrooms in hot pursuit?

Pretty damned well, I'd say. The nature of the F800GS is to stay out of your fun-havin' way. About a hundred pounds dropped away every time I let out the clutch (could have been those fairies again), and it steered with confidence through the dirt — with one exception. In a naked attempt to make me feel at home and suitably annoyed, some wiseass had imported hundreds of tonnes of Iraqi "moon dust," the sifted flour of steering disaster.

Relying on dim flickers of memory from 28 years previous, I had come to terms with setting the GS into corners with its handlebar and steering it out on the rear tire but that lunar dust was a different story, so loose and greasy that neither end was connected to control. The only hope was to lean back, twist its neck and supplicate Buddha with all the desperate sincerity my panicked heart could fake. The deficiency of that tactic lay in the relentless acceleration of the bike. Riding out an 80 mph tankslapper is not my notion of dirty delight.

Turns out I wasn't the only one who noticed. Ron, who after bolting his brakes back together had been roosting my sorry butt all morning, said, "Y'know, for awhile there I was thinking these (Metzeler Saharas) were completely amazing. Then I got into that loose dust...

"They're *good* tires, but they're not amazing."

Following a spirited descent from the stone ridges of Utah onto the high plains of Colorado, lunch was served on brilliant linen under a white awning at the Gateway Colorado Auto Museum. As chefs flourished their toques over unpronounceable savories, all our brake calipers were perfectly torqued by preventive maintenance pixies. I'd never really imagined such a distinct juxtaposition of hard riding and soft living. Bavarian moto-gnomes had stitched us a tapestry of luxury, sport and security on the order of a presidential candidate's snow boarding trip.

Falling into my seat, I took a breather, 800 mg of ibuprofen, and stock of the situation.

Lessons learned: if you're gonna ride a long adventure loop in the desert, best be a skilled off-roader or in stunningly good physical shape — *not* neither. The first question you should ask yourself is, "Self, can you stand up on the pegs for 150 miles?" If the answer isn't well north of "*maay-*

be…," you should probably go anyway, but in the full knowledge that you're going to get your ass kicked firmly and continuously.

It came down to a Hobson's choice of pain. Stand up and immolate my knees like beeswax candles, or sit down and get my can pounded. Either way, I'd be all right. Sore knees and pounded asses are well-documented risks of freelancing.

After a lingering look at dozens of the world's sexiest cars — like Sophia Loren, a '32 Auburn Speedster never goes out of style — we remounted for post-prandial larking about.

What a truly good badlands bike this is. We fled fluid and fast across the open range, tearing out of corners on silky crescendos of torque. I can't report our average speed or fuel consumption, as the bottoms of my bifocals fuzzed out the clever LCD menus of the optional computer. Besides, I hadn't brought my 13 year-old son along to explain the functions to me. At least the engine was easy to grok.

Like an original Stoner rifle with the selector set on rock'n'roll, the saddletwin opens up smooth and steady and just keeps on cycling faster if you hold the trigger down. It lugs, it guns and it raps out clean. Back in the pre-Corinthian era when I rode dirt bikes, they didn't weigh a quarter-ton or have radiators bolted to the front — but they didn't make 85 hp, either.

Climbing into alpine territory again, we were all having a high old time scooting through tree-lined roads when we rolled up on an M&M-red minivan parked in the dead middle of the road. Standing next to it was 324 lbs. of shivering Fine American Woman tightly squoze into four strained ounces of cinnamon-peach double knit, surely the most terrifying sight of the day.

I watched her Scottie dog leap and snap at the three bikes ahead of me while the mountain woman videotaped an unmoving box canyon and jabbered obliviously into her cell phone. Miraculously, all the guys ahead got through without squashing the darting fur ball. I missed it, too. Note to self: next time, pack the Savage into checked baggage. A .32 ACP dust shot cartridge is just the ticket for dispatching antagonistic terriers at close range.

I cherish a working theory that to each of us is allocated a measurable daily dose of stupidity — and that this is not a per-capita percentage. No matter how far you venture from the endlessly teeming stupidity of town, your personal inanity quotient will track you down. Even the Legendary Motorcycle Mavens of Germany couldn't plan around it.

That episode was our Calvinistically predestined moment of transcendent hell, and the Fine American Woman was dropped right into the middle of Freakin' Nowhere specifically to provide it. She and her dog may actually have vaporized after the last bike disappeared back into the woods...

Two turns later, I slid out of a corner and blasted onto a veritable esplanade lined with even more glorious, golden aspens. Bursting into the sound of music was my first impulse, but it turns out off-road helmets don't have the same lovely resonance as full-face street lids. Also, rain hurts your face. Who knew?

Previous to this trip, I had been unaware that BMW engineers were capable of fine-tuning the weather. The rain cooled me down, woke me up, showcased the many virtues of my Fieldsheer Adventure jacket (not just lots of pockets but pretty darned waterproof, too) and dampened the roads and trails just enough to improve traction. Joseph Smith smiled as we worshiped reverently at the Church of the Latter Day Supercrossers.

By this point, I was sitting most of the time. On open dirt roads, the tall, flat seat of the GS lets you slide up close enough to bejewel the fore-mounted air/battery box, stick down an outrigger boot, cross up the bike and flat track it through the sweepers. That, friends and neighbors, is the king of fun.

There may be no bad motorcycles, but that doesn't prevent there being some *very good* motorcycles. The hornet yellow (actually, "Sunset Yellow") GS gave me the confidence to run hard on unknown roads with changing surfaces. It is a very good motorcycle.

My squawk list was short. The shock (innocent of linkage) could use more rebound damping, and I wondered if an Öhlins unit would be optional.

As an aside, the swingarm is a pretty thing, made lighter than *Afrika Korps* boxer GSes through the wonders of shaftectomy. Its countershaft sprocket aligns with the swingarm pivot. Perhaps BMW will finally be the outfit to successfully patent this notion.

Heavy rear peg risers that stick out should be unboltable, not welded to the frame, because pillion pork merits a line-item veto. Say "no" to earmarks for extra pegs!

Mid-morning, I experienced an odd midrange fueling gurgle for about six minutes. Could have been a slurp of water in the gas, or a panicky throttle hand. The sticker on the subseat fuel tank demands high-test, but if you need to ride through Somalia (or Newark) the bike's gas-huffing computer has the olfactory judgment of an oenophile. It allows the bike to drink Third World gas at the cost of a squib less horsepower.

Worst gripe: the skid plate is inadequate. In a curious engineering decision, the 8GS has a plastic plate that doesn't wrap up in front of the engine and seems insecurely penetrable. Surely a thicker engine condom wouldn't impair handling feel… The plate needs to be able to resist the bike and rider's full weight dropping onto a sharp rock.

It also needs to wrap a few inches up in front of the engine. One rider sucked a rock through his oil/water heat exchanger just an inch above the leading edge of his skid plate. For the record, that bike quit steaming and finished out the day in a feat of magical self-healing worthy of a Messerschmitt limping home over the Channel.

What is good? The transmission is good. I've owned three German bikes and ridden dozens, and this is the first BMW that shifts like buttered silk even through my bolted-up kluge of an ankle. It felt Japanese enough to send shivers of Axis worry down my padded spine.

The riding position is variable and good. Better riders griped about the plastic wings forward of the seat, but when standing I was mostly too scared to notice them.

Spiffy pegs have rubber street tops that pop off, exposing useful croc teeth.

The engine is very, very good. An F800ST mill tipped up to near-vertical, it has a dummy rod to ensure that the tasty little snarl it makes isn't translated into Magic Fingers grip vibes. Torque and power claims of 61 lb.-ft. at 5,750 rpm and 85 bhp at 7,500 rpm make for a modestly exciting streetbike and a king-hell off-road snorter.

The best feature is BMW's heretofore unannounced Autopilot Rider Replacement (you read it first in *Motorcyclist*), which trumps ABS and traction control with a robo-*gestalt* solution for rider safety.

Mid-afternoon, I entered a downhill, off-camber, decreasing radius left-hander. Too sexy for my skill set, I was coming in hot when the surface transitioned inconveniently into moon dust and I realized for the forty-sixth time that day that what you can see can hurt you.

And was about to.

I poked out a boot and was levering at the handlebar like a pellet-crazed rat when I slid past the apex and straight across the bow of an onrushing Dodge Ram pickup.

Aiming for a narrow strip of road to his right, I missed completely and segued nimbly into a nasty high side. By the time I finished wincing at imminent traumatic amps, I was deep into a bar-banging tankslapper and headed for the rocks.

I don't know what happened next. Suddenly, I was rolling gently along the ditch bottom. A little burp of throttle eased 'er back onto the road, and off the bike and I went, both of us shaking our heads in wonder. This year's Gelände/Straße is like a jet pack for adventure squids. Near as I can tell, I crashed two or three times right then and there and Chitty Chitty Bang Bike just refused to cash the check.

If BMWs can do that, maybe they don't need skid plates at all.

Overall, my bike was as quietly disciplined and relentlessly competent as a Special Forces expense claim. When attacking paved twisties at a pace that was moderately short of "madman," tipping it into 90 mph sweepers resulted only in a tiny hunting sensation as the front knobby squirmed in protest.

A short straight saw 115 very blustery mph indicated. Although there's a sit-up sweet spot of around 70 per, road wind made me want to test the accessory touring windscreen. With its stout brakes and modest weight, a GS on streetier tires and perhaps with stiffer fork springs would make a fairly fierce road assault weapon.

Factory reps indicated that supermoto wheels aren't contemplated, but I don't think that's this bike's mission, anyway. A gender-bender bike with the 800's motorvation and an upgraded "650" chassis might really star in the streetside hack-&-squirt role, but this horse was built tall in the saddle for gazing over the top of your commute traffic, all the way to a distant horizon.

Utah blessed my sight with interesting fauna all day long. My critter count for the ride included morning deer, enough squirrels to feed a whole trailer park, one golden eagle fattening nicely on squirrel meat, two jackrabbits and one streaking lynx. Plus a fine and beastly bike that never ran away from me all day. Like a young but smart horse, it put up with my shenanigans long enough to make it back to the barn for fresh oats.

Is it the horse for me? I don't know. The GS was sumptuously comfortable through every inch of off-road, but I paid for my fun on straight paved sections as my spine, momentarily undistracted by survival concerns, peevishly ran down the litany of my every episode of foolish living. Hard to say how that would play out for in-town riding and let's face it: I won't be spending 90 percent of my riding life haring around Moab. Besides, it's only 14 lbs. lighter than my R1200S street bike, and I can make up half that difference by unbolting Black Betty's passenger pegs, and all the rest with her Akrapovic pipe.

But the F800GS is almost *50 lbs.* lighter than its big dual-sport brother — and about a thousand pounds narrower. If the mid-F is a two-wheeled jeep, the R1200GS is a Land Rover station wagon — and the ginorphantine R12GS Adventure is a Unimog.

My wife can't get over the sexy singles scene. I know lots of folks like that. "Some of my best friends," etc. Like many of them, she rides a 2004 BMW F650GS.

Make no mistake, you can strap coffin-sized panniers to an Aulde Academie 650GS single — washing machine motor and all — and flog the thing to Prudhoe Bay and back. Many have.

With a team of mules and a modest DoD grant, you could also wrestle an R12GSA up the Rubicon Trail, although I'd hate to watch.

But an F800GS would make those things fun, and I came home to an unused Shoei dual-sport helmet that cries out to be field-tested.

I hear Argentina is nice this time of year.

January 2009, Motorcyclist

Hacked on

Pretty Wife was soaking in the tub when I tapped gingerly at the door, mumbling. "Good news and bad news.

"Which do you want first?"

Prompted for the better news, I said, "There's one S/TEP course scheduled before Boomershoot."

"Damn it, Jack." I heard a long sigh from the other side of the door.

"It's the weekend you promised me a vacation, isn't it?"

Tire warmers were insufficient. Pushing through our 27-degree fogbank, I wanted asphalt warmers. A lousy morning to be up on two wheels, but just right for sidecar frolics.

Boeing Space Center hosts several ranges of riding instruction administered by the Evergreen Safety Council. Holding the contract for Washington State motorcycle safety instruction, Evergreen is the elegant avenue to buffing up your endorsement collection. Completion card in hand, you belly up to the DoL counter, pay 25 bucks for yet another lousy picture and walk away with another skill set franked onto your license.

Once you pass the course.

Evergreen's S/TEP (Sidecar/Trike Education Program) instructors are serious people packing a detailed syllabus. Riding a three-wheeler isn't rocket science, but it's remarkably unlike any two-wheel experience. Like SCUBA or skydiving, you must absorb unnatural knowledge — tip line equations, accelerating against your brakes, and sudden shifts from truck steering to countersteering.

Like college, there's no money-back guarantee. For 125 bucks, you get a one-weekend opportunity — come rain, shine or hyperborean fog — to grasp something new and demonstrate competence.

Can't hack it? Try again in a few months. Because this constituted my only chance to S/TEP up before a planned Ural adventure, I paid close attention to primary instructor "Krash" and tried not to smart off too much.

Starting with ballast monkeys, we progressed through basic turning and braking to complex maneuvers, throttle-brake balancing and emergency evasions. Once our monkeys climbed out, vehicle dynamics instantly became less balanced and more interesting. Like youth soccer, swerving a sidecar outfit amuses onlookers more than participants.

I spent my weekend on a Ural Tourist, a demilitarized (i.e. no machine gun mount) Soviet army M-72 sidecar rig. The beast carries more ferrous metal than our hatchback, and a pair less horsepower than my 1969 BMW "Slash Two." Fortunately, our instructors were good enough to point out where the transitions lurked between "riding" and "driving," because this was like no motorcycling I've ever done.

Left turns — performed on the gas with front Brembo dragging, power wheel spinning and car wheel drifting — were a cross between snowmobile shredding and sprint car driving. Hard rights were like wrestling, ever so politely, with an amorous alpha sow. You do *not* want to wear a hat with a 717-lb. dry weight.

After a written exam on Saturday night, we took the performance evaluation around noon on Sunday so the instructors could cut our two trike guys loose, then proceeded to dessert: flying the car.

That part is a curriculum bonus, not a testable item. Lofting the hack, like spinning an aircraft or sliding a motorcycle, is something you can either practice under control or learn on your way to the crash site.

Finding the balance point to live that long, delicious moment as a gravity scofflaw is epiphanic. So nerdy it's cool, it's the white guy's Funky Chicken. Cage drivers are outraged by sidecar riders lifting their leg at the world. It looks like cheating.

Maybe, on a bleak January day featuring black ice on the road, it really is.

May 2009, Motorcyclist

BOOMERSHOOT

Pretty Wife anticipated Boomershoot approximately like this:
"Skitchy vet who's got about five minutes of sidecar experience
borrows someone else's Ural to ride across two states, hang out
with armed strangers, and shoot at exploding targets.
"What could possibly go wrong?"

My grandfather knew good technology when he tried it
— and he tried it all.

In the 19-teens, Grandpa flew the U.S. Mail in de Havil-
land biplanes. He roared through the Twenties on a Harley-
Davidson J Model, beating a set of Slingerland Radio Kings
with his jazz band on the weekends.

Gramps liked good gear. When he finally got tired of
horseback hunting, he bought himself a Willys pickup,
the first 4WD in McCall, Idaho. Behind the seat rode his
trusty Model 70, a "rifleman's rifle" that emerged from
Winchester's New Haven works around the time the first
Ural rigs shipped to the Soviet army.

By the time that rifle came down to me, it was field-
scarred and scruffy — and nothing like cutting edge — but
it still shot better than I could on my best day, long before
the shakes and flinches set in. Even so armed, however, I felt
woefully unprepared when a drinking buddy invited me to
check out Boomershoot '09, a long-range shooterpalooza in
north-central Idaho.

My *kamerads* at Irbit Motor Works had promised a lend-
lease 2WD Ural Safari, brand new and tarted up in desert

camouflage with fuel can, ammo carrier and spotlights. I was rubbing my hands together with anticipation when Pretty Wife arched an eyebrow and said, "Don't you need an endorsement for those?"

Much scrambling around resulted in my taking a sidecar class in frozen fog, which would prove appropriate preparation. Meanwhile, back at the national distributor, my fully optioned loaner was sold to some cooler guy to go the Long Way. When I showed up to kick start my big adventure, they led me instead to a seven year-old test mule, decked out in rust-bubbled olive drab.

Smacked around for 66,000 kilometers, an '05 mill in an '02 frame with '0-everywhen dings, the shop beater was a blueprint match for Grandpa's old rifle.

Some assembly was required. Factory hackmeister Sergei is on the short side, and his solo perch positioned me like a shy boy at the urinal. We unbolted it in favor of the standard loaf, an excellent all-day saddle.

I asked about maintenance.

"No, nothing."

I pointed at the dipstick. Sergei just shook his head. The man is a believer.

After admonishing me to shut off the gas at every stop lest hydraulic lock shear the crankshaft in two (don't laugh — this is actually possible), Sergei sent me wobbling out into eastside traffic.

I signed nothing. They held my black Beemer hostage. Everyone was nervous. Only I was armed.

•••

The next morning at oh-gray-thirty, Pretty Wife bustled around packing double-bagged electronics, extra duds and road snacks into the capacious trunk. I contented myself with wrapping boxes of match-grade ammo into a double-rubber *Wehrmacht* bag strapped to the outboard nerf bar.

Finally, Pretty Wife approached the sidecar as gingerly as a virgin ascending *Tlaloc's* altar. Bundling her into fuzzy blankets, I tossed two cased rifles across her chest and we were off.

Pulling off for a health and safety check in Issaquah, I executed a tight left spin for Pretty Wife's amusement and popped her neck out of joint. Although it's still sore, her nose has recovered fully.

"Don't worry!" I bellowed, "it won't rain in the mountains!" And it didn't.

It snowed. When my marble-white fingers quit working the Ural's manly control levers in the vicinity of Snoqualmie Summit, we stopped for a long enough breakfast to wrap them around a series of hot coffee cups. It was still 32 degrees after breakfast, but at least the snowfall was harder.

Saddling up in a spring blizzard inevitably provokes commentary, and everyone who spied the Ural wanted to talk. With our rig broken in to ratbike perfection, folks assumed we were midway through a world tour. A Ural curries instant credibility among the type of people who travel in school bus conversions, and seems a precious curio to everyone else.

Freeway speeds exceeded the car's trim and turned the throttle-balancing joy of slow curvy roads into monotonous rightward pull. My left shoulder was gunny-sacked by the time we pulled off on the dry side for gas and a cleaning kit.

Spinning around to reverse into our spot at the Kittitas Sure Shot Guns & Pawn brought the proprietress skipping out, clapping her hands under her chin. She never saw no motorsickle do that before!

Turned out she stocked not just kits to fettle old Winchesters, but also an EDM Windrunner chambered in .50-cal, .338 Lapua and .408 CheyTac. Only Pretty Wife's stern refusal to hitchhike with the Windrunner strapped across her back prevented me pawning our borrowed steed and two rifles on the spot.

Now wary of the interstate, we nosed along secondary roads halfway to Vantage before rejoining I-90 to knife into the Columbia Gorge. Millions of years ago, cataclysmic releases of pent-up glacial water warmed by the Idaho Batholith blasted a channel through the hard rock of eastern Washington for the express purpose of luring optimistic truck drivers into running out of fuel on the Vantage grade. Two Class 8 tow trucks based by the river do a brisk business.

Burbling downhill, we effortlessly dispatched a VW Bus and two sport bike riders interviewing with the State Patrol. Across the river, we ascended back onto the high plains and followed the 26 past the legendary speed trap of Washtucna and La Crosse, where once I left my totaled KZ1100 shaftie — but not Grandpa's rifle — lying by the roadside because I was going hunting that day. A buxom lady in a bright blue Caddy picked me up and took me all the way. You do what you have to do to get a buck.

With the sun setting behind us, there was no chance of catching our shadows. We plugged along, me wishing for a windshield and Pretty Wife huddled behind the car's tonneau. Wind blew bitter over the hilltop as we honored an irregular pilgrimage to Colfax Cemetery where I'm always cold, even in full summer.

A better bike to visit ghosts on, I could not imagine. Among the trees edging the careful lawn our Patrol sat timeless as granite, ready to bear us back into the present. Pretty Wife climbed in silently. With marble-white fingers, I opened the petcock and was grateful when the engine caught — as it would every try — on half a spin.

At Texaco station #306327 on South Grand in Pullman, the clerk watched Pretty Wife clamber painfully out of our sidecar after hours on the road, chilly and sore, before announcing that he ran the only service station in Christendom featuring no public restrooms. Too bleary to think of shooting him on the spot, we silently resolved to dis-recommend the place to friends and decamped for a planned dinner stop in the Russo-philically labeled burg of Moscow, Idaho.

Dead-set against buying college town pizza, we took a chance on the empty Old Peking joint and were promptly rewarded with spicy beef platters and delicate egg drop soup.

"We'll bivvy here," I announced, happy and warm for the first time since Seattle. We were a day up on our itinerary and I was looking forward to a scenic morning run to Orofino.

"Here!"

Pretty Wife had other ideas. She shook out her long brown hair, which is unfairly distracting, and pegged me with a blue-eyed look. "It's not really that far, is it?

"Maybe you should call. See if we can get a room tonight and just settle in."

Getting no answer at the Konkolville Motel, I left a message and smugly tucked into my chow. We were all the way to fortune cookies before my jacket rang and a cheerful voice said they'd leave our room unlocked with the heat on. *Bastards!*

Pretty Wife smiled pretty.

With the hollow-eyed look of a condemned man, I backed out into 38-degree traffic, passed a Harley rider cruising with shorts, sunglasses and half a six-pack on his wrist, and set course for Lewiston in the pitch dark.

Merry as an escaped parade float, the Ural pulled us tirelessly south. Although I had kicked off the right side manifold for the fifth time, sucking extra air on the right didn't bother it at all. Cutting edge technology ain't everything. Sometimes, you just need things to work.

I thought of musician Charlie Ryan as we tipped into Lewiston's widow maker grade, where the race that inspired "Hot Rod Lincoln" actually took place. Tires sizzling over chilled blacktop, we plunged past truck runoff after truck runoff, but we weren't scared. Our brakes were good, tires fair.

Pulling into the Flying J travel plaza near the river confluence saw both ambient temperature and my mood rise by ten degrees. Whistling to warm up my teeth, I fueled the rig, screwed the right intake boot on again, and ignored the dipstick as instructed. We were due for a beautiful piece of road, our first of the trip without traffic, snow or rain.

Winding east along the Clearwater, stars reflecting off the river and the boxer mill droning like bombers over the English Channel, was hypnotic. Inside my hat, I sleepily chanted the ground rules: "Gas goes right, slow pulls left, watch for deer…"

Ten minutes before midnight we crossed the bridge into Orofino, home to a state prison and the Night Force tactical optics company, murmured through downtown and hove to at the Konkolville's parking lot in the lee of a pickup truck flotilla flying Police Benevolent Association bumper stickers. Stumbling in, we stood rifles in the corner, pulled off each other's boots and collapsed. No need to lock up in a motel garrisoned by armed White Hats. The world is divided into the good guys and the bad guys, and the good guys decide which is which…

•••

Morning blossomed crisp and fair to river sounds courtesy of G-d's country and fresh waffles, hot coffee and fruit courtesy of proprietors Joe and Sherrie. Blotting syrup off our riding suits, we took weapons in hand and headed out.

Passing the fishermen below the Dworshak Dam, we mounted the Ahsaka Grade, a rattlesnake spine of a road featuring pastoral beauty on the right and to the left, a fall long enough to take postcard pictures of the approaching river. Like motorcyclists, Idaho hills are graded on a curve and Ahsaka's eight percent grade makes Lewiston's hot rod hill look like the bunny slope.

Feeling snorty, I charged up at the limits of chassis, traction and recent hack training. We were getting right into it, me throwing my weight around and sliding against brakes, Pretty Wife tilting her head left and right like a bobsled brakeman, when I detected a strange thumping. Slowing down to check for damage, I let the rusty Chevy Citation ahead stretch its lead.

Pretty Wife lowered her rifle and quit punching me.

Boomershoot's shock and awe is discreetly professional. Small white signs with neat red lettering led us off the highway at Cavendish toward the Huffman family ranch, where Friday's clinic was getting underway. Waving to the safety scout posted on the approach road, we idled up on a scene of careful organization.

Shooters moved up and down the line with actions open and muzzles reliably pointed downrange under supervision by range safety enforcers. Below a rain fly, retired Special Forces officer Eugene Econ calmly expounded on the subtleties of trajectory, mirage and quarter-minute winds to an attentive group.

These weren't your father's rednecks. Boomershoot draws from every profession (attorneys and tech geeks are over-represented) and social stratum.

It's a family event, too. My buddy Ry's adorable daughter wasn't the only kid on the firing line, and some guys' wives outshot their hubbies.

Boomershooters aren't leftover Cold War survivalists. They're serious precision shooters, with gear as refined and carefully maintained as any MV Agusta. They came in shiny trucks with onboard custom storage, broke out bull-barreled rifles with bipods and adjustable triggers, and stoked their chambers with handcrafted ammunition.

Range days are their track days. Boomershoot was race day, and I felt like Little Fauss on a dyspeptic Hodaka. It's a poor craftsman who blames his tools, but only idiots and journalists go up against a roomful of Snap-On rollaways with a rusty Boy Scout knife.

Meanwhile, up at "The Taj," volunteers happily mixed mayhem with Kitchen-Aid blenders. Taciturn Boomershoot impresario Joe Huffman supervised manufacture of enough explosives to level three or four middling Idaho townships. Fertilizer, antifreeze and disinfectant, sweetened with sugar, stirred (not shaken!) with a twist of lime builds a lovely cocktail *flambé*, but we couldn't play.

Everyone in the chemical kitchen held a BATF explosives license. When your recreation can kill you — and can anything else truly be called sport? — it's not actually better to be lucky than good. It's better to be good.

So we unqualified amateurs folded thousands of boxes for the cause, to be stuffed with explosives and disseminated for participants' shooting pleasure. Boomershoot's closest targets are set on a berm at 380 yards. Most are much further — and they're four inches square. You won't hit one by accident or luck.

For closer work, there is the joy of "cleanup." A slight additional fee lets Boomershooters wail on exploding targets from 30 yards out (eye protection recommended).

We left the range by a different route, the vertiginous Old Ahsaka Grade, composed of pea gravel over hard dirt wound around curves coiled tighter than an M16 buffer spring. We tiptoed down between native cherry coppices, standing on the brakes. If further proof is needed that Idahoans can do anything, it is this: there are school bus stops on that road.

Partway down, we pulled into an old feedlot to gambol through nearby woods on the surefooted hack. It's colossal for a dirt bike, puny for an SUV, just right for what it is: distilled escapist pleasure. Pretty good workout, too.

For Saturday morning's ride to the range, I stuffed my ego into the trunk and tooled up the hill in relaxed fashion, rediscovering the Lost Secret of Hackdom: slow is easy, easy is smooth, and smooth is fast.

OK, actually I learned that on a military rifle range, but it works for sidecars. We made it in less time and without leg punching. I'd have to collect my bruises elsewhere.

At the range, our Ural stood out like a kitten in a kennel. The big dogs sniffed at it gently, inquiring about hunting utility. We calculated the Patrol would easily carry two whitetails or a shedload of geese.

Like a motorcycle training course, our clinic opened at 0800 with a safety briefing and goal definitions. I paired off with a quiet fella named David to shoot steel targets until lunch, then try for our boomers.

When I pulled the old Winnie out, instructor Gene whistled. Most of its bluing was rubbed to silver. The red rubber recoil pad was crumbling. Dad replaced Grandpa's pre-Jurassic Lyman Alaskan scope with a Leupold Vari-X, but I hadn't zeroed it since the late 80s. When I unscrewed its turret caps, dust snowed off the elevation screw.

David, studiously preparing his custom M1 Garand, politely said nothing.

Nothing for it but to do it. I spotted a few rounds for my partner and we got the Garand onto eight-inch steel at 400 yards, then switched up. With many misgivings, I laid a round into my Model 70, closed the bolt, wrapped its thick leather sling around my left arm and said, "Shooter ready."

"Send it."

We kicked dirt eight inches left at 400 yards with a two-minute wind from the right. My old scope had held zero through 19 years and seven household moves. Two minutes of windage adjustment got us a reliable chorus of "Send it." BOOM! *Bong*.

I should have packed better excuses, but every miss was mine. Grandpa always did know his gear. I would like to have hunted with him, ridden with him, or been his wingman. I'd like to have known him past kindergarten age.

I'd like to have inherited his Harley. Somehow, though, I think Grandpa would have favored my high-compression Beemer over his own hawg, and reminded me that a man buys the best he can afford and performs the best he can with it.

With David spotting and Grandpa whispering in my ear, we rang steel out to 680 yards in a stout quartering wind, the best I've ever shot. Joe Huffman really does make a bit of magic out there, just back of the river bluffs.

The day was not without glitches. I scope-cut my nose and beat my throttle arm to a livid pulp, but we got our share of boomers and 158 rounds of validation.

The rest is details, but they make pleasant memories. On Sunday, Boomershoot proper saw many fine explosions, some respectable .50-caliber shooting by Pretty Wife, and the traditional Launching of the Anvil. Participants whooped as they tagged boomers across the hillside.

•••

We met one other motorcyclist at Boomershoot — an Aussie on an SV650 — but he wasn't shooting, just fascinated. We rode with Tenchi for awhile, cantering over Palouse blue roads, and count him a friend.

At the banquet on Saturday night, we'd purchased 25 raffle tickets to support Soldier's Angels and collected too many prizes to pack. A friend volunteered to schlep them back in his van and we tossed our rifles in, too — Pretty Wife having previously informed me that her chest was not, in fact, a "rifle" rack.

Unburdened by schedule or armory, we upped our two-lane percentage to relax the travel hours. Gamboling along at 35-55 on a curving road with your sweetie in the sidecar is like ice cream on a sunny day.

All weekend, the Ural just worked. It gave zero trouble on-road or off and opened travel options rarely available to standard commuting apparatus, such as chugging straight through a boggy bar pit when I arbitrarily punched out of interstate traffic in favor of a calm frontage road. When curiosity finally wrestled me into pulling the dipstick, it was coated with clear golden oil right up to the full mark.

It's a better bike than I am a mechanic; a better magic carpet than I am a pilot. The old Winchester is a better gun than I am a shooter, and it just may be that Grandpa knew better than all of us.

At a faux-retro coffee stop in North Bend, an old man stopped by our table to talk. He couldn't take his eyes off the bike out front.

"What's that, about a 1942?"

I squinted at the bike, a time-traveling contrivance if ever there was one, decided the front disk brake was probably invisible, and answered up on behalf of Grandpa's Winchester.

"Close. Nineteen-forty."

"Ah." The old party smiled a little, out of one side of his mouth, and his eyes crinkled. "They don't make 'em like that anymore.

"Russian, is it?"

The Ural has German gears, Italian ignition, Japanese carbs, U.S. wiring harness. "Actually, sir," I said, "that bike's from everywhere."

He put one hand on Pretty Wife's shoulder and one on mine, but he never looked away from the bike. "And where are you two going?"

Home, I thought, *back to work, back to routine.*

But Pretty Wife didn't wait for my answer. She spoke right up and if she didn't make the old man's day, she surely made mine.

"Everywhere," she said. "We're going everywhere."

We were on the right road, all along.

March 2010, Motorcyclist

BIKE ZONING

This smug little fluff piece turned bittersweet a couple of years ago. We had flown to Indiana to buy a savage, unpredictable, marvelous little motorcycle. It's a corker. I looked forward to showing it off to my neighbor over beers and brats and agreeable lies, but Tony passed away abruptly before we got home.

I bought my dream bike on that trip, but missed my chance to show it to my friend. Without riding and friends and wrenching and bench racing, motorcycles are just things. Pretty, shiny, static things.

That's the puzzling aspect of "community," see. Like "motorcycle," it's actually a verb, not a noun.

Thank G-d for the housing crisis. If it weren't for the ineptitude of the Masters of the Universe, we'd probably live in a much worse neighborhood.

Oh sure, we'd still be in this school district. Kids have to come first. But if we hadn't damped down our borrowing expectations — after all, the Fed's never going to bail *us* out — we probably wouldn't have stooped on the cheapest house in Shoreline like vultures onto road kill. Our house is to your house as basket cases are to running motorcycles — not a functioning house, but a kit for a house. The credit crunch coupled with the cost of demolishing the shack we now live in prevented developers from snapping up this double lot, so instead of a perfectly decent tract house we ended up with the worst imaginable dump on a wonderful street.

Here's what's great about our neighborhood: we have no HOA. All the houses look different. Like everyone else on our block, we have a real backyard — even if we did have to export 70 cubic yards of trash to find it. We found some fruit trees, too, plus a great place to park a bike or five.

When we needed a temporary solution to stow our motorcycles because our garage is stuffed with flooring and drywall, Tony from across the street didn't just loan us a pop-up rain fly; he came over and threw it up for us. Tony gets it about motorcycles.

See, that's the other great thing about our neighborhood. Tony keeps a couple of Interceptors in his garage, a sweet 500 ("does great wheelies") and a first-year Rothman's edition 750 in mint shape. He's also got a quick-draw XR200 on the back porch, and a loanable bike trailer with working lights.

"Guess I'm an early 80s Honda guy," Tony says. Yep. More to the point, a motorcycle guy.

Tony hangs out with Moon, Eastside Harley's sales manager who races Buells and who used to live a block and a half over. Their bikes sport white-on-black, racing-style NESRA fork stickers for "North End Street Racing Association," an in-joke for riders living in the Seattle pseudopods oozing towards Canada. If anyone asks, though, NESRA stands for "North End Sport Riding Association."

Across the fence from Tony live Dick and Mo. Their yard features a hodgepodge of axles and front clips randomly distributed among hot rods including a flamed '41 Buick and a purple T-bucket. When we first looked at what would become our house, the listing agent glanced across the road and mumbled about zoning and land use codes.

"Are you kidding?," I said. "They've got a Studebaker pickup over there! You don't see those every day.

"I think we'll get along."

So now I do see a Studebaker pickup every day, and Dick and I get along fine. I don't bitch about his car parts, and he doesn't interrogate me about my qualifications to take on This Old Dump.

In the summer, Dick takes long trips on a cherry red '61 panhead FLH and comes back griping about alky bikers who can't get their rides or their brains running in the morning. Turns out we prefer the same brand of leathers, still handmade in Oregon from carefully inspected hides.

There's a kid down the block with a sparkly new GSXR. Haven't met him yet, but we wave at each other from time to time. He's an ATGATT guy ("all the gear, all the time"). At my age, I shouldn't need a mid-twenties guy to remind me to shrug into protective equipment, but I'll take my examples where I find them.

Sometimes our neighbors stop for a chat over our broken-down front fence. Joe, a retiree from kitty corner over who peddles acacia juice to stay busy and makes zombie movies for fun, used to ride Hondas and can draw from a deep fund of road stories. Steve from around the corner stopped by one day with his "pups" (a pair of brobdingnagian Great Danes), spied a bike parked out front and said he'd bring his Harley by sometime.

"I've got it stored around the place somewhere, rusting away," he told me. "Should probably get it out and fix it up some."

I figured that was the last I'd hear of that. Everybody has a someday project, waiting on a round tuit.

A few days later, Steve came chugging cheerfully up on a mint-condition, root beer brown '81 Sportster XLH needing nothing but a fresh front tire. We talked for a half hour or so before he went to crank it up, and I snickered quietly to myself as I settled in to enjoy the promised entertainment of an elaborate starting ritual. Steve sat down on the bike and thumbed the button.

His Sporty cranked up in half a spin, settled into a rumpety idle, and he toodled off down the street. I wish my '07 Beemer started that well. That's the way old bikes should run. Heck, that's the way new bikes should run.

This is the way a neighborhood should feel.

February 2009, Motorcyclist

Classic Rock

If the music's too loud, you're too old.

Daddy did a bad, bad thing today. Following a doctor's appointment for my back (yep, still disintegrating), I slid by Seattle Ducati for an iced double shot of midlife crisis.

The dealer didn't have a standard Streetfighter. Their only demo was an "S" with more carbon fiber than the paddock at your local track. No virgin, it had been around the block a time or two and gone down on a couple of guys already. It knew the score.

Their Streetfighter wasn't red, either. It didn't need to be. An olive-black lasagna of speed and aggression and cheesy testosterone, it was a Monster's monster that was a better bike than I am a rider — or you, either.

My description for Black Betty, my BMW R1200S, has long been "old man's touring bike." Before I met the Street-fighter, I thought that an ironic turn of phrase. Betty may not be a real sportbike, but she's got a glint in her eye.

I didn't expect to be impressed by the 'Fighter. It looked long and ungainly in magazine shots. I figured it for a spine-curling agony with all the leg room of a Mini Cooper's trunk, snatching and jerking at any speed under 30 mph and idling like a funny car on Mexican gas.

One should expect the unexpected. Pictures of Moto Guzzi's Griso once struck me as the pure essence of *dolce del motocicloto* but in person, its tank plastic bulges like Big Mama's arm giblets. On paper, Ducati's own Hypermotard

S is a hot chili recipe for thrills, but it tastes a little bland from the saddle.

The Streetfighter is different. It made my S-bike hackle up and back away, alpha bitch no more. Packing 30-odd horsepower more than Betty, it weighs a hundred pounds less and has brakes that would stop a runaway Kenworth on Cabbage Hill. Right. Now.

It starts easily, sits right and has room for a full-sized American. It looks good from the side and invisible from the saddle, but slashing this bike through in-town traffic is like hunting butterflies with a .416 Rigby. Work it hard enough to interest the bike and you court a roadside tasing.

And it may just be that, like weightlifting juice and belly shirts and Rottweilers on logging chains, Streetfighting is a younger man's conceit.

Ever have the sudden realization you walked into the wrong club? Ever hit the dance floor anyway, just to see what happens? Did you pretend you weren't really the creepy old guy, or just get jiggy wit' the "place thumbs here" tattoos?

Ducati's Streetfighter is too much bike for me. There, I said it. I'm not man enough to keep up with it. Hardcore romping fun it may be, for a few minutes of remembering my twisted youth better than it ever really was, but two consecutive hours on it would ruin me for days.

This is possibly the first bike to qualify for a Powerglide transmission. By the top of second gear, you've outsped every legal highway speed and the riding position as well. What the other four gears are for, I have no earthly idea. Feeling like a grandfather driving a ZO6 Corvette, I crunched a few gears just to prove I knew how.

Mages from the Öhlins works had anointed the bike with pothole erasure potions, and the high leverage bars let me work it like a man half my age. I was living that dream where I star in a Buell commercial, but I wasn't limited to riding a Buell and I'd progressed to the third stage of tequila: I was rich, good looking *and* bulletproof.

Then I woke up tired and sweaty and groping for ibuprofen. Twenty minutes into my ride, I remembered why old ballplayers trade in their shoulder pads for the sofa and remote. Sexy and dripping with power it may be, but the Streetfighter is ten pounds of tomcat in a five pound bag and feels about three feet long. Tweak its erectile throttle and the wheel pops up faster than a porn star in the bonus round. If you slap the Brembo trigger with both fingers, you'll instantly comprehend Ultimate Ro-Sham-Bo.

And it's too damned loud.

The problem with committing to the dance floor at that club you should have stayed out of is there's no graceful exit once you're dizzy and out of breath. The youth will stomp your tattered carcass into the parquet, laughing and shakin' it down.

I wanna want a Streetfighter, but mostly I want to re-visit that place in my life when I would have killed for 20 minutes with a young Duc, when I circled Ducatis at a reverent distance, wondering how to talk to them; when my reflexes didn't tick slower than a rusty metronome and fighting in the street sounded cool and tough, not dung-candy stupid.

The 'Fighter immolates the shreds of my mental overhead the way an escort service burns through walkin' around money. It's Angelina Jolie at 19 when my tastes run more to

Sophia Loren at 36… and my doc prescribes Kathy Bates, more fiber and gentle constitutionals.

And ibuprofen. Lots of ibuprofen. Who needs kidneys if you can't walk to the latrine?

For the first time, it occurs to me why Harley-Davidson names so many of their bikes "Glides." Might not be so bad to ease back and glide around, smooth as Clyde Drexler working the key. Maybe geezer clichés exist for a reason.

Sure would be nice to ride a Streetfighter now and then, though. I want one bad — just not right now.

I want this bike 27 years ago. Why, if I'd had this bike when I was a teenager, instead of my 40-horse RD400, I would've… well, okay, I'd probably be dead. Long before "back in the day," I used to wonder why silly old fossils rode mighty torque beasts like the GS1100E when they should've been plopping their bran muffin-bloated butts over Gold Wings and Super Glides. Weren't they embarrassed?

Well, no. They were buying the overdog bikes they wished they could afford when they were lean. Because they could, that's why. Anyway, nothing really embarrasses you after the first endoscopy.

Stopped at a light while headed home from my test ride, I watched a girl sashay across the parking lot, honey-blonde hair swaying heavy and rich, and reconsidered whether the Streetfighter should make an old man want to try again.

My insurance rates are much lower than they used to be. Maybe in a few years, when the kids are grown and the mortgage is beaten back… A full-pate helmet ought to cover my bald spot, and ear plugs are cheap.

Then I smiled down at my own Black Betty, grumbling under me, always ready to go, low maintenance, comfortable and pretty.

Curving sweetly under my hand, she took me right on home.

November 2009, Motorcyclist

HOLY HARLEY

In the midst of death, they are in life. There may not be a single safe place to ride in Israel, but has that ever been the point?

On Holocaust Remembrance Day, I picked up a kosher hog in Tel Aviv. This is no easy thing.

You can import any bike you want into Israel, provided you're willing to pay 190 percent VAT on top of the import fees. That pushes the Israeli market value of a Dyna Street Bob (MSRP $12,999.00) up around fifty thousand bucks. Back home, that money would buy two and a half MV Agusta F4s or a nice used Ferrari with gas money left over — so go ahead and google for rental bikes in Israel and see how far you get.

On the clutch hand, I've always told my daughter that asking nicely works pretty well all over the world. Talk to enough people and sure enough, someone will square you away. The friend of a patron of an ambulance service had an uncle who knew a guy... And so it came to pass that the guy, Eitan Ben-Arie of Tel Aviv Harley Davidson, had a Vivid Black Dyna waiting with bags on.

At 10:00, as we talked traffic tactics, air raid sirens sounded and every single citizen stopped and stood with bowed heads and folded hands as the horns of *Yom Hashoah* continued for two minutes, mourning six million irretrievable victims. In my country you may witness such universal respect nowhere outside military reservations. Only in Israel does every citizen hide a soldier's heart behind a veteran's smile.

Two minutes later, Eitan was reminiscing about blasting through Miami on a plus-size hog with a chrome Iron Cross adorning his noggin.

"Seriously?" I raised a goybrow. "A Nazi helmet?"

He spread his hands and grinned. "Hey, why not?"

The rhythm and flow of Tel Aviv traffic functions like a messy cultural collision of Seoul and Milano. Police cars run around with their lights flashing constantly, and thus are universally ignored. It's no wonder Israelis won't be pwned by terrorism; they commute to work as combat maneuver elements.

From Tel Aviv H-D to the Mercure hotel on Ben Yehuda takes seven minutes, unless you get solidly rear-ended by a van when you chirp your brakes because another van yanked out in front of you. Then it takes seven minutes plus the time to pull over, check damage and cuss while both vans drive away, honking at each other.

Bending the saddlebag frame of my $50,000 charge back into shape, I rode on to the hotel. The fresh scuffs on the left bag matched the old scuffs on the right bag. When every car sports color-swatched mirror edges, it's hard to take these things personally — but now I know why AAA won't cover rental vehicles here.

•••

Tel Aviv itself is aquiline Europe with a Brazilian wax; a curly, Levantine cosmopolis of shining, *kohl*-eyed vitality; Madrid in a miniskirt with rolling acres of party cleavage shading tanned sandaltoes, no additives or preservatives required. Beach bars pour Maccabi lager into schooners the size of a governor's arm. Men accessorize with chunky chronographs, aviator sunglasses and sidearms showing holster wear; women with skin, tight; all must buy their t-shirts from the same disco gift shop.

The next day, I pointed the black hog southeast. First paved by Ottomans in the 1860s to connect the Arab port Jaffa with the world headquarters of religious strife, Highway One is Israel's mother road. In 90 minutes it takes you through Tel Aviv suburbs, between industrial parks and across farmland until mounting the hills toward the golden city. Serene as Jerusalem stone, my Harley plunged casually backward through time from Tel Aviv's beach party future into Jerusalem's defiant, conflicting histories.

The toughest biker in Jerusalem is a diabetic stroke victim with Government Press Office credentials, motorcycle gear and a pistol permit. About my height and tattooed with the scars of four open heart surgeries, he's built like a No. 2 Dixon Ticonderoga and animated by the comfortable humor of the damned.

"Four people in the Western hemisphere have my cluster of symptoms," Alon Tuval told me, chaining off a smoke. "And the other three are dead."

Then he tore through a pile of armored vests and tele-photo lenses to find his motorcycle helmet and a corpsman-quality aid kit ("If I bleed, I don't stop"), hopped onto the pillion behind a rider he'd never met, and smacked me on the shoulder for GO.

"Did we touch down?," he yelled a few minutes later. I shook my helmet, unwilling to admit crunching my mid-control pegs into the oily streets.

"Do it again!," he demanded.

If you want to write a motorcycle story in Israel, you need your own Alon — not only to gain access to special police units and the best bar in J-town for expats to suckle *arrak*, but literally to show you how to get around. The secret, in this high power-to-weight country, is cheerful aggression. In a land where the top predators tailgate through construction zones at *triple* the 50 kph limit, traffic is not for the timid.

"Steal the lane!," he'd yell in my ear. "Move up! You have to learn to ride Israeli style!" Small wonder the bastard's had two heart attacks and a stroke.

Alon may have taught me to squeeze the Dyna through where angels fear to lane split, but he couldn't teach me how to get around Jerusalem's antique, thumpbird warren of roundabouts, alleyways and bazaars without getting lost 11 out of 10 times. We rode that Harley to the Old City, the West Bank, the American colony, the Dead Sea, the "Nazi colony" where Alon lives (look it up), the Mount of Olives and even the Western Wall. I have the pictures to prove it, but I couldn't guide you to a single one of those places on a rich bet.

"You get lost a lot," Alon observed. "That's why you're a good rider.

"Extra miles."

•••

I gravitated to the Negev Desert without too much trouble. Follow the blue signs to Be'er Sheba ("Seven Wells"), then make for Ben Gurion University, perched on the lip of the world's largest *maktesh*. At night, the Negev is quiet the way the Mojave is dark. If Yahweh vacations in the Holy Land, it's more likely here than in theocultural

Jerusalem. I'm betting G-d, like most Israelis, ain't overly religious.

Israel's weekend is one day long: Saturday for Jews, Sunday for Arabs. On Shabbat, when the scooters go into hiding and the sport bikes come out to play, tripling the speed limit suddenly looks conservative. You really want to see G-d, skip pious tourism and try hanging with these guys. If you're riding a Street Bob with large feet, your boot heels will make serviceable lean angle indicators…

Although I'd planned to ride with Eitan's H.O.G. buddies on Shabbat, I predictably got lost again and sailed into a fuel station featuring every flavor of bike from a 1942 Triumph sidehack to a fresh Hypermotard. Every type, that is, except Harleys.

What would Alon do?

Preferring to believe that you're never really lost until you run out of gas, I taped one of their rally maps to my tank and flocked together.

We stopped in a suburb a few miles from the station, where a burly man with a grey crewcut and Legionnaire's beard stood in front of a lamppost where a wreath hung, solemnly addressing the crowd. On the nearby highway, the Harley group I failed to meet boomed past like a missing man formation.

A pretty woman touched my elbow and asked, "Do you speak Hebrew?"

When I shook my head, she frowned. "Then you do not understand anything?"

"Not a word," I said, sure that I did and dead wrong as usual.

Further on, at an "Active Recreation Area" surreally enough sponsored by the Oakland East Bay Community Group, I learned that the rolling party was thrown by Yankele Weintraub, the spade-bearded roadside speaker. When his son Roi died on a motorcycle several years ago, Yankele vowed to get even with life.

His vengeance is simple. Every year, with a couple hundred buddies, Yankele takes a ride to celebrate the joy he felt when riding with his son. Smiling, hugging and shaking hands, Yankele greeted everyone there like long-lost family, even to the point of ladling up a mug of cardamom coffee for the stranger from America.

I was gonna need that caffeine. Our ride was just beginning, and Israelis are adventure riders by predisposition and default.

Burbling along with the "wrong" group, the Harley and I bumped and ground through the valley of the shadow of David slaying Goliath, up cracked military roads along the Jordan border fence to "Peace Island," a cooperative Jordanian-Israeli oasis where in 1997 seven pre-teen Israeli girls on a school trip were shot by a crazed Jordanian soldier. Afterward, Jordan's king personally visited the girls' hometown of Beit Shemesh, getting down on his knees to beg forgiveness in the name of his country.

"He was our sworn enemy," said John Markow, a Honda TransAlp rider who made *aliyah* (emigrated to Israel) from South Africa, "but King Hussein had class."

Our parade of Super Ténérés, ratfighters, maxi-scooters and one lonely black Harley bounced up dirt roads between olive orchards to a mountaintop overlooking Golan with the Sea of Galilee shimmering beyond. There the Parliament and Israeli Motorcycle Club, Israel's two biggest "bike gangs," noshed on Turkish coffee and oranges, listened to wind caress the peak and spoke of the perennially favorite subject in a country so small that every place in it feels like a border to somewhere:

Peace.

"The land laughs at us," said rat chopper guitarist Magen Dahari. "It says, 'Because you are fighting, you will come to be inside me very fast.'"

Israelis laugh back, and riders laugh best. If tomorrow is not promised to us, then today we ride.

October 2010, Motorcyclist

Jack wishes to thank Eitan Ben-Arie of Tel Aviv Harley Davidson and Alon Tuval of ATP Productions, without whom this story would not have been possible.

Launch Sequence

R.I.P. Uncle Tony.

The little one was still off at camp when I eased up to the house in our rusty Ford half-ton, a pair of stubby handlebars barely visible over the side of the bed. Our neighbor Tony sidled out and grinned big.

"You didn't."

"I did!"

Tony helped me unload the little blue missile, asked if we had pro gear for the sprout, then promptly proposed a training mission to his mom's three acres outside Stanwood. We were still grinning like idiots when Pretty Wife came outside and her eyes lit up in sapphire sparkles.

"Oh, that's *much* cooler than I thought!"

"It kinda is, idnit?"

It was because we couldn't help ourselves that we helped ourselves to a few laps up and down our quiet street, butter-knifing the air with the murmur of a very polite chainsaw. Pretty Wife discovered it's the only bike in our stable she can flatfoot on both sides, and it turns out that a used Yamaha PW80 cheerfully hangs respectable wheelies with a full-sized American male aboard, despite having no clutch to pop. No pictures of such unhelmeted lawlessness will be published here, of course. This is a family magazine.

The neighbor kids ran out in the street to stare. Little Emily from over the road immediately decided, "My daddy's gonna get me one o' those." Emily is rather forthright. Last week she asked me, "Why don't you have a job? My daddy has a job."

Yeah? Bet he has to pay taxes, too.

Four more blasts up and down the street and we shut 'er down to leave a little oil in the reservoir for its intended recipient. Pretty Wife shot me a stern look.

"So we're agreed," she said, "we don't tell her until her birthday?"

Smalldaughter's birthday is in November, the cruelest month.

"Ah, sweetie, c'mon. Look at the weather!"

Pretty Wife had not run out of looks. She speared our neighbor with one.

"Are you in on this?"

Tony scuffled one sandal toe in the driveway, looking like an embarrassed middle schooler. "Well," he said, "it *is* summer."

"You guys are terrible!"

The ayes had it.

One week later, on a sunny afternoon in late August, our seven year-old soberly accepted a handwritten note initiating a multipoint sprint around the neighborhood, under her special willow tree, under the cover of her mom's Moto Guzzi, inside the truck and finally down to the mailbox to find a clue reading, "Silly girl! Go ask Tony. Maybe he knows."

Tony stocks him some Hondas, not one or two but fully a few. Nosing around his Interceptors and XLs, our sprout finally stumbled over the covered mini. Ripping off the moving blankets, she looked up, sparkling from teeth and eyes.

"I *knew* it!"

For adults it's only a figure of speech, but seven year-olds actually can *jump* into their gear. It's something to see. Smalldaughter perfected it some time ago, scrambling like a tiny firefighter. Every time I walk out to my bike, I find her already suited up and tapping her foot by the back seat, impatient and excited and grinning.

This was different. Our daughter — the kid who nonchalantly hops off her moving bicycle, shucks her shoes and is in the kitchen eating a snack by the time it falls over — sat on that little Yamaha with a deadly intent look, listening and absorbing. Chunking it into first gear, Smalldaughter hesitantly cracked the throttle and off she plonked with me trotting alongside, gripping a fistful of her leather jacket like a briefcase handle.

We made few tentative runs up and down in front of the house. Her blue eyes never lost their gunfighter glint, but a little smile grew behind her chin guard as she smoothed out her stops. Pretty soon she was braking for corners, throwing a boot out on the inside and gassing it around the bend, and I couldn't keep up anymore.

Limping off to stop and pant with my hands on my knees, I watched her putt-putting away from me on her little Yamaha. Two weeks ahead of second grade, she was already charting her own course.

That's what Lewis daughters do. One state south, her big sister pilots a vintage Honda Hawk to classes at an urban college — in between organizing political actions, holding down two jobs and tuning up a social network that would give a White House protocol chief the vapors.

All a dad can do is watch and smile, dream and remember and hope. Their job is to leave us behind. Who would have imagined they'd be so good at it? As Louie Armstrong sang, "They'll learn much more, than we'll know."

What a wonderful world, indeed.

April 2010, Motorcyclist

THE LONG AND WHINING ROAD

Wherein our tattered protagonist requires days of hands-on instruction to comprehend the obvious: Harley-Davidsons are real motorcycles.

If you're a real motorcyclist, that is.

The following is a paid announcement:

Harley-Davidson and Best Western hotels sustain a warm, group hug of polyamorous co-branding.

There is no story here. Had there been a story, no doubt a real journalist would have been assigned. Instead you get an errand boy, sent by grocery clerks to collect the bill…

"Why me?," I angsted. "I'm not a Harley guy. I ride motorcycles, not Tractor Glides. I don't even drink *beer* from Milwaukee — it's down on horsepower and still overpowers my chassis."

"Haven't you ever ridden a Harley?," asked Pretty Wife.

"Uh…" It occurred to me that in thirty-odd years of street riding, my sole Harley-Davidson experience was on the Aermacchi-built Sprint that broke me in. As a hog virgin (quite rare in certain Alabama counties), I experienced bruising cognitive dissonance between cheap prejudice and avid bike sluttery. If sailors were motorcycles, I'd date the Seventh Fleet.

And I do like my wine…

•••

In San Francisco, Fisherman's Wharf beckoned with salt breezes and tourist gorp only four blocks from the Best

Western Tuscan Inn. Turning Japanese in my plaid shirt and Nikon, I headed out for the waterfront.

My mind no longer manufactures useful new memories. After fifteen years away from The City, the fishing fleet was just where I remembered it — but it took half an hour, a 4-1-1 Hail Mary and a twelve-block hump to navigate back in time for supper. Along the way, I found a genuine Harley-Davidson store with plenty of black t-shirts and no actual motorcycles.

No bikes at SFO's Tuscan Inn, either; it's not in the BWRider.com network. It did feature sleek GILFs parading unselfconsciously across the lobby, serenely rationing their power... is it just me, or are Californians a little sexier and healthier than the rest of the country? And louder, but not in a Texas way.

Sipping the iced chardonnay that materialized in my room that evening, I phoned up Pretty Wife.

"These people seem really nice," I said. "What if I hate the bikes?"

"What if you love them?," she asked.

Damn these conundra.

The next morning, we picked up a bevy of baggers at Bob Dron Harley-Davidson. I bounced up and down on my assigned White Gold Pearl / Pewter Pearl Electra-Glide, squinted at the bar pods, wondered what all the indistin-guishable liquorice buttons were for and prayed I wouldn't drop it in the parking lot.

Moments later we headed out for the Bay Bridge and I realized what funeral escorts and parading Shriners have always known: the Electra-steering was steady and torque lolloped out rich and lumpy as heavy cream. Ride the

Buick-style brake pedal and you can circle inside the diameter of a garbage can lid at less than 1 mph.

Skirting the Central Valley, I spared a thought for Stockton, where a once-Best Girl grew up to take over the world. Scheduling conflicts and my severe buckshot allergy prevented stopping over.

I was predisposed to slag Sonoma for a tanplastic-breasted theme park of fauxthentic nostalgia, snooty wine cellars and gimcrack stores for brain-checked tourons. It is all these things, of course, but it is also rolling hills of vineyards unsullied by subdivisions. It is sun-kissed California attitude. It is old trucks, time-warp hippies and choo-choo trains.

Who doesn't love choo-choo trains?

Weekday traffic was cask-mellowed. Our bikes chuffed along, unstoppable as logging elephants. Sixth gear (sixth! What is this thing, some kind of MV Agusta?) is the Overdude, geared for 362 mph at 2,500 rpm. On the S-bike I'd have been screaming into my helmet and munching fistfuls of VA ibuprofen for my limpish wrists, but on the Bike-a-Lounger I could just ease back, wish for a soft passenger against whom to lean, and watch the vineyards roll by.

Porcine or no, the two-bagger sows have moves. After lunch, three of us took a rapid detour down an untrafficked creek gully to plumb the limits of touring talent. When neither banging the floorboards nor scotching front tire darkies at corner entries upset the massive chassis, I resolved to steal me a Harley.

•••

Swapping keys with Toph, editor of Hot Bike Baggers, I took the Road King at its name, skipped the winery tour program and un-assed upscale Napa for Sunnyvale. Ninety-five miles south, friends who had no idea I was in California were hooking up for Thai food. If they didn't see me coming, they couldn't switch restaurants on me...

Unfamiliar with the area, I ran 80 miles south along I-680 and remembered why I moved to Washington: We may have potholes to bottom a new bike's suspension, but they're not decorating interstate freeways.

One of the bikes gathered for *pad thai* was a Mission Motors development mule. Conforming to software guru Seth LaForge's strict double-secret probation, I burned all the negatives in a white-hot digital blaze to prevent you from learning that their rolling skunkworks strongly resembles a 750SS Ducati, that it wears a rear sprocket bigger than your head and that its ammeter runs up to "several hundred." Hawg-rollin' into that parking lot felt like cruising a '57 Chevy onto the Microsoft campus, where geek chic trumps jock boy swagger eleven out of ten times.

After supper, the Road King and I got lost, criss-crossing three of the two bridges and picking fights with deep-tinted Oakland traffic, finally stumbling back into the Elm House Inn around midnight. The next morning, Heather (think pre-surgical Drew Barrymore) told me she dreamed I'd abandoned the group because they failed to conform to my Christian values.

I get that a lot.

•••

Nothing perks a guy up like running along coastal pastures and ocean-hugging highways, smelling salt and pine and discovering a dozen places like Dogtown (pop. 30), an artists colony smack at the mountain-coast interface where I'd move tomorrow, given money enough and time. Like owning a big, red biplane, that's one of a hundred dreams I can't live yet… but pretty people were loaning me bikes, buying me drinks and pretending to like me. Strange it is to have everything you want, and still want things.

Like motorcycles — how many could you possibly need? Just one more, and maybe that a big, sweet Road King with callipygian saddlebags and fat bob cleavage. You ride that honey and you are the king of all you survey through its detachable windshield.

Along NorCal's coast road, you can ease into a no-brakes flow and watch the hills unfold, or just go for it. Toph and I chose to go.

Playing bagger tag along Highway One was as joyful as wrestling puppies. Speed is relative, and doubling corner limits on the King is approximately as exhilarating as tripling them on a sportbike. Floorboards were my bitches until I grounded the frame so hard that I levered a half-ton of bike and schlub into the air and had a brief view of the troll waiting 200 feet below an onrushing guardrail.

Yes, speed is relative. And Harley builds stout, predictable frames. The troll can keep waiting, for now.

Later, I asked Toph how he kept his rhythm so smooth on the Grandissimo Glide. He raised his eyebrows and blew Lucky Strike smoke at me. "Ya gotta hang off."

Hunh. Heavy flywheel means revs build slow, so you carry speed through corners. Hanging off allows this. Seems I had misjudged the essence of these baggers. They're snap-crackling racerboy platforms thoroughly padded with middle-aged comfort.

Just like me!

•••

Our third day of riding took us up Highway 9 at a freshening pace before trickling us over Skyline Boulevard behind a docilely driven Tesla. Along the way I almost spattered a sport bike rider onto my windshield when he early-apexed and skittered 18 inches over the centerline. Dang kids!

Then again, I've been over the line more than once. Some folks never go over the line, but I do not envy them.

Now herding a Road Glide, I had leisure to fiddle with its harman/kardon stereo on the way to Alice's Restaurant, where my order of a "BMW Burger" with Jack cheese met the same gung-ho perkiness we enjoyed throughout the trip. Waitresses don't love Harleys just for the motion. When you burble in on $150,000.⁰⁰ worth of shiny new bikeware, you ain't the Fringe, baby. You're the Tip.

In our diminished age of extended warranties and Harleys that don't even leak oil, biker intimidation seems a distant anachronism. Our sole authentic biker, Boozefighter Bill, nearly became our One True Casualty when a Mercedes SUV cranked a no-look u-turn in front of him while we were clicking along at (elided) mph. Pounding the brakes, Bill jumped the Benz's wake, pulled up alongside and addressed its driver in no uncertain terms. With hand signals. And *feelin'*. When I passed her moments after she nearly killed biker Bill, she was still laughing.

Be careful out there.

•••

Mission debriefs should end with lessons learned. Here are mine: The Road Glide rode tightest, the FLH was easiest to pack, and I was wholly smitten by the Road King. H-D's new frames are rigid and their 96-inch fuelie engines are dope-proof. Whine-*crack*-BOOM-thumpa-thumpa, drop 'er into gear and meditate on down the road. Big Twins shift like Kubota tractors — i.e. *much* smoother than BMW twins.

While riders of any marque are welcome to polish rags and wash stations at 1,250 "rider friendly" Best Western hotels, Harley folk get H.O.G.-tied into extra spiffs (almost as many spiffs as we over-indulged journalists), plus "Gold Elite" status and pointage galore.

Wear earplugs to cut down the windshield buffeting. You'll hear the music better.

California's water sickens with every sip. Ambrosia by comparison, Washington's water explains why Northwest wine is superior and every decent Californian has already preserved their precious bodily fluids by migrating north.

Oh, and this: Harley-Davidson knows something motor-cycle journalists forgot long ago, which is that riding never was just about the bikes — ask a cowboy sometime, or a fighter pilot.

All motorcycles go to Heaven.

January 2010, Motorcyclist

The New Minutemen

Because Alon Tuval is connected to everyone in Israel worth knowing, I was privileged to meet representatives of every type of Israeli emergency services, from emergency medics and parade cops to ultra-Orthodox grave tenders and special warfare soldiers, and spend time with all of them where their rubber meets the glass-slick, Jerusalem stone road.

A finer, friendlier, more resolute group of people I have yet to meet.

Thou shalt not go up and down as a talebearer among thy people; neither shalt thou stand idly by the blood of thy neighbour: I am the Lord.
— Leviticus 19:16

These are not your domesticated American house Jews. They're what Americans used to be, what our *Ur*-myths tell: settlers, frontiersmen, Manifest Destiny, one nation under Yahweh. Fearless but shy, they smile like gunslingers. They're rude, swaggering, cheerful, egalitarian underdogs, and at some level of bumper sticker brain rot, we hate them for it.

Meet the New Minutemen.

"We are surrounded by enemies all the time, who have missiles aimed at us," said Yisrael Rosset over platters full of pickles and chopped salad, bagels and salted fish. "Israel is the hard nut of the world."

I met Rosset when he chugged up to my hotel on his ZAKA emergency scooter, looking like the Fiddler on the Roof in a flip-face helmet.

I was ready for him, maybe. My black Harley-Davidson Dyna Street Bob was fueled and carried water bottles in its saddlebags. Bumping off the curb, I shadowed Rosset through evening traffic. He paddled cautiously along in his black knee socks as traffic blared past us on both sides.

"ZAKA - Identification, Extraction and Rescue - True Kindness" wasn't so much founded as assembled *ad hoc*. Following a carnage-bespattered 1989 terrorist attack, nearby Orthodox Jews followed their rabbi's directives to gather, honor and return all human remains from the site. As the Palestinian *intifada* stacked bodies around the country, they coalesced into an organization unique in the world: wielding plastic bags, spatulas and towels, ZAKA volunteers literally pick up the pieces of life's unexpected endings.

Logging well over a million volunteer hours per year, they operate in every Israeli police district and several countries around the world. Their example of even-handed veneration — returning even the remains of suicide bombers — earns ZAKA cross-cultural respect in the tinderbox of the Middle East.

Street shorthand is "Nokia connects you; ZAKA collects you," but during the al-Aqsa *intifada* they expanded their toolkit to pack bandages along with their body bags. When they formed a Rapid Response Motorcycle Unit in 2001, Rosset was among the first to apply.

Sedately meandering toward his flat in a north Tel Aviv suburb, Rosset suddenly slapped a hand to his ear and wobbled to the curb, punching responses into his MIRS satellite communicator. Before I even got my emergency winkers operating, Rosset burned a screaming "U" across the Ha Ta'arucha Bridge, bubble light blazing.

Game on, then.

With Israel's nationally integrated emergency dispatch, a call to one is a call to all. Besides, Dreamsicle-orange scooter and archaic buckle shoes notwithstanding, Rosset is one fast old man.

With Rosset's siren wailing and blipping like a clock-sprung metronome, we slashed through HaYarkon traffic like Moses parting the Reed Sea. Jumping a curb near Shlomo Lahat Promenade, we snaked our mounts down brick walkways to a segregated *Haredi* beach where ultra-Orthodox bathers had dialed for aid after dragging a boy out of the surf. Just far enough past his *bar mitzvah* to swim with men, the kid was nearly drowned by the stormy waves busting against the breakwater.

Israelis devised the innovative one-handed pressure bandages we all tried to score for our vehicles in Iraq. The respirator, defibrillator and epinephrine in Rosset's scooter box also put U.S. combat lifesaver bags to shame. Hopping off his scooter, Yisrael grabbed an O2 bottle and his jump start kit and shouldered through the crowd, face shield up and locked.

Response time from call to attendance: two minutes flat.

The swimmer crowd gathered for a golf clap as Rosset carefully repacked his top box. Just as we got turned around to leave, Magen David Adom's ambulance van pulled up. Bucking moderate traffic, their response time was ten minutes.

When breathing stops, it's a four-minute trip to irreversible brain damage.

•••

We tootled cautiously on to Rosset's flat, where he calmly sliced up our dinner. "I am *cooker*," he bellowed happily from the galley-style kitchen.

An uncommon man even in this uncommon country, Rosset answers several calls each month on his Honda Silver Wing maxi-scooter. He attends regular refresher training with the national ambulance service, and is a major in the Israeli Defense Forces.

Despite the lifelong work exemption given to *Haredi* (ultra-Orthodox) Jews, Rosset also holds a day job managing the largest cemetery in Israel. He manages all this with a balance of reverence and corny humor.

"I'm the mayor," he said of the cemetery, "and I never get any complaints from the citizens."

Then he unfolded a scrapbook and showed a snapshot of his IDF unit, taken just before a mass casualty evacuation performed under fire in Gaza. They took the picture because they didn't expect they would all come back.

Everyone is smiling.

Three languages of laughter poured out into the warm night air as we talked for hours about city riding, army service, middle age (we're a few months apart), and our names: "Yisrael" is analogous to "Jakov" which is close to "Jack" and in Hebrew, "jack" means "kickstand." Rosset's lovely mother-in-law explained how her parents charmed their way out of Nazi Germany by posing as Episcopalians. An inveterate roundballer, Rosset was crushed to hear of the Sonics abandoning Seattle.

Although otherwise dissimilar to Tel Aviv's ongoing party by a millennium or five, Jerusalem also is thick with New Minutemen. I rode to the Jerusalem headquarters of Magen David Adom, Israel's state-affiliated ambulance service, near the highway's entry to that city on a hill. Facing a small Arab town across the Seam Line gully, the building has only gun slit windows well above head level to reduce the chance of successful potshots. Safe in the basement, connected by fat snarls of hasty rewiring, MDA's tactical center coordinates EMS calls for multiple agencies.

Michael Iflah has responded to MDA emergency calls for over ten years, moving to a scooter two years ago. Now he proudly rides a Piaggio MP3, which he said rides like a regular bike "but if you have oil in the road, you don't fall every time."

The Harley I was on found oil patches all over Jerusalem streets, not to mention the oil-based paint slathered onto every crosswalk and lane line. Jerusalam is so skittery that even walking over the ancient stone of the Old City can be treacherous. Three wheels good, two legs bad!

Also important, skipping sidestand deployment cuts 20 seconds off Iflah's response time. A surprising number of Israelis think this way. After nearly 6,000 years of fighting for cultural survival, that Jew Minuteman gene is bred in the bone — and shared across Semitic cultures. Both Qu-uran and Talmud explicate the point: to save one life is to save the whole world.

MDA's Jonathon Feldstein recounted the time a nearby *yeshiva* full of Orthodox boys was shot up by terrorists. The first responder on the scene — who had to return fire with his sidearm while treating his patients — was an Arab medic.

In the north, both ZAKA and MDA employ full units of Druze responders. Arab doctors serve in Israeli hospitals, and MDA sends ambulances to retrieve the sick from Gaza.

"The best coexistence of Arabs and Jews," Feldstein said, "is in hospitals."

Israel has a six-day work week — unless you're a medic. Then you're on call every day.

"Except Purim," Iflah reminded me. "You have to drink at Purim."

ZAKA's moto medics ride to more than 16,000 incidents per year, saving hundreds of lives and palliating thousands of injuries. Iflah himself has rendered CPR about 300 times and delivered a dozen babies, but even the saltiest moto medics suffer occasional miscues. Shortly after he was issued new Spidi Air Bag armor, Iflah jumped off his Piaggio and forgot to untether his jacket.

There was a loud POP.

Iflah grinned. "Suddenly, I was so *beeg*!" He waddled in like the Michelin Man and calmly resuscitated his patient, an Arab shopkeeper who collapsed at home after *Jumu'ah* prayers.

"I'm going to the call and I'm not caring if he's religious or what color," said Iflah, himself *Haredi* Orthodox, "only if he's human being.

"I like helping people."

Not every patient is saved, and some days aren't so funny.

"Some things are not depending on me," Iflah said. "Some things are for G-d."

Down in the parking lot, my Harley was a swarming anthill of *Haredi* boys, sidelocks just starting to curl. Conspiring to corrupt their tender futures, I let them scrap over who got to twist the throttle and make the black beast roar, while Iflah showed them his medical kit.

A few blocks from MDA sits the headquarters of United Hatzalah, originally founded in the U.S.A. to access New York's Hasidic (ultra-Orthodox) neighborhoods.

Pikuach nefesh is the Torah's commandment to put everything aside to save a human life — not an Israeli life, but any life. At the risk of their skins, both Hatzalah and ZAKA volunteers rendered aid at the Twin Towers on 9/11.

Because no good deed goes unpunished, Jewish aid service in New York fed internet rumors of an Israeli conspiracy to destroy Islam's good name. ZAKA also assisted after the explosion of our space shuttle Columbia, possibly indicating the presence of strategic Israeli space lasers…

Matan Nitzky made *aliyah* from St. Louis in 1996. He studies at *yeshiva*, rides for Hatzalah and carries only an Israeli passport.

"This is the Jewish home state," he said, echoing a familiar theme. "This is the only place on Earth where I don't have to feel like a second-class citizen."

David Dahan, a frosty-cool Moroccan Jew who blatted up on a chrome-encrusted, 1800cc Honda, said every day riding the streets of Jerusalem is an adventure. A computer tech, Dahan never pauses for apologies on the occasions when he leaves his job at a dead run, heading for a call.

"It's 24/7," he said, "not 24/6."

Their boss, Hatzalah bike captain Zeev Sofer, is a native-born Israeli who logs about 1,000 kilometers a week on his kitted Suzuki V-Strom. What drives him?

"My bike," Sofer grinned, explaining that lifesaving motivates him but he dreamed of motorcycles since he was a kid.

Didn't we all? But while I remember biking to the Grand Canyon, through green river valleys and over the Continental Divide, Sofer's scrapbook rides have been to terror attacks, a wedding hall collapse and a three year-old girl hit by a bus.

Stoically, Sofer disclaims bad dreams. "It's part of my daily life."

"We jump in, we jump out," said Dahan, claiming his heart was protected by "Israeli armor."

"Otherwise," Matan said, "we wouldn't be able to continue."

The famous Israeli smiles turned rueful while each rider reached for words.

"Our wives know," Sofer finally said, "that if we have to hug the kids a bit more, we've had a hard day."

•••

It's hard to imagine what might constitute a hard day for Jerusalem's mounted Special Police Unit, a special corps within the storied YAMAM elite force. Soft-spoken infantry veterans, they carry no handcuffs, ticket books or Tasers. Counter-terror shock troops for a living, they also serve as IDF reserve paratroopers. Police spokesman and British expat Mickey Rosenthal never calls his YAMAM stalwarts "officers" or "patrolmen." That's not their job.

He calls them "fighters."

Following a tactical syllabus comparable to U.S. Delta Force training, YAMAM's bike jockeys spend another week in the dirt, learning to rear-steer and ride gracefully over obstacles, riding two-up with weapons and ammo for hours on end.

SPU guys live near their partners, park duty bikes outside their homes and never turn their radios off. Toting CQB-sighted M4 carbines and Jericho "Baby Eagle" handguns, they course fluidly up and down stairs and prowl the narrow, cobbled alleyways of the Old City to put the fear of Yahweh into potential terrorists and the "adventure" into bone-stock BMW F800GS bikes, a recent upgrade from Kawasaki KLE500s.

They don't have a drill team. They never ride in parades.

Unshakably calm and matter-of-fact, YAMAM fighters wear flip-up Nolans and riding suits — but no bullet plates. "If we do our job right," Sharon Ashtamker explained, "nobody shoots back."

Cut *that* onto your adventure mirror and snort it.

We shadowed a squad of YAMAM around Jerusalem for an hour. They politely circulated the town, rarely splitting lanes, signaling every turn. They don't always ride this way. Like the medics, Special Patrol's response time from initial dispatch to Red-Direct averages less than two minutes — and for the same reason. If YAMAM is late, Israelis die.

For a treat, they gave us hoplite escort to the Western Wall, where I found it challenging to ride an understeering, 600-lb. hog two-up through pressing crowds across pavers slickened by millennia of sandals. On their dual-sports, the counter-terror cops idled quietly through, feet on the pegs, expressionless behind their tactical shades.

Outraged by insolent bikers snapping pictures with teenage girls, the supervising rabbi sent police to eject us from hallowed ground. When the patrolmen encountered our YAMAM standing quietly around the bikes, they practically curled into fetal positions.

Surrounded by cool professionals, I stifled my unseemly giggle. For the next two days, wherever I went in Jerusalem, a YAMAM bike murmured around the corner. I confess I was a little relieved every time they smiled and gave me a thumbs-up.

Israeli Defense Forces military police also field a mounted unit, composed of soldiers riding custom Harley-Davidson 883 Sportsters out of the Tzrifin IDF base south of Tel Aviv.

Not every MP gets a ticket to ride, said Maj. Amir Lazover, unit commander for the past year. Motor MPs are never first-hitch conscripts, and must show an exemplary service record before they may apply.

"They usually ride alone," Lazover said. "They need to be relentlessly professional."

IDF MPs are not YAMAM, though. Although they take a two-month train-up where they're taught never to scrape a peg, the units I saw were well scuffed by tipovers.

Tom Gery, a thick-set, soft-spoken 21 year-old MP, fought hard for his job because he loves bikes. A Harley guy to the bone, his ambition is to someday buy a big twin, grow a big beard, and get a big helmet with a spike on top.

"I would ride it around and around my house," he said reverently, "around my heart.

"How you call these angels — Hell's Angels? I like these the best," he said, carefully stubbing out his cigarette so it wouldn't show up in a picture.

"Because my mother," he said, blushing a little as his commanding officer silently nodded approval.

•••

Riding for ZAKA's Jerusalem office, Shimi Grossman averages 80 calls per month and he's not slowing down. A realtor by trade and a hyperkinetic exclamation point by nature, Grossman explained (more with hands than voice) why he never turned off his pager, took off his medic jacket or left his helmet behind. One morning, the omnipresent MIRS directed him to a neighboring house to find a friend crushed under a fallen wall.

"Femoral artery bleed very fast," he said. "I am there less than two minutes. I stop with — what is word?"

"Tourniquet?"

"Yes! *Tourniquet!* And he *live*! I see him later, and he is walking." Hopping around, Grossman grinned the trademark Israeli smile. "Hospital give him two plastic legs. He go back to hospital and show them, 'Look! Can dance!'"

"He is happy. He have reason. Nothing is better than this!"

Sometimes, even New Minutemen take their pagers off. Grossman only takes his off when overseas. His last two trips — to Thailand after its tsunami and to Haiti for earthquake relief — were vacations only in the sense that he wasn't on call all the time.

He was just on duty.

Grossman's devotion isn't unique among ZAKA riders. Four years ago, medic Aaron Gross left his bride standing under the *chuppah* to resuscitate a heart attack victim outside the wedding hall, then returned to crush the glass.

Despite the MIRS pager on his nightstand, he remains happily married.

On our way to the pizza parlor where ZAKA's scooter arm originated, Grossman took a call for heat prostration in an Orthodox synagogue. Suffice it to say that riding rapidly through Jerusalem gridlock is quite a lot like blasting your bike through Tel Aviv, only with orders of magnitude more roundabouts, oil on the street and obdurate pedestrians in beards and black tailcoats.

Deep in the Orthodox quarter known as *Mea Shearim*, Yaakov Uri runs a pizza parlor unlike any you've seen. Men and women wait in separate lines at Pizza Uri, and young men without families of their own eat in a separate room. Other than that, it could be a Chicago neighborhood joint: hot, greasy, clamorous, and the pie is angel-kissed. Uri, round-cheeked and smiling, extended his hand much in the manner of a Catholic cardinal. Resisting the urge to kiss his ring, I shook it formally.

"Sit," he said in the gentle wheeze of Brando in *The Godfather*. "Please, let me serve you."

At a wave of his finger, huge wedges of kosher pizza appeared. He waved me off from eating it until he could personally slather it with a spicy, off-white sauce. Great slices apparently do not require pepperoni.

Wearing six layers of black wool in 90-degree weather doesn't faze Uri, but watching people die while waiting for an ambulance to arrive stopped him cold. What could a pizza restaurateur do? In 2001, Uri's simple, perfect inspiration changed the game for EMS in Israel.

"I looked at these," he said, pointing at his delivery scooters, "and I thought we could use them."

Uri emptied out a delivery box, rode across town and pitched his idea to Yehuda Meshi-Zahav, chairman and founder of ZAKA and a running buddy of Uri's in Orthodox political circles. ZAKA's been splitting lanes ever since.

In Jewish tradition, it's a *mitzvah* or righteous deed to keep Shabbat holy, but a greater *mitzvah* to honor the dead properly — and the greatest of *mitzvot* is to preserve human life. ZAKA's speed into action gives them a place at the table for emergency medical response, just as their devotion to skilled handling of the dead makes ZAKA teams a welcome sight around the world.

Underneath the conflicting agendas of socialist ideals, *Haredi* purism and the dream of Zionism, Israelis are a pragmatic lot. Occupying a nation about twice the size of the county I live in and surrounded by governments sworn to destroy them, they shrug their shoulders and conscript most everyone to military service. Parked on perhaps the only piece of Middle Eastern desert with no oil, and with seven million Jewish, Palestinian, Bedouin and Druze mouths to feed, they task their engineers with creating the world's biggest desalination plants. To the New Minutemen these are viewed as practical matters, transcending politics.

And when their ambulances can't punch through traffic, they listen to pizza shop wisdom from the Orthodox Godfather to dispatch medics on two-wheelers. You can't carry litters on scooters, but salt enough of them into the community and you can push a respirator, defibrillator and bucket of bandages anywhere in Jerusalem in about two minutes.

I wonder if we could do that here.

•••

In 2007, Harley-Davidson offered eight free bikes to New York City for an EMS pilot program and the fire department turned them down flat. "Unsafe," FDNY called it — even as NYPD sewed up a million-dollar purchase from Harley.

Here in the States, we don't have a problem putting police on bikes for revenue enhancement. But when the payload is ventilators and pressure bandages instead of guns and ticket books, suddenly motorcycles are "too dangerous." The opportunity cost is lives — but then, with some 300 million citizens to Israel's seven million or so, maybe we just have more lives to spend.

Or maybe we've decided it's more important to fine speeders and escort politicians than to rescue our countrymen.

While you perused this article, an Israeli scooter medic from ZAKA, MDA or Hatzalah cheated Death by cutting the track during rush hour. Back here in the States, somebody's four minutes expired while an ambulance driver pounded his steering wheel in frustration, desperately trying to imagine a way through, over, between the lethal gridlock.

Because motorcycles are dangerous.

October 2010, Motorcyclist
(abridged version)

The Niemöller Principle

"The only way to have a friend is to be one." — Ralph Waldo Emerson

"Ninety-nine percent of motorcyclists are law-abiding citizens, and the last one percent are nothing more than outlaws."

Nobody knows who said that. Maybe it's apocryphal.

What did happen as a matter of record and history is that "One Percenter" became a badge of honor for "outlaw" clubs, its outlaw brand celebrated with delicious terror in a thousand pulp mags and a handful of Roger Corman B-flicks. Sonny Barger may (or may not) have been the first guy to get "1%er" inked onto his pelt, but surely he wasn't the last.

Herd nature drives us together against common threats, or what H.S. Thompson branded "The Menace." The same flocking instinct requires The Menace to provide for their common defense against, um… "Us."

And who are Us? We're the good guys — conscientious, ATGATT ambassadors of the sport. We meet the nicest people on our Hondas. We put our best wheel forward. We sneer at the unwashed and the ign'ant. Our tire pressures are perfect.

That arrogant patch holder with the tattooed arms, loose-meat pillion bitch and cherry bomb drag pipes who won't so much as nod at our cheerful wave from our kickass Hyperbusa? When he gets lit up by the law, we snicker up our armored sleeve as we elegantly zip by, firmly wrapped in fail-safe technology.

Better him than me. He makes us all look bad.

When a Suzuki rider recently got popped clocking 122 mph on I-205 south in the small hours of the night, his harshest judgments came from fellow riders. The intertubes lit up with digital pitchforks and torches: *he makes us all look bad!*

That heinous crime allegedly occurred at three in the morning. What's 122 on a modern sportbike — top of third gear? On a long, wide, straight, well-lit, untrafficked expressway at 0300. No one to hurt but himself, unless a deer wandered out.

He lost his bike and license for that, if it makes anyone feel better.

Still think they're not coming for you? A few months back, a couple on a Gold Wing hit a mule deer on I-5, backing up traffic for miles. Wearing armored clothes and full-face helmets, herding a shop-tuned, late model touring rig along the slab at the speed limit, they were nearly killed by a woods rat. Public comment consensus was that they deserved it for riding that damned donorcycle in the first place, how *dare* they hold up everyone's commute for a Life Flight… and was the deer OK?

Even Wing Dingers make us look bad!

•••

Riding a bike brands you as the minority, and discrimination against minorities is automatic. It is instinctive, but we riders should be better than that. If we ostracize every rider who doesn't meet our personal purity test, *e pluribus unum* goes straight into the toilet.

When they came for the one-percenters, I didn't say anything because I wasn't a one-percenter (besides, colors are for clowns). When they came for the squids, I laughed at those brain-dead punks. When they came for the sport tourers, I... hey! Wait a minute! It wasn't *me* making us look bad!

Then the LORD said to Cain, "Where is your brother Abel?"
"I don't know," he replied. "Am I my brother's keeper?" (Gen. 4:9, NIV)

If you refuse to wave to scooterists or three-patch bikers or squids or whomever, you're a dick. They face the same blind cagers, get hassled by the same LEOs, and get frozen by the same sleet. Asphalt burns us all the same shade of red.

Think about this the next time you blare on about how young stuntahs ought to take their tricks to the track (and what track would that be, exactly?): when you were a kid, could you afford a newish sportbike, full leathers and track day fees?

Or did you get your kicks where you could? Be honest.

It was several years ago when Ex2 and I were passed on the right by Little Joey Rocket in the diamond lane of westbound SR 520. Doing about 80, he stood on the seat so he could see over the flying front wheel. As the lane ended and the floating bridge began, he set it down softly, slowed, signaled and merged seamlessly into the flow of traffic.

It was beautiful.

"My God," said Ex2. "That's *crazy!*"

Yeah, OK — *crazy* beautiful.

I hope that kid lives to be a cranky old fart, querulously wheezing on about "kids today." I hope someday he stops to help a brother on a busted old Harley. I hope he aces an expert riding course, and raises a litter of bright, daring kids who understand that "outlaw" never was a synonym for "criminal."

You grown-ups are making *too much noise*! Go play Outside for awhile.

February 2010, Motorcyclist

SWEATBIKE NORTHWEST

Looking back at this story now is possible only through the lens of friendship. Photographer Michael Pierce and generous host Ken Morton subsequently became dear friends... with one of them since lost to time and fate. I remember the roads, the countryside, the bikes, and especially the friendships. Very little sticks of the event itself. SBNW remains, if nothing else, a fine excuse to get on your bike and ride.

If you need an excuse.

We're a gathering sort of species, and riders are more gregarious than average. As for me, I ride alone.

I ride alone to work, to lunch, to parties, to meet friends... and to all kinds of places where complete strangers want to talk to "the guy on the bike." Really, I ought to just find a few good roads and go riding with my buddies.

Tom Mehren, the publisher of Sound *RIDER!*, had that idea in 2003. He found a few more roads, invited a lot of folks, and dubbed it Sportbike Northwest. Base-camped at the Skamania Fairgrounds outside Stevenson, Washington on the banks of the Columbia River, participants can scamper west into the hills if it's fair, or blaze east across semi-arid wine country if it rains on the wet side.

At Sportbike '09, fairing-mounted beer cozies, chewed frame sliders and leather g-strings were in short supply. These rally cats incline more toward GPS-guided, low-altitude mileage missiles saddled with tank bags full of protein bars. By the time we got sealed into our orange plastic Bracelets of Admission, riders were emerging from the Small Animal Barn carrying small sandwiches of pulled pork (NOTE: not included in admission), while other barns full of tailored bikes offered better browsing than a three-ring dealer showroom.

•••

Saddled up for the week on a K1300S courtesy of Ride West BMW in Seattle, I wasn't shopping too hard. Dipping south into Portland to link up with pro cameraman Michael Pierce, the Orange Krusher proved itself deceptively swift and smooth. It even had the GM's personal tank bag strapped on for a little unearned sport touring cred. It's good to know things, but it's better to know people.

It's especially better when June's thermometer spikes well north of 100 degrees Fahrenheit. Crazed by the heat, Portland pedalers fluttered and spun into our armored shins like moths sizzling against Coleman lanterns. Who commutes on a mountain bike in 114-degree heat? The K1300S may not be precisely "green," but its meticulously catalyzed exhaust smells better than any bicyclist.

Brains bubbling inside our helmets, we chose commuting from a buddy's Vancouver home over tenting on the ol' fairgrounds. That added 300-odd miles to our rally tally, but while the hard corps unrolled their creaking bones onto scorched Skamania grass, we were filling our Camelbaks out of Dread Pirate Kermit's icemaker and lingering over chilled cantaloupe and *café au lait*. We later heard from a diehard tentizen that campers queued up hundreds deep for a single, 50-cup urn of tepid brew.

Friends can last a lifetime, bikes for years and brekkie for a couple of hours if you're doing it right, but a road is new just once. Undiscovered roads are to track days as gunfights are to target ranges. Well-provisioned, we sallied forth with a glint in our eye.

Promptly lost in the horse acres outside Washougal, Michael and I stopped to soak our heads in a stock tank and talk horses with Melissa, a sandy-haired, green-eyed pixie who's cowgirl enough to make an old motorcyclist reconsider his mount.

North out of Amboy runs a choice road wriggling with sun-dappled curves. It sails into a town where you can leave a $700 jacket and $500 helmet hanging on your bike with a D-SLR in the tank bag and stroll into the Cougar Café without a care.

In retrospect, it might have been better if someone had stolen the camera. I needed shelf space for my gut after piling through a chili cheeseburger plate the size of seven McDonalds combos, washed down with half a gallon of sweet tea.

"Ultra-size me, honey."

The geeky goodness of BMW's Electronic Suspension Adjustment let me toggle over to the COMF setting until I finished belching 200 miles later. The K may not have Black Betty's everyway-adjustable (and *shiny!*) Öhlins dampers but really, aren't wrenches for the underclass? SPORT mode tightens the chassis right up to let you steer the rear without fear, but the real fun lurks in its electronic quick shifter.

Inhumanly smooth and quicker than any hand can fan the clutch, the shifter works best when you're hard on the gas. It also works better the higher you rev it, which can lead to naughty behavior. Whoop-*burp*-whoo-OOM-*burp*-WHOOOM! Damn thing's a gateway bike…

•••

On Friday afternoon, the mercury finally dropped to a frosty 91° F at the pass junction where we decided against pushing our rocket sows over 50 miles of gravel to Berry Field. Instead, we plunged our steaming feet into Rush Creek, a fast-flowing trout stream of runoff water cold enough to seize up toes. Suffered a few gnat bites, but we'd wreak bloody vengeance on their tribe later with our Headlights of Death.

A couple of miles above Wind River Road, practicing trail braking into downhill sweepers, I gazed off into the treeline for a moment and kissed the gravel-frosted fog line. I don't mind Death tapping me on the shoulder occasionally, but I wish he wouldn't distract me when I'm searching for my mislaid front wheel traction.

"Pin and grin," I reminded myself, "not pin it and bin it."

Just as I was reestablishing the kind of sweet rhythm that loosens up my lower back, we cranked around a right-hander to see a car yanked over and a tall woman waving us down.

In a ditch to the right sat a narrow fella in his early 40s, unzipped and perched disconsolately on his pretty, red, capsized bike. I pulled up my visor.

"Y'alright?"

"Yeah. Collarbone."

"Got ibuprofen and water if you need some."

"Nah. I'm okay."

With EMS summoned and the site secured, we eased on down the road. Screaming uphill came a fire truck, an aid car, a deputy, a two-ton aid truck, another deputy and an ambulance. The helicopters must have been deployed to an ankle sprain site.

•••

Inevitably, our brunch-enabled morning laziness was punished. Alongside host Kermit, Michael and I rolled out at 0415 on Saturday for our fourth day of road burning. Bleary and blinking, we had a sunrise date with Stonehenge Memorial.

Their names inscribed on small bronze tablets, spirits of soldiers past greeted the warm dawn breeze as did our three-man patrol of former soldier, sailor and airman: quietly. But only we could still look out over the vineyards lining the Columbia by the pink early light. The dated plaques divulge no history, only stories' ends: boys by their ages, men by their deeds.

Three middle-aged men, grateful for another day's chance to improve, bowed our heads, walked slowly out, and rode into the future on our once-unimaginable toys.

Few experiences are finer than strong, swift bikes on good roads in the company of skilled friends. Motorcycles aren't actually better than women but they are, as Secretary Rumsfeld once said of American soldiers, fungible. Swapping mounts around reminded us that all men may be created equal, but all literbikes are not.

If Ferrari built a tractor, it would sound like Kermit's IBR-farkled Tuono R. While the big orange K scratches that occasional itch to revisit 175 mph, the Tuono is a KTM for grown-ups, with build quality that makes the Super Duke look like a high school shop project.

Michael's Yamaha FJ1300 did everything the Big Beemer did for 20 percent less money, sitting straight up in the saddle and dragging the saddlebags. When Michael sits straight up in that saddle you may as well be following a bus for all you can see, but the big bugger is too sneaky-fast to get around, even with Ride West buying me tires.

Delicious road days call for exquisitely crafted desserts, and Maryhill Loops Road is as rich and refined as Napoleon torte. Laid just prior to WWI by Sam Hill (patron of the aforementioned Stonehenge Memorial), Maryhill was Washington's first paved road and remains a peerless playground, so tight and steep and sweetly cambered you could shred the wheels off a skateboard.

An improved section of Maryhill can be reserved for special events. It packs 25 turns — including eight hairpins — into 3.6 miles. On Friday, it was reserved for runs by rally participants (reservation required). We had passed up our chance to trade paint with Friday's horde of scrabbling squidlings, instead meeting professional instructor Rolf Vitous for a private clinic on Saturday. It's good to know things about motorcycles, and even better to have expert friends.

Nearly binning my high-ticket Beemer half a dozen times on the sighting lap relaxed me enough to slow down until I could speed up. Our ATC clinic graduated from line-picking exercises to one-gear laps to coasting laps, then to coasting laps without touching the brakes.

A 600-lb. K-bike will *schuss* brakeless down Maryhill like a toboggan on afterburner, but not without tracing peg lines around the hairpins and shagging its tires to the edge lines. Brakeless coasting on steep twisties is eerily peaceful. Like glider aerobatics, there's no sound beyond whistling wind, grinding teeth, and the squeaky squinching of seat vinyl.

Around two p.m., asphalt now sweating as hard as we were, we decamped for Mexican food in Wenatchee. Burning west after lunch, wind turbines on the bluffs appeared suddenly as alien tripods, standing ready to alert us to any threat of wind. No such menace was reported. I watched the K-puter readout climb steadily from 109 to 114. Then we dropped into the Klickitat River Valley and it hit 116. Yanking bottle after scalding bottle of water out of my tank bag, I poured it into my riding suit, bemused. Northwest riders spend most of the year trying to keep water *out* of our clothes.

•••

Back at the fairgrounds, we ambled past dealer pavilions and aftermarket booths where evaporative vests sold like coldcakes, test-rode a couple of KTMs (no wheelies allowed!), and eyeballed tables jammed with silent auction items and raffle prizes. Running up another 400-mile day, we had missed supper but were right on time for dessert. Ride stunning roads all day, then eat ice cream. This is the sport for me!

Because Sportbike NW is part of Sound *RIDER!* Rally in the Gorge — a constellation of events including Sport Touring NW, Dual Sport NW and (be still, my heart) Maxi-Scoot NW — there's a lot to tie up at the closing ceremonies. We learned that two or possibly three participants had crashed out on Saturday; no one seemed quite sure. Mention was also made of "boo-boos" on the poker run, prompting a woman who'd tipped over to yell, "'Cause ya dit-n't have no *sign!*" I wondered how one might word a sign advising poker runners not to belly-flop their bikes.

Sponsors were thanked, attendees exhorted, and Mr. Mehren's contributions exalted. Raffle giveaways featured everything from beer cozies to a BMW Street Guard 2 to instant karma: the same guy who coughed up his KTM-specific prize to a grateful KTM owner won the BMW riding suit about four minutes later.

No one begrudged him, but the crowd remained sluggish. After four days riding through convection oven heat, cold beer and a live band could have brightened up the vibe had someone thought to lay them on. Mehren grabbed the mike to announce that attendance dropped from 550 in 2008 to 400 in what participants were by then calling "Sweatbike Northwest." He blamed the weather and the economy. If global warming doesn't get you, Goldman Sachs will.

That June, $99.^{00} bought you the plastic bracelet, a fistful of route maps, poker run, admission to various seminars and sound-impaired movies, four nights of camping, some reportedly meager chow on Saturday and a Sunday morning sendoff from the Christian Motorcyclists Association.

Choose you this day whom ye will serve, but as for me and my buddies, we will worship the road. There will be more runnings of Sportbike NW, but you won't find us bivouacked there.

Look for us out on a secondary road, happily lost and running on fumes, or arc around a bend to discover motor-cycles parked by the creekside. Pull over if you feel like it. You don't need an invitation to stop and talk bikes.

And we don't need a ticket to ride.

July 2010, Motorcyclist

The Bike that Changed My Life II

"A mule has neither pride of ancestry nor hope of posterity."
— *Robert Green Ingersoll*

It wasn't the Harley Sprint that I blasted down the parkway at Evergreen State College, sneering through the bugs in my teeth at the poor collegiate denizens trapped in the smoky confines of their microbuses. Nor was it the *pur sang* IT (for "international trials," dontcha know) that did its pipey best to cripple your devoted scribe.

No, it was a mannerly, medium blue Yamaha of the "enduro" persuasion. "Enduro" is an archaic term that used to mean, "I can ride this damn thing anywhere." They're now called "dual-sports." That seems… limiting.

I bounced on its black loaf seat in the parking lot of my dad's business while he negotiated the price downward from several hundred to a few hundred dollars. By that evening, our garage sported a low-mileage DT175, the world's shiniest All Areas Pass.

The unbreakable engine had seven moving parts in a low state of tune, but a reed valve gave it a modicum of two-stroke cred. Six forward speeds were a 50 percent increase from our Harley's four-cog box. My maintenance ritual was to tank up, check the Autolube reservoir and go riding. If the battery was dead dry, I never noticed — the kick-starter and rectifier got the bike going just fine. If the uniblock tires were more or less round, I hopped on and went. Rode it for a year before I learned about chain lube, but it didn't make enough power to stretch the chain much.

Carpet never came more magical. The DT would putt through tight woods, wail up and down sandy quarries, and get me to school late every time. It had rear pegs and just enough seat for a date if she was lean, flexible and possessed of the requisite sparkle-eyed sense of adventure. You could ford a tank-high stream w/o stalling if you were reasonably expeditious about it.

What did I learn from the little blue Yammie? Sliding, for one. Half the riders I know these days have never ridden bikes off road. Consequently, the least slip wads their panties tight. That makes as much sense as a pilot who never takes spin training. Muscle memory is what you fall back on when only the seat of the pants will save your ass.

Wheelies and jumps, for another. Trivial goofiness it may be, but it was revelatory to a clumsy kid with bad balance that I could get away with those little stunts intact. My areas of teen competence were few. One, actually.

Safety gear was a big lesson, absorbed in the time-honored fashion from my dad: "If I see you on that bike without a helmet *one more time*, I'm selling it." Alrighty, then! Less hardheaded these days, I'm happy to be in the armored hat habit.

Respect for law enforcement. Not always for the law — our speed laws are criminally draconian — but for the guys who have to walk the line between humane and authoritarian behavior. I was pretty pissed about pushing my Yamaha three miles home after I got busted riding to freshman two-a-days, but in retrospect it beat hell out of an impound.

Lack of respect for limitations. That little bike was slower than a CB750 — unless you were dodging muddy roots. It wouldn't jump as high as an RM250, but I could ride mine to high school on the public roads (well, after I got my license and endorsement, anyway).

It was a real bike, with a real kick-starter, because that's how dreams are cranked.

Not previously published

Going Gently

Do not go gentle into that good night,
Old age should burn and rave at close of day;
Rage, rage against the dying of the light.
— *Dylan Thomas*

I have no great history with trikes.

My first one was red and white, came from Monkey Wards and had a temperamental habit of getting its straight-linked pedals ahead of my fat little legs on steep downhills, whacking me in the Achilles tendons and tossing me over the high side in a toddler-style Fosbury Flop.

Yeah, I rode fixies before fixies were cool.

I was still a single-digit tyke when Dad brought home the not-so-legendary Blue Bullet and Red Racer, a pair of Honda ATC 90 three-wheelers. If you recall the zero-travel suspension and solid axle steering of those pristinely engineered deathtraps, it's probably because you have a good-sized scar to remind you. In my case, it's about a three-incher across my left thigh.

Nope. Not a good history. Still, when the editor wants a story, a freelancer asks, "How high?"

In this case, the answer was high enough to break a leg, scrub half the summer's motorcycling and evaluate Harley's new trike instead.

Why "new trike?" Since the 2009 model year, Harley-Davidson has offered their FLHTCUTG Tri Glide Ultra Classic, a three-wheeled big twin for those who don't want to give up the wind in their faces when knees or hips go. In Milwaukee's lineup, the Tri Glide (NOTE: not a personal lubricant) displaced their factory sidecar rig that moved units on the order of negative figures per year. While the 2009-10 tri-wheelers were assembled by Lehman Trikes in Spearfish, SD, the 2011 run moved to H-D's York facility. The current model is thus the first all-Harley three-wheeler — other than sidecars — since the putt-putt Servi Cars manufactured from 1932-1972.

Local twins racing legend Scott Moon looked at me funny when I hobbled into the showroom at Eastside Harley-Davidson in Bellevue, Washington to pick up a zero-mileage Tri Glide that retails at $30,499, but the staff brought the bike around promptly. While they bolted up an accessory rack suitable for lashing on a pair of crutches, I eye-molested an unridden XR750 from the late Evel Knievel's stable. Innocent of stoppers at either end, it boasted the world's best torque-to-brakes ratio.

•••

GM Scott Cook wasn't feeling the gimp love.

"Are you *sure* this is a good idea?," he asked Pretty Wife at least three times as I stumped around, examining the beast from all angles. "Is he gonna be okay riding?"

Her Mona Lisa smile was the silent reply of one who pays the life insurance premiums.

Harleys combine time-honored styling licks, carefully engineered vintage-appearing powerplants and certain funky touches that either make you smile or drive you bats. The Tri comes motivated by a luscious 103-c.i. Twincam engine, dressed up in an Electra batwing fairing ahead of a leather sofa cushion. The signal indicators are calculated to kill you as you fix your eyes firmly away from the road to seek their tiny green confirmation, but you soon discover they shut themselves off without help.

All Geezer Glides should come with self-canceling signals. Endless blinkering is for Airstream-hauling Suburbans, vintage Plymouths and Rascal scooters. Harleys are too cool for that.

Even this one, maybe. Trike it may be (and at 4.3 cubic feet, that capacious rear trunk is right-sized for a Costco bale of Depends), but this is a for-real, manly mo'sickle. Mine was Vivid Black — the only proper color for a non-Italian bike — and its alloy rear wheels packed the same blocky intaglios found on the latest Blackline factory customs, deep and malty with undertones of the Bat Signal...

They looked at me funny when I asked if it came with a jack.

"This is a motorcycle."

•••

Like all Harley-Davidson motorcycles, the factory recommends dealer servicing for any flat tires. We departed Eastside in proper biker attire — i.e. leathered up like The Gimp in *Pulp Fiction* — and sallied forth directly into the teeth of a late spring storm. Characteristic that the Leisure Glide shares with its two-footed, progenitive Electra Glide platform: excellent weather protection. Six-footers will get damp knees and a dribble over the tops of their helmets only, which militates against helmet laws because the hardhat is just one more thing to get wet.

Characteristic that it does not share: being a motorcycle.

The first thing a three-wheeler course will teach you is to never put your boots down (or in my case, your fracture dressing). This is to prevent you suffering the Massey Ferguson-style embarrassment of maxing your style points by running over yourself from behind — kinda like so many of us did on those little Hondas of yore. Still hurts when I limp about it.

The first thing you learn on your own is to consciously dispense with the instinct forcing you to steer down the wheel tracks. Just plant its nose wheel in the greasy middle of the lane, and leave it there.

There are other contrasts. The bike(ish) does not lean. Not even slightly, although H-D's people claim a round-shoul-dered front tire is necessary to lighten steering and because there is a non-zero amount of sideward tire roll during cornering. I grew to dread the notion of heavier steering as I built up my arms over the next few days.

During a hard stop, you stomp the brake pedal with Kenworth authority to haul down car-sized rear tires — the Triflow packs more contact patch than an L.A. lowrider. One wonders whether skinnier tires wouldn't open up the option of drifting the chassis and perhaps improve fuel mileage, perhaps at the cost of appearing overly retro.

Did I even say that? In the age of the Springer, Road King Classic and the 48, can a Harley possibly appear overly retro? We say bring on the wide whites, skinny tires and chrome spokes! Maybe pimp it out with a spare tire in a Continental kit…

It may be no motorcycle, but the Gimp Glide is every inch a Harley in the universal attention it attracts. On our first two-up foray with Smalldaughter, a darkroom denizen of the North City Tavern lurched across 15th to learn whether Harley's triple threat had a reverse gear. At my admission, he exploded in mirthless laughter.

"*Hah!* All you Harley guys make fun of my Gold Wing 'cause it's got reverse!"

I smiled my gimpiest smile. "Maybe we're just tired of being called 'barhoppers' by Honda riders."

He stumbled backward before I could gout-test his toes with the rear wheel. Can't be too harmless, lest they take my rumbling Rascal for granted…

Mumbling casually along on the Tri evoked memories of college days on the Palouse. Shifting at 2,200 rpm, two hands firmly on the wheel, stomping the pedal to slow and "apexing" wherever traffic engineers painted the line: these weren't memories of my '86 Yamaha or even my '52 Beeza. They were memories of a grain truck.

Or of an army deuce, famous for an emergency brake you couldn't release (or even see) without opening the driver door. Similarly obscure, the Tri Brake hides under the right passenger footboard and fouls it on release.

These are trivial things. Real men don't fuss about buttery shifting. We make our gearboxes do the whining for us.

Dick's Burgers (aka "Chez Richard's") is the PNW's grunge analog to the chipper neon of In-N-Out. Small-daughter took over my seat at the drive-in, the better to get Dad to hold a chocolate shake at her elbow, and I surmised the canniness of Harley's strategy for spousal buy-in: the pillion is not only the more comfy perch, it also has rear volume and channel controls for the 80w harman/kardon quad-speaker stereo (the better to keep her chauffeur in line).

Shipyard Larry pulled into Dick's on a Wing-based trike that looked about nine feet long. Nice fella, about six-three with two canes and a patch that reads "IF YOU DON'T LIMP, YOU AIN'T SHIT." Larry's building a V-8 trike back home, now that he can't really ride his chopped Triumph anymore. As his other patch explains, Larry is "Free On Three." We talked about all the typical, tough-guy biker topics: kids and dogs, mostly. His grandkids love his trike.

We stopped at a park to rummage the last of our fries. While Smalldaughter dashed off toward the swings, I lay down in the grass, trying not to think about my leg, and watched the clouds leave without me. A fiftyish voice intruded politely.

"Are you okay?"

I struggled up onto my working foot. "Uh, yeah… sure. "Just waiting."

I gestured vaguely toward the play area, hoping the distinguished gent didn't think I was some kind of slow-moving playground pedo, but he was raptly caressing my Tri Glide.

On the other side of his beige minivan, a teenager tapped her pretty foot impatiently. Looking carefully away from her, I tried not to think of myself as a playground pedo.

"This is beautiful," he said, half under his breath, then looked up brightly. "What's it like to ride?"

"It's…" I thought for a moment about being stuck on this non-bike, then surprised myself with the truth. "It's… kinda neat, really."

Beaming, he flashed vintage orthodontia through last week's Mazatlan tan. "I *knew* it!"

"Da-ad…"

Without taking his eyes off the Ultra Tri, he clicked the doors open for her. Shaking his head gently, he repeated his chant.

"Sure is beautiful… sure is beautiful…"

•••

The next day, we embarked on a family expedition. A lovely, two-ferry peninsular swing brought us to the solstice-timed Wetleather™ Goat Roast on Vashon Island, where the only way to earn more scorn than pulling up in a car is thumping up the dirt drive on a three-wheeler.

Still, our flats of PBR have mostly given way to Dram Club arcana and even stud(ette) riders grow up to collect bridal trains of orthopedists, oncologists and cardiologists. With Wetleather™ approximately the only cohort aging more swiftly than Harley's fishtailed Boomer demographic, we indulge in fewer capering goat dances, practically no street bike races in the dirt and much more standing around, sipping acacia juice and fulminating about the lapsed condition of the world.

It ain't the end of the line, but we can see it from here — and either worry about it, or find a way to keep riding. As Phil's sig line reminds us 17 times a day (we older folk can be repetitious), "Ride 'til you can't!"

For all the good-natured rebukes, I found myself talkin' trikes to a surprising number of old, bold riders. Stealth sidebar topics included steering (heavy, and non-counter), mileage (car-like) and the virtues of "heel-and-heel" shifting for the cast-bound.

Trikes are great for summer tramping and Smalldaughter, who had turned her nose up at tenting behind our house, was very excited about "real camping" in Daughtergirl's backyard. All yards are not created equal.

We stuffed food, clothes and gifts into the trunk; staged camera, water and snacks in the top box; strapped bedrolls, tent and crutches up top; then bailed south toward Portland. Pretty Wife mocked us gently with the curvaceous agility of her middleweight.

Twenty minutes into the trip, surprised by an unaccustomed level of podiatric comfort, I looked down to discover that my weakest ATGATT link was a black, slip-on shoe. Loafer Glide! I laughed so hard I slipped a disk in my back…

•••

Our destination was a friend's memorial. Alone at night on a Nebraska highway, Kermit was likely hit by a "supercell" storm. He went out quicker than an Ali jab. The last thing Ken heard was probably something from iTunes. We disagreed about riding with music. I prefer road rumbles to tinny pop, but with the miles Ken put up, who was I to tell him how to roll?

Near Kalama we saw a red-tailed hawk lying on the shoulder in a tattered discomposure of feathers. It probably got smacked by a semi. I choked a little in my helmet, and turned the radio up.

In Vancouver, we celebrated Kermit's life with a rev-off, wherein I elected to blip the Harley off the bottom rather than voiding its warranty with a resonant Motoman break-in. Even amid a fury of shrieking triples, zinging sixes and ringing two-smokes, all bass notes go to Heaven. From our pipes to G-d's ear…

Wakes are timely reminders to get over yourself. No can ride bike? Well, here's this three-wheeler, all wrapped up in silky black, scratch-resistant paint, ready to rumble you a little further down the road. Is the point of all this to travel a ways further through the world, to be resuscitated one more time by the kiss of the wind — or is it mostly to look cool while we pass up the guy in front of us? Either way, it's a lead pipe cinch that the difference between bungee-ing crutches onto a motorized milk stool and never riding anything again isn't one hundred percent.

It's infinite.

•••

With Pretty Wife riding scout on her GS, we stole through Portland's exurbs with the glint of rural freedom in our eye. Just for the memories, we ran up and down Germantown Road, where decades ago I learned to drift in a '64 Chrysler without ever having visited Tokyo. It's since broken out in a rash of Texas speed bumps, for which I suppose I must share blame. Holding her arms out like wings, Smalldaughter yelled for more speed, cheering every time we hit one fast.

Not far past Sauvie's Island is the Crown Zellerbach mill town of Scappoose where I've been more times at 0200 than in daylight, staging teammates on the Hood to Coast relay. Some promoter's bright idea lit off their "Worldwide Peace Candle" (no doubt you've heard of it). On the western outskirts, Seventh Day Adventists and Jehovah's Witnesses faced off across the highway in a catfight for the affections of Jesus.

Refusing to take sides, we eased pensively through the green and grey countryside, passing a representative sample of '69 International pickups more or less identical to the one for which I once traded, in a spasm of uncontrolled pique, a bike with more chrome than go. Although the 103 Twincam this day was more than willing to run up the speed, everything — wind protection, mileage, handling, stereo tunes and my attitude — worked better at 60 than 70.

Tri Clydesdales can do one thing no mere motorcycle can do. They can pull lateral Gs. Squealing with laughter, Smalldaughter braced her arches against the backs of her footboards as we slalomed along the river road. She didn't care that we weren't on a "real" motorcycle, only that we were having real fun the best we could, with what we had, where we were. Teddy Roosevelt smiled down out of the past.

How much better was that than not riding? All the way better.

•••

Past Deer Island and Goble, we wound on through Rainier, where churning tugs pushed freighters around like border collies working particularly recalcitrant pieces of livestock. We changed states on Highway 433, sailing over the Columbia River to Longview and its comforting array of feed stores and logging supply houses. Wrapped up for painting, the Lewis and Clark Bridge looked like a gigantic Japanese lantern.

We changed rivers there, too, winding north along the Cowlitz on what I remember as Greyhound's milk run north out of Portland. Sunlight broke through to warm our backs. Silhouetted against the western sun, three red-tailed hawks swung in the sky. I smiled into my helmet then.

Smalldaughter tuned into a country station, but I turned it up anyway.

Between Winlock and Napavine, we crossed the interstate for a rest stop at Spiffy's, which sells Nature Cure World Famous Bee Caps although our family unanimously prefers the pie. We went with banana cream.

Smalldaughter's enthusiasm was well-matched to the long summer day. Running lines that I used to scout in a beat-down diesel lift truck, we hove east toward Mt. Rainier National Park. Even Ansel Adams couldn't do that landscape justice.

Turning north at Morton, we burbled through a thousand photo albums worth of scenery until we were stopped by the narrow-gauge tourist train at the intersection to Elbe. Behind us, a chubby sportbiker twitched impatiently. Places to *go*, man! On the way out of town, he wailed by us on the double yellow-lined straight and I winced as he nearly clocked a farm truck.

Highway 7 to Eatonville is as generously endowed as any hip-hop princess and its cliffhanger curves are all-natural. Pushing a Tri Glide until its tubular handlebar shakes leaves a rider with three options: 1) slow down (yes, really — and right-damn-now); 2) plow the front wheel into the outside bar pit (sub-optimal); or 3) lean down hard over the inside handlebar and goose the snot out of it at 3,000 rpm. If the highway gods and its open differential smile upon you with favor, this will break loose the rear in a brief spasm of golf cart athleticism.

If not, see 2). If Pretty Wife is watching from behind you, better stick with 1).

On the third sweet Easter basket of twisties, we caught up with Mister Sporty Pants. Seeing as there weren't any cars in front of him, we bathed him in a warm, friendly shower of illumination from the Tri Glide's floods, which are Harley-Davidson's functional equivalent of a log truck's air horns. *C'mon, man!* We got places to go...

Somewhere out there rides a young man, wearing blue and white racing leathers, on whom late-model Suzuki sportbikes are entirely wasted. Although he urgently needed a countersteering demonstration, we couldn't be his examples that day, because trikes don't work like that.

Do as I say, not as I gimp...

It was a good day to be out, perched in warm air to share the ride with family, forest, pasture animals — and another rider, even if I was jealous of that whole "balancing and shifting" *schtick* of his.

Sometimes, on a rural road under the sun, you can feel your personal rings seat as you settle into the rhythm and flow of the road. If you require a state of the art "master-bike" to make that happen, maybe you're doing it wrong... I backed off the young man on the sport bike, silently wishing him a long, happy road.

Piling west toward McKenna, we were looking straight into the sun and I nearly missed My Precious sitting pretty behind a bobwire fence. There aren't many '39 Ford pickup trucks spatted up in root beer float colors. Actually, I'd never seen one — of any color — that wasn't a picture on an old trade poster. Centerfold incarnate, she wore a grille fair as a racing hull, bodacious as a Jacobsen radial, pretty as possibility.

Gimping around the truck, I thought about constant maintenance; thought about "Armstrong steering" and foolish parking brakes, ill handling and puny horsepower; thought about the stacks of money I didn't have. No honkin' Hailwood Replica but oh my, was she a pretty thing. She could keep me enjoying the road for a long, long time.

Of course, I have no great history with trucks, either.

Row, row, row your boat,
Gently down the stream.
Merrily, merrily, merrily, merrily,
Life is but a dream.

November 2011, Motorcyclist

UNEXPECTED CONSEQUENCES

Ken was a friend and a fine rider who took care not to harm others while drawing pure delight from coloring outside the lines. This salute to him collected more hits than anything else I've published on my website, less because of its luminous literary quality than because of Ken's remarkable, global network of friendship. At his memorial rev-off in Portland, at least a half dozen states were represented by the plates present.

Vaya con Dios, mi amigo.

There's an old story about Chinese luck. It's probably B.S., which is why it belongs here...

An aged farmer's stallion kicked down his stall and ran off. The farmer's neighbors commiserated.

"Ah, bad luck!," they said, but Li Chien only shrugged.

"Good luck, bad luck," he said. "Who can tell?"

Shaking their heads at his absurd fatalism, the neighbors walked away, chattering about fortune. There were ways to propitiate the gods, offerings to earth and sky and river and underworld. Everyone cherished a theory.

Don't they always?

Three days later, the farmer heard a quiet snort in the flossy grey light of predawn. His stallion had reappeared in the pasture. By his side were three strong mares, one pregnant. Without a word, the farmer and his son, Li Cheng, set about repairing their corral fence as the four horses grazed quietly inside. His neighbors watched, impressed but not impressed enough to lift a hand to help.

"Such wonderful fortune!," they agreed among themselves. "Three new horses, and one with a colt quickening!

"Surely the gods have smiled on you, Li Chien. You must render offerings."

The farmer said nothing. They all stayed late at his home that night, singing and drinking and rubbing elbows with the blessed man until he finally snapped at them.

"There is no unmixed fortune!" He glared at them, eyes glittering black through the smoky lamp light. "Have you learned nothing?

"Nobody knows what tomorrow brings!"

Startled, they drank off the dregs of his rice wine and slouched off into the night, muttering about his ingratitude to Fate. The farmer and his son watched them go.

"Tomorrow is not promised to us," Li Chien told his son, "so we must remember to enjoy its blessings as they arrive."

"I will remember, father."

The next day, breaking the second of the three mares, Li Cheng fell hard and broke his arm badly above the elbow. As the farmer splinted his white-faced son's terrible fracture, first pulling it into place as Li Cheng bit down on a bamboo stalk and tried not to scream, the neighbors proffered their wisdom once more.

"Terrible," they said, shaking their heads, "terrible fortune. You have angered the gods this time, Li Chien. It will go ill for you now."

No one offered to help break the mares. Li Chien offered them no wine. He reminded them only of the obvious fact that the world spun beyond the control of men or sprites or house gods.

"Good luck," he said again, "bad luck... who knows?" But he wasn't trying to reach them anymore. His mantra had become just a resigned murmur, backbeat to their chatter, a quiet carrier wave to the white noise of the world.

"Who knows," he hummed to himself, gently dressing his son's arm, "who ever really knows?"

Chien Li looked up at the most vocal among his expert fortunetelling neighbors.

"You, Jun Hai," he ordered, "bring wine for my son."

The fat neighbor pulled his chins back, indignant.

"But I may run out!"

Based on his recent experience, the farmer was forced to agree that this could happen to anyone.

The next day, a cavalcade of soldiers entered the town, resplendent in sparkling, richly embroidered dress armor and preceded by trumpets and criers. Awed by their presence, every family from the town and its surrounding farms gathered in the public square to see them and hear whatever magnificent message they might bear... perhaps from the Emperor Himself!

In hushed tones, they all agreed it was a most propitious moment. The most richly arrayed officer among the soldiers unrolled a scroll. His tone was peremptory, his attitude commanding, and the scroll's message short and to the point.

Save for Cheng Li with his useless arm, every young man was promptly impressed into the service of the Royal Armies of the Son of Heaven. They were herded up, lightly armed, and marched away to battle Mongols that very afternoon.

"Ai-eee!," Chien Li's neighbors shrieked, tearing at their clothes. "What miserable fortune has befallen us! Why do the gods punish us? Will we ever see our sons again? How will we bring in our harvest?

"Why is this happening to us?"

Palms up, the old farmer had but one thing to say. Perhaps it was wisdom. Perhaps he was only simple. Perhaps his neighbors listened to him, although that seems unlikely, does it not?

"Who knows?"

•••

We were supposed to ride to Laconia Bike Week last month, followed by a motorcycle camping trip through B.C. and Alberta this month. That seemed a fine plan, right up until I slipped in one extra trip to ride Triumphs around San Diego County's Pine Valley area, tipped one over and took a frame rail square on the medial malleolus.

Crushed that sucker good and proper.

Riding with a busted shank is bloody inconvenient. Worse, putting weight on a broken ankle can displace the bone, resulting in longer (and even *more* bloody inconvenient) healing times. I know this because the orthopedist told me so. I know this because orthopedists past have told me so, more than half a dozen times so far. And I know this because I've been a hardhead and screwed up my rehab before. That proved to be a boo-boo...

So no weight bearing, and here it was the beginning of summer (FSVO "summer" as expressed by virtue of a warmer troupe of steely clouds than bears on us during the other three laughingly named "seasons" experienced by Northwesterners).

What*evah* was a moto boy to do? It's hard to tell what the meaning of events is. Probably depends on how we construe them as much as how we react to them. What did a broken ankle mean to our summer?

Well, for one thing, it meant we were at home when our buddy Ken rode into town for the start of the 2011 Iron Butt Rally. He wasn't riding in it — chose to go with the Utah 1088's "extended bonus round 72-hour version" instead — but Ken knew just about everybody in the LDR community and was there to help out, encourage and generally cause that kind of trouble, being cool like that.

Pretty Wife baked him a scratch-made pizza and we dug out a Tecate Light lager 'cause Ken didn't drink no pretentious, micro-brewed ales. I remembered looking at that crappy-ass Tecate after a friend left it off during a house party, and asking Pretty Wife what the hell we'd do with it.

"Who knows?" She shrugged. "Somebody will want it."

Being off regular bikes also meant that I could (finally!) follow my editor's instructions and go test Harley-Davidson's three-wheeler, the ever-genteel "Tri Glide Ultra Classic." Thanks to Eastside Harley-Davidson in Bellevue, Washington, we were able to get our mitts on one in time to ride it to the annual Wetleather™ Goat Roast out on Vashon Island. Creaky bones or not, I tanked up on ibuprofen and we enjoyed a beautiful two-ferry route to Vashon where we sucked goat marrow, single malt and MGDs, cuddled the indigenous poodles and had a generally lovely time at the first Goat Roast in the past few years that was wide-open sunny. Turned out to be our first nice family ride with Smalldaughter this summer, and it wouldn't have happened if I hadn't crushed the ligament-bearing knob on my ankle.

The law of gravity is a capricious variable compared to the universally overwhelming Law of Unexpected Consequences.

I felt like a goober pulling up on that chromed golf cart, but what the heck… it was good for a laugh and a lot of conversation. Moreover, in a group that lately discusses our cardiologists and oncologists with the same fervor and precision as lap times and tire compounds, it's entirely possible that the trike revealed a glimmer of extended possibility. Chrome hips and plastic knees aren't universally conducive to stoplight stands on a two-wheeler.

Laugh-a while you can, Monkey Boy! Time and chance happeneth to us all…

•••

The next morning, Pretty Wife's dad was scheduled to visit. Given that he tattooed his cardiac trace around his biceps just to freak out any doctor who catches sight of it, we always make time for him. Pretty Wife bustled efficiently around, preparing brunch and cleaning meticulously while I desultorily browsed email with my bungled foot propped up on a cushion. Pretty Wife was visibly annoyed when I suddenly cried out.

"What?"

She always hates it when I do that; shoots the adrenaline right through her, it does. This time, it wasn't because I had moved wrong.

"Ken is… Ken's…"

She came and looked over my shoulder, crushed my trapezius unconsciously, and then we both agreed to talk about it after her folks had left. We would talk late into the small hours that night, finally changing out the pillowcases for dry ones.

Details were scant and some will never be known, only guessed at. This year's Utah 1088 started before the Iron Butt Rally finished. There was a *huge* bonus offered to "long form" 1088 riders who lit out on a 4,000-mile detour to get their picture taken with an Iron Butt competitor at the IBR checkpoint in upstate New York. For those of you playing along at home, that's one helluva side trip that required maintaining a 55 mph average for three solid days.

No problemo, señor.

Ken was in shape, he was cookin' along on a well-sorted DL Maximus, and he knew practically every real competitor running the IBR. Ken loved him some bonii, and that one probably smelled like good luck from the saddle.

Maybe it was, for him, even if G-d knows it was tough for a lot of people who cared about him. Smacked abruptly into the next life, Ken went out at the top of his game, known to virtually all long-distance riders as the notorious Dread Pirate Kermit who somehow posted an official finish of the 2005 IBR... on a CX500 Silver Wing. He was "doing what he loved" (to quote the old cliché), healthy and happy and basking in the love of his beautiful wife. When he was here for pizza, practically all we talked about were great rides, pretty wives, and our kids.

Ken's buddy Tedder and his wife Tamara led a dedicated band of friends who threw a helluva memorial for him, one week after Ken met (a truck wake? Tornado? Standing water? Sandman?) his final mortal moment on a lonesome highway in the Nebraska panhandle, all by himself in the dark with no one but the night to see him off.

He was impressively skilled, rigorously prepped, physically fit and thoroughly experienced. The Dread Pirate Kermit didn't just know what he was doing; he knew how to do it better than almost every other rider out there.

The wake was a ride-to call, of course. Purely due to Eastside H-D's generosity with the Tri Glide, I was able to get there on a kind of "bike" with Smalldaughter perched on pillion, Pretty Wife scouting along on her F650GS and my crutches strapped to the top rack. It was a simple affair with more hugs than ceremony, featuring Ken's precisely worded request from an online conversation months before: friends gathered around a cheap keg, a little food, a lot of memories, and a rev-off of the assembled bikes. Ken's brass plaques and rally towels decorated the walls, his ashes sat on the memorial table next to a great picture and a can of crappy beer; his friends were everywhere, all over the world but especially concentrated there, in that suburban *cul-de-sac*, remembering.

Tedder green-flagged our rev-off at four p.m. Others would later send cell phone video of individual revs performed simultaneously in the midwest, Canada and the Oregon Desert. Because I happened to get dented the week previous, we got to do ours there in his driveway. Trike or no, the Harley acquitted itself well, making much more noise off the bottom than pinned at redline because (as every session player knows) all bass notes go to Heaven.

From two-strokes to sportbikes to hawgs, it was something to hear. Not only did the neighbors not complain, some of them joined in. I don't know that Ken's ashes rolled over, but then again I couldn't see them through the box.

•••

He'll never suffer from prostate cancer, diabetes or heart disease. On the day Ken died, he was 51 years old. He could still bicycle a hundred and fifty miles with his sweetie for fun, ride two weeks at a thousand-mile-per-day clip, and knock out a hundred sit-ups without a rest. He declined a third slice of pizza when he was here, and I couldn't get him to drink the last can of that lousy Tecate, either. That's how it ended up on the memorial table in his garage. I'm not proud of that but unlike Ken, I don't always play fair.

Good luck, bad luck…? Ken never had a chance to watch himself crumble; good looking corpse and all that. I may envy him that some day, as the future becomes increasingly foreseeable and the open chance of life devolves into creaky-boned iterations of Groundhog Day.

We like to think that the last thing going through Ken's mind was a thought about his sweetie. Chances are good; he never could stop talking about her, and he was generally grinning like a lovestruck fool when he did. It's a misery for her to lose a man like Ken.

It's a misery for everyone who knew him. Ken was that guy who never made you earn it. He acted as a friend without ever a thought to do otherwise, and you suddenly felt like you'd known him for decades. We would have done anything for him, and by "we" I mean to include hundreds of people, most of whom I don't even know, have no right to speak for — yet am correct about.

There's no good luck in losing such a friend, such a father and fellow rider and husband and pet owner and all-around *mensch*. What malevolent, undiluted misfortune — and yet, how much less terrible than never having known him.

Good luck, bad luck…

We may not have tomorrow, but today we remember our friend. The worst luck that Ken brought us was the day he went down and didn't get up. The best luck that he brought us was the reminder to ride it out until the last, gunning toward one more sunrise to clear our night-bleared eyes.

July 2011, jaxworx.com

RIDE LIKE A GIRL

I'm lucky enough to know a surfeit of female riders, in and outside of "the industry," who ride well and manifest the situational awareness of the queen snakes that so frightened Linus of "Peanuts" fame, but the actual estate of my luck is best measured this way: three of them are family.

There was a boy once. In the time-stained manly tradition, he learned to gun it down public roads at age 13, trying to concentrate through the sound of his dad yelling "daggone it, quit killing it" from the side of their shuddering, sputtering Harley-Davidson Sprint.

Once underway, punching through the gears proved eminently easier than the launch itself. A dozen seconds after clutch drop, that helmetless boy was steaming 75 knots up the Evergreen Parkway with tear-drenched ears, wondering what to do next.

By the time he'd figured out how to stop (some) and turn (sorta), his father had chased him down in their dented Sportvan Beauville, lights and horn going like some demented highway patrol junkman. Pulled over with the engine killed again, the kid shivered like he'd just finished his first fight.

My first words on motorcycling were, "Can I ride it home, Dad?"

There was a girl once, who wanted to ride. Finding a safety course, she squeaked through by a single point on the first motorcycle she ever rode, a Team Oregon loaner.

She didn't ask to ride it home.

Oure Faire Rider found an experienced rider's list on the Intertoobz where she got gang-FAQed into oblivion. Say what you will about motorcyclists, we serve generous helpings of lore. Sifting through data for women, beginners, and short riders, she determined to spend a tidy sum on quality gear — and start on a lesser bike.

She also found Joy, a mentor who whispered down the wires of freedoms still unexplored and materialized one day on her own learner, a well-thrashed 1981 KZ440. Like some Kobe-birthed Skin Horse, that little hoopty had most of its chrome loved off, but its valves were on spec and the oil topped off clean.

Our gallant lass declined a neighborhood ride.

"Go ahead," inveigled the pusher-woman. "I've dropped it. Not like it hasn't been around the block before."

Her first moto cost that girl $750, a car ride home and one encumbrance:

"Someday, sell it to another woman learning to ride. That's KZ's purpose."

On the way home, Joy nudged our heroine into a bike shop visit, helped her score proper gear at good prices, brandished her own riding club discount to lighten the hit on a single mom's credit card, then disappeared back into the ebb and flow of the riding world.

The tenderfoot apprenticed herself to parking lot practice, strafing lampposts and planter beds until that hand-me-down Kwacker responded like wings on her lifted Lady Daytona boots. She shunned townie traffic to steeplechase over blue-gray Willamette Valley highways, faster and smoother by the day. When she first grazed a peg in an uphill left-hander, it felt Zen-like as a proper trigger squeeze.

By the time I met Joy's protégé, she had passed KZ along and graduated to Sal, a voluptuous Moto Guzzi Mille. Sal crouched, dragon-like, over a treasure pile of chrome vanadium sockets and a greasy wooden stick used for disciplining fork seals.

The Mille taught new lessons — endless Lombardian maintenance, mostly, but also the two best ways for purdy li'l gals to right foundered motorcycles: A) squat down, back-to-bike, and hoist with legs; or B) snatch the damned thing off the ground before anyone sees it lying there.

On a sun-dappled river road, she danced with an older rider to the double-bass melody of her megaphones. Notwithstanding a 160-bhp ultrabike and the attention span of a caffeinated ferret, I wasn't bored. On another fine day I married that woman, and she hasn't bored me yet.

She bought a scorching yellow 2004 F650GS named "Tweety" to slide around trails and gently foist on newbies. She also helped me find girl gear for my offsprout.

One autumn day, Daughtergirl borrowed Tweety to join me on a short loop. Scaling our vertiginous driveway, she executed a counterclockwise snap-doughnut, quickly followed by recovery technique "B)."

It wasn't her first ride. Daughtergirl already owned a Honda Hawk with a slender Euro tank that hit reserve every 85 miles. She aced her Basic RiderCourse by riding "Hawklet" an hour down to the Tri-Cities MSF range, pre-endorsement. The nature vs. nurture question remains thus unresolved...

Five years older than its owner, Hawklet wasn't fast ever, but ticked along cheerfully, made Daughtergirl smile, and unleashed her mordant streak.

When a rawboned teenager came on hard about his bad-azz Ninja 250, Daughtergirl opened her baby blues wide. Softly, she breathed, "But… mine's *bigger*."

Like Tweety and KZ before it, Hawklet came along from another woman rider, a Certified Flight Instructor and cowboy action shooter who's not boring, either. Nor is Daughtergirl destined to dullness.

There was a girl once, who wanted to ride. May there be many more.

April 2009, Motorcyclist

MOOSE GLIDE

This accidental tour should never have happened. The gig was offered first to Jamie Elvidge, who prudently turned it down, leaving it to me to pick up the "Hard Way" trip where Joe Gresh left off (after riding all the actual hard parts). Luggage amounted to riding suit pockets and eventually a gym bag from Wal-Mart, photography support came from my pocket camera, and about half the weather was horizontal rain.

It was glorious.

The Moose Glide passed me when I stopped for pictures. A root beer brown, dreadnought-class metric heavy, it was clad in flapping, buffalo robe bodywork, tastefully embellished with spoon antler handlebars. I saw her again at a gas station thirty miles on, but I was showing three fuel bars and only 129 miles on my odometer.

I kept going. That big horny babe was probably just Sarah Palin filming another segment, and I had miles to go before I ate. Back in Anchorage, the p.r. professionals had assured me that Joe Gresh got 280 miles to a tank, all the way across Russia.

Forty miles out of Glenallen, the Wee-Strom's fuel gauge dropped to one bar and flashed a fuel pump pictogram. With 178 miles elapsed, the flashing bar developed a hole in it and a boldfaced "E" appeared. Tucking into the draft of a Super Duty Ford, I resolved to shorten fueling intervals to 150 miles and wondered how long before anyone would notice if I dropped out.

The bike had been an afterthought from the get-go. This trip was all about cars, Suzuki *Kizashi* (bless you!) sport sedans celebrating "Tokyo to Los Angeles the *HARD WAY*." Each two-man car crew carried iPods, iPads, GPS, SPOT tracker, special maintenance mats, comprehensive tool roll, electric compressor, industrial first aid kit and satellite phone (plus the obligatory weapons, ammunition, clinical opiates and prophylactics).

"Will I have a flat repair kit?," I asked, over a dinner of braised sablefish and large crystal pots of The Macallan. They told me not to worry. The tires on the DL650 were new, and specially chosen.

"Uh, is there any luggage on the bike?"

They pushed a small manila envelope across the glossy tabletop. I counted it, looked up.

"What should I do for emergency communications?"

They looked at each other, then passed over another, thicker envelope. Looking inside it made me feel much better prepared, but when I walked out to the bike the next morning, it was fettled for a 4,000-mile pavement tour with Continental TKC80 knobbies. And a cable lock.

The Wee-Strom proved a capable trotter. Even on Specially Chosen Tires, five-hundred mile days would slip by fairly easily if I kept an eye out for special test sections, woombahs and wabbles.

At speeds over 95 mph, my knees gently patted the tank sides. The wabble, which went *thunk... thunk... thunk-thunk-thunk*, was a serviceable speed governess.

Woombahs were road features sometimes marked with cones, sometimes not, as befit the playful caprice of highway crews. On asphalt mixed from permafrost and prayers, "frost heaves" are consequential. At 83 KIAS, the bike would pump up and down, preparing to take flight. Gathering herself at the penultimate hump, she would crest the final peak, temporarily — and, it must be said, with evident joy — shedding the fetters of gravity to soar with aching, mechanical heart toward yonder rainbow. *Whoomp... whoomp... whoomp... WOOM-BAH!* Go toward the light, little bike...

Special test sections are best enjoyed by sailing around a corner at Alcan Cruise Speed, helmet screwed down tightly over a speed-stupored grin, only to find the asphalt ended in a straight cut across the road. Note to Editor: wrong Lewis! Should have sent Jimmy.

The true mother of invention is pant-squeezing fear. De-clutch, grab *all* the brakes while dropping three gears, then let out the clutch as the front drops in, stand up and gas it. Kind of fun, once you get used to it, though I think I'd enjoy it much less on a Winnabikeo.

Into Glenallen with just 188 miles on the trip clock, I bought five and a third gallons of regular, chastened to learn I'm fully 100 miles fatter than Joe. Pretty Wife says it's my big knobbies. I rubbed the editorial rump and thunk about it.

Only 3,800 miles to go.

•••

Since Caribou Lodge manifested the B-list chic of a Sun Valley log condo, I accepted the toothless Chevron attendant's advice and repaired to the "The Freeze," a burger shack where I listened to two boys brag to their big sister, or maybe their mom. When the days get short up here, it can be hard to tell.

"A trooper shot it, but he didn't get it, either," said the towhead. "It was a bear."

"Wha'd you do to it." She sounded bored, checking her eye shadow for seismic fissures.

"Shot it," said the other kid. He chewed his fries thoughtfully. "It got all mad."

Those boys were maybe nine years old.

It's hard to explain why I've dreamed Alaska dreams so long; harder to excuse myself for never visiting in the nearly half-century I've lived in upper left CONUS.

Maybe it was Dad's stories of moose hunting and salmon fishing on Air Sea Rescue drills, flying his Albatross home belly full of chops and filets.

Might have been the stories of Mom's grandfather and my great uncle coining a fortune selling produce to gold-crazed Yukon miners. Hand-tinted postcards show them standing in fields of hundred-pound cabbages. The white wolf hide on Grandma's basement sofa and plaster-bleeding moose head in our garage bespoke a moldy "durring don that longeth to a knight."

Always I doubted my worthiness to stand with my forebears. Those two boys, all four-foot-two of 'em, wonder no such thing.

Having waited 46 years to see it, I left Alaska after one day's ride, entering Yukon Territory from Alaska's Glenn Highway at about 8:30 with magic light firing the golden leaves of aspens and the temperature reading about 10 degrees C (50 degrees F). For 90 minutes I'd navigated a refractive funhouse of rainbows: half and full rainbows, short-radius rainbows, ultra-bright rainbows, double and even triple rainbows.

Occasionally, the glory of rainbows was mitigated by a lurid, knobby-tires-on-pavement, two-wheeled slide as my attention to the horizon overcame my survival instinct to keep a close eye on the morphing road surface. Those tires hunted a little but were otherwise fine in the dry. In the wet, they secretly planned to kill me.

The first time it happened, I was staring off at a low, particularly intense rainbow. Rounding a 90 mph sweeper (kindly devoid of woombahs), I was startled to note that my bike was scrithering.

No motorcycle should scrither. Really, not ever. A throttle-induced slide is one thing; scrithering is right out. The problem with a two-wheel drift on wet pavement, on a street motorcycle, is that just about the time you get it sorted out, the wheels catch traction and launch you on the loopily random trajectory of an Iraqi Scud.

This is considered suboptimal.

Owing more to fatigue-level reflexes than mastery, I stayed in the throttle and rode it out, waking right up and yodeling into my helmet. The helmet remained inexplicably unimpressed by my bravado *fortissimo* — it was, in its defense, a Shoei and thus inscrutable.

A pressing need was conceived. From a photogenic pullout, I wobbled into the middle of Highway One and cocked an ear to nothing but the gentle white whisper of wind through stunted, cold-country branches. Then I dug the silicone putty out of my ears.

Still not a murmur of traffic noise. The north country has about the right traffic density: one vehicle every six to 15 minutes coming head-on (note that Alaskans are competent at driving long distances over empty roads, thus closing speeds hover around 160 mph), and a vehicle or two overtaken and passed about every 20 minutes to an hour if you pace the road confidently.

I waited. Sure enough, after a couple of minutes, two things happened: my adrenaline subsided and a motor home pulling a trailer (does every single Alaskan and Alaska tourist have a trailer with boats or four-wheelers on it? They're *burning up my gas!*) puttered past with a desultory wave.

Alone again, I breached the machicolation of my armored trousers and saluted the road with everything I had in me. "There," I noted confidently, "is one clean spot on this greasy damned road."

It took quite a while. No family drove by to be scandalized.

There were no guard rails there, no runoff areas, no shoulders and no cell service. Plop the Wee into roadside muskeg and they might never find a gobbet sufficient to identify DNA.

Shortly thereafter, the highway turned to dirt and my knobbies came right into their own. Beating the cars into Beaver Creek by nearly an hour, I followed a rainbow of particular intensity straight to our motel.

On their last night open, Beaver Creek's young staff were lax on policy. We schlepped schooners of tap beer to our rooms, checked email on their back office computer and made unseemly suggestions to half-smiling waitresses who tucked Suzuki's money into their aprons, dreaming of younger men and home. Over Yukon Arctic Red ales, Todd Lassa of *Motor Trend* asked why I kept passing the car crew and running out in front.

"Well," I lied truthfully, "I don't have comms, first aid, tools, riding partner or a flat kit. Anything happens, you guys'd be two hundred miles south before anyone thought to look for the idjit on the bike."

Sure, I would have liked more conveniences — at least a ditty bag — but couldn't envy the car guys. It's gotta be dull, watching hour after hour of postcards slide past, boring as B-roll shots with the mute button on, isolated from the feel of the place like divers trapped in a glass-bottomed boat; to pelt past a thousand two-tracks leading into the woods and never once wonder not only what you might discover down that road, but also what it would *feel* like to ride it and whether you had skill and stamina enough to win your bet against injury or breaking the bike; to never shout your gratitude for cool rain on a hot afternoon; to lay a thumping MP3 template over this lively vastness that is no substitute for the mournful and proper wind.

I motored out front because it was freer there, because that is what Alaska and the Yukon became for me long before I was privileged to see them, to rub my skin against their fierce and feathery air and remember what my Neanderthal progenitors knew without learning. To run and throw yourself into the world: there is liberty that requires no document, no government to grant it. Nothing can take it from you but fear.

It's dumb to just get on a bike and ride, and I'm foolish about it: anywhere, anytime and most likely too fast for conditions. But it's hard not to imagine, pelting south through the onchilling autumn air, that I really was born for this.

Of course that's easier to imagine when someone just hands you a key and says "meet us at the hotel."

At a Haines Junction gas station, I gave my spare gloves to Marcello, who was headed into the teeth of the north with a leather vest, open helmet, tent and bedroll. His gloves, windproofed with duct tape, were tattered from a trip out of Uruguay. On a stock Street Bob. My Tinbutt pretensions have rarely left me feeling less worthy.

•••

Chased by the ghosts of my grands, I dropped downhill into territorial capitol Whitehorse to browse the MacBride Museum of Yukon History, picking up a carpetbagful of social history and an eyeful of antique erotica, but few direct insights into forebears.

RVs and I chased each other south. I'd pass half a dozen every hour or two before they blew past my fuel stops with 300 gallons of diesel in their bellies and movies on the big screen. The fuel/RV park/hotel/restaurant properties populating the Alcan Highway every few dozen miles increasingly were shuttered for the season. Logging chains stretched between stone cairns enforced caution of twilit driveways when jonesing for coffee or urgent about fuel or the men's room.

The Continental Divide Inn, no doubt as famous as its sign suggests, offered no fuel, no coffee, not even the cold solace of a wrapped sandwich. A few kilometers down the road I found the Rancheria log inn offering hot coffee, a sweet roadhouse waitress worn to a thin strip of woman jerky and, importantly, gasoline.

While I chatted with Jürgen and Tilde from Stuttgart about their R1100GS, the car guys rolled up. They convoyed out well before I ordered my ninth cup of warm-up coffee, but cars are rarely difficult to catch.

With 1,350 miles on them, my Contis were substantially smoked. Before the rear could melt off its last knob, I whiled a few hours pooting around enough dirt tracks, gravel pits and logging roads to discover that a V-Strom 650 is what you might expect off-road: a cumbersome fat chick with a sweet personality. At least I got some value out of those ridiculous tires.

Laughing my way out of a mudhole where I'd foundered the long-suffering beast again, I looked to the far horizon: pretty far, alright. Then I looked to the opposite far horizon. It seemed pretty far, too. Then I looked at my cell phone, which showed zero reception and little time before dark. Realizing how annoyed Pretty Wife would be if they didn't find my coyote-gnawed bones before spring thaw, I slither-whomped back out to the highway and lit the smoking lamp, safe in the loving embrace of motor homes, RCMP and onrushing Kenworths.

Slowing for a corner marked EXTREMELY DANGER-OUS CURVE, I couldn't help noticing the young moose lying dead in my lane. Good signage, that. I waved a warning at a wasp-colored, carrier-class F800GS. He stared at me, probably because I was in BFY without so much as an ADV sticker. I stared at him because he was heading north.

The Forest of Signposts in Watson Lake was originally planted by Carl Lindley from Company D, 341st Engineers in 1942 and since replicated by GIs from Korea to Qatar.

Outside the Alaska Highway Interpretive Centre, I exchanged weather reports with a pair of Calgary riders on an '84 Venture Royale and some generic 90s big twin. I told them it was raining north. They told me it was raining south. When they asked how to get my job, I lied inventively. That is how I got my job.

Inside, a breathy brunette with liquid eyes insistently particularized the area's attractions for me, laying panegyrical emphasis on the Liard Hot Springs.

"Especially on a day like this," she sighed, laying fingertips gently against dripping grey panes, "if *I* were on a motorcycle, I'd just want to get off and just... just be *in* there, all deep and warm." She looked at me in a way that suggested she hadn't actually been on a motorcycle — yet.

"I'm going there later today," she added helpfully. "When I get off."

I looked at her in a way that suggested she was around my daughter's age.

If I were much younger, I thought, hopefully not out loud, *more Canadian and a lot less married...*

On the way out, she smiled enough BTUs at me to soften my back protector.

Liard made a well-timed lunch stop. I received gasoline, soup and coffee from the earnestly helpful Scots-Irish proprietor; cold looks and change from his First Nations wife. After lunch, I smilingly begged loan of a dish rag to debug my visor. She stared fully ten seconds while I basked in the café's heat.

"Can't you use a napkin."

"'Fraid it would scratch my faceshield," I said, still smiling.

A 20-second wait ensued. Holding my gaze unsmiling, she bade her husband fetch one.

I considered their interpersonal dynamic as I reinserted bits of stuff into various pockets, peeled ibuprofen tablets off a wad of silicone putty and ate them, squished the anti-inflammatorized putty back into my ear (NOTE: may not actually reduce earaches), then strapped my freshly polished helmet back on. Such bemusement distracted me from leaving a tip, which I nearly always do and why not? It was American Suzuki's dosh.

The road out of Liard sidehills along a river canyon through the Muncho Lake Provincial Park and into Stone Mountain Provincial Park. The Liard River bridge leads directly to a series of curves that could only have been more fun if either A) the road were dry or B) the bike weren't shod with tattered knobbies. Or both, in a perfect world, but you could die waiting for one of those. Bonus tip to End Timers: live your life now. G-d didn't put you on Earth to spend all your time imagining someplace else.

Shortly after the road opened up, a pair of woodland caribou materialized on the right shoulder. With the sublime grace of wild creatures, they spun in opposite directions, bumped into each other and leapt like startled cats. One crashed into the woodline. The other landed in my lane.

Whoa, I thought, scrithering around him, *that was WAY more exciting than this morning's wild horses and wood bison.* I chuckled a little under my breath, or maybe that was the stutter of my heart slowing down.

Presently, the highway crossed a plain bordered by lateral moraines, each of which generated its own brutally abrupt crosswind. I was wrestling with one of those — being of the school that asserts anyone blown off the road was *de facto* deficient in their situational awareness, I was reluctant to prove the point on someone else's brand-new motorcycle — when a six-point bull strutted up the left bank. Squeezing the "pro-lock" brakes hard enough to force an unearthly howl from the front knobby, I watched as he made a decision and bulled across the road, nose up and horns back, legs pumping like Michael Johnson at the tape.

I have never been so close to a wild elk, pre-bullet. Had my hand been less busy with braking, I might have reached forward and stroked him as he thundered past. Giving passing thought to how long it would take to gut him with a Leatherman, I realized he would have been far more likely to walk away from it than I. There are well-armored garments and there are superbly armored BMW Streetguards, but there are *no* elk-proof riding suits.

When a spike bull wandered out of the woods seven sweepers later, I knew exactly what was coming.

My prediction proved inaccurate. Failing to yield the right of way, he pulled into the southbound lane and accelerated. I turned on my flashers and we promenaded companionably on for a couple of miles before he took his exit up a steep bank of glacial till.

Stone Mountain Provincial Park, just down the road, seems to exist primarily for housing the chubby mountain sheep that capered all over the road. After dodging my third flock, I gave a "horns ahead" signal to an oncoming pickup/caravan combo. He laughed, rolled down his window and jerked his thumb toward the mother and kid browsing by the roadside behind him.

•••

Riding suit pockets overflowing, I stopped at Prince George, B.C. for custom motorcycle luggage. For $19.95 CAN, Wal-Mart supplied a six-pack of bungees and a nylon gym bag. I stuffed it with jerky and (finally) a decent store of drinking water. Also gifts, tools, receipts and thermal layers — with temperatures now over 80 degrees F, I was still dressed for Yukon autumn.

Right about Buckhorn the temp slouched twenty degrees, cold water rolled down like Justice from clouds foaming black over the Cariboo Range and the wind smacked me around like a latex slave girl. Over a railroad and up a mud road, I made *cabana* at a farm shack to zip my liners back in. Ten minutes later, brilliant sunshine split the roiling clouds again.

I wicked it up then, so grinningly happy that the fuzz-mustachioed Royal Canadian Teenager who pulled me over couldn't help but celebrate the weather with me. We talked bikes and cars, weapons and women, work and family. He didn't bother writing a warning, but I was danger-close to civilization now.

The next constable was hollow-eyed, jumpy and 100 percent less accommodating. He asked about Iraq after he spotted my ID, grieved his recent officer-involved shooting, and wrote me a demerit that cut a healthy slice off Suzuki's largesse. Following an obligatory safety lecture, he strongly hinted that I purchase fresh tires.

Few things are better than new friends when you need 'em, and I found mine in Williams Lake. John at New Life Cycles, who stocks rear tires for GSers coming out of Prudhoe, snap-sold me a new Battle Wing before rushing off to a funeral. Spectra Power Sports down the road not only levered it onto my rim for free, but shop owner and race driver Heino Seibert took me on a demo blast in a freshly race-prepped Polaris RZR. With upgraded suspension, 12 psi of boost and Haino's maniacal slope attacks, if we didn't see G-d it wasn't from failure to jump high enough. Since neither dealer had a front streetie in stock, I would have continuing chances to visit G-d that very afternoon.

The Fraser River Canyon clove the Coast Mountains under unbending iron skies. Shafts of late sun glared off ferrous cloud bottoms. Tunnel to tunnel, the updated Cariboo Wagon Road is as dazzlingly dimensional as low-altitude aerobatics. I rode it half-blind, with rain splooshing through my chin vents and an unscuffed rear radial pushing my shagged front knobby, wailing out "Why Don't We Do It In The Road," occasionally throwing out a bootrigger and grinning 'til my face broke.

The only thing better than new friends is known friends. In Vancouver, Newfie Dave had already procured a Michelin 110/80R-19 to match my new Bridgestone better than the toasted TKC. He also made reservations for midnight microbrews and seafood at the Sand Bar on Granville Island. The next morning, Newf gave me a directional tow to Bayside Performance for a Sunday morning tire change. The Wetleather™ cabal (google it) had struck with a seen hand.

•••

With that it was only a hop, skip and a border crossing back to home and a barbecue with friends. I had another thousand or so miles to go, but that was just a ride to the office on new tires. Bent and rusty lance securely socketed, I'd already finished off the main windmill.

"Aren't you awfully hot?," people asked at every stop, or, "Aren't you really cold?"

Yeah, usually.

Once every long while, though, for a fleeting glorious moment, conditions are ideal. Rainbows blaze out between squalls, three corners in a row aren't just great but *perfect*, and you catch the flash of a wolf's eyes as your headlight sweeps the trees.

If you're not already out there — dodging trucks, navigating gravel and fending off the weather — you'll miss all those things. They won't fit on the widest screen; never manifest, swirling with golden light, over a cubicle farm. This is ephemeral magic, some of the last that's left.

Russian loggers pulp the Siberian taiga as fast as they can run their saws; Chinese soldiers sedulously secure Tibet for Chinamen; Canucks and Yanks cooperate to make their great World War II project, the Alcan Highway, straighter and safer. Cutting the natural curves out of roads is as appealing as grafting fake curves onto women, but reengineering that road will get trucks to Fairbanks a couple hours quicker.

It may not take you to the same place at all. Maybe you shouldn't wait as long as I did.

December 2011, Motorcyclist

World's Toughest Riders

This wasn't the hardest, the rainiest, the coldest, the longest, or the most boring tour I ever took, but it constituted a fair percentage of all those things, all at once.

Who are the world's toughest riders? If you believe their license plate brackets, it's the Iron Butt Association.

Sure, there are those who disagree. Ask a 1%er if he's "IBA-tough" and he may feed you your beaded seat cover. Ask a rescue rider and he'll probably tell you not to bug him while he's working. Ask an ADVrider and he'll consult his Bluetooth smart phone for the GPS coordinates to a smart-ass reply…

I have no earthly idea what Travis Pastrana would say. He has effectively transcended the argument. His big, brass bucket holds more than most.

Although not a Butter myself, I know a few IBA members, including a couple of high-placing competitors. Regarding their riding, they're workmanlike, efficient and specialized in the quiet manner of professionals at any complex task. That's one definition of toughness. I'm not sure it's the only one that applies to motorcycling.

Bucket lists are funny things for a couple of reasons, one being that by the time you know what's on yours it's usually too late to fill it out (and maybe that's part of the point). The other is that you never need excuses. Job, kids, money, time and health considerations righteously trump the punchlisting of dreams.

If one day you wake up without an excuse, what must you do? Scramble for more excuses. The closer you come, the more impossible your chance looks as the shimmer of distant mirage resolves into the gritty focus of a big, hard wall.

But I had this motorcycle, see? A comfortable, easy-natured bike with new tires. Plus an 1,186-mile commute to work. The opening ante to IBA membership is a Saddle Sore 1,000 ride — i.e. 1,000 miles in 24 hours. I've wanted to knock one off for years, but my excuses hadn't failed me yet.

Maybe my wall had a door in it.

Electing to sledgehammer through the wall, I resolved to launch for L.A. six hours after arriving in Seattle, following my 2,000-mile bimble from Anchorage. Though I wasn't sure I could pull it off, a spat with Pretty Wife helped settle my nerves. It also took 18 hours to resolve.

Now I had exactly one day to deliver the bike to its expectant owners timely. Gentleman, start your engine.

Why was I nervous? I'd been riding 30 years on the street (legally) with no help from the IBA. I've launched thousand-plus-mile trips on single-cylinder bikes, other people's bikes, and vintage bikes. They generally required better prep than "Hey, here's a motorcycle!

"Let's go, then."

An SS1000 requires documentation, though, and everything's harder when someone's watching. I found myself overwhelmed by the syllogistic inevitability that you never know if you can do a thing you've never done.

Pretty Wife and the Toucan (IBA #10456, with brass Bonneville plates on his ZX-many-R) signed my dance card after a stout launch breakfast of bacon, eggs, coffee and scratch biscuits. IBA documents chastise the use of stimulants, but also officially pretend that members never ride while fatigued. Kneebone's legions are a human organization. Humans are weirdly contradictory. Calling every other rider on Earth a big pussy, then whinging on about safety like a PTSA meeting? Weird, contradictory... and human.

Anyway, I never go to the office without coffee.

Despite my tawdry descent into the hellish grip of caffeine, my trip was successfully uneventful. Having discovered that a DL will stoppie at need on street tires, I didn't sweat braking or handling — especially not on Interstate 5. Monkey hold bar; monkey ride to L.A.

Hours of drizzle in Washington preceded the 150 miles of hard Oregon rain precipitating a fatal multi-car accident near the North Umpqua River crossing, but rain and bad driving are standard features of NW riding. Sometimes no cage is stout enough to keep the spirit from moving out.

In opposition to my best instincts and the good guidance of others, I took no tools but the onboard kit — not a flat kit, or even a Leatherman. Due to the worldwide shortage of demo bikes for freelancers, I'd be returning on a flight with only a carry-on luggage allotment, and I didn't want to donate gear to TSA again.

My "toolkit" consisted of a credit card, cell phone and AAA account with their RV plan. I also took a half-empty, six year-old can of chain lube subsequently to be abandoned in my hotel room. As the wise women of Wetleather™ implicitly know, lubrication is the key.

If I try to certify another IBA ride, I'll switch to a flip-face helmet to avoid dealing with spectacles under sunglasses under a helmet that had to come off for drinking. I'll wear the same magnificent riding suit — for lousy weather, a BMW Streetguard 3 is basically cheating, and its back protector makes a nearly adequate picnic table mattress — shorter gauntleted gloves than my Shift Torrent Storms, and hopefully will munch on Pretty Wife's bacon drop biscuits again. They are the 21st century hardtack of choice.

The accidental goodness of finding myself on a Wee-Strom was not to be overlooked. In 4,000 miles, it never put a tire print wrong without the insistence of the punch-drunk monkey at the controls. If you always pack a couple of torn rotator cuffs, assorted zipper scars and a resume of old fractures into your Ironbaggage, this is the bike for you. Neither too heavy nor too light, not too aggro nor too slow, it's Goldilocks' warm porridge on wheels.

With 21 hours elapsed, I hit the office at 0820, charmed my way past the receptionist ("Hi, I work here — where's the men's room?") and was promptly introduced to the building head of security. Turns out we have pretty nice offices. That's how we dominate international motorsports information. That and being the world's toughest riders, of course.

Somewhere around this cluttered house is an ammo box holding a SCUBA certificate, skydiving picture, a couple of old medals and (x-1) divorce decrees. I call it "The Bucket." Not everything has to go up on the wall.

Provided my breakfast coffee wasn't grounds for a DQ, The Bucket probably has room for the world's toughest styrene license plate frame.

April 2011, Motorcyclist

MOTHER OF ALL BIKES

When I was young and convinced of my need for more motor than had ever been seen before, motorcycle magazines regularly broke my heart by anguishing over the impending death of the superbike. Gas prices, safety-obsessed bureaucrats, and spiraling cost were sure to profoundly, permanently neuter performance.

It was the best sales pitch ever. Riders looked at what had happened to cars — the Camaro was suddenly a four-cylinder in base trim — and mourned the tragic future of performance motorcycles. Get one while you still can!

Reality, as it often does, refused to accede to prognostication. Computers and all, today's literbikes make about 100 bhp more and weigh about 100 lbs. less than the mighty Honda CBX, which in 1978 shocked the world with its wretched excess.

I hate waiting for the future. I want to live there immediately. Looking around me now, I'm pretty sure we do.

Stop me if you've heard this one: Japanese tool firm ships new drill bit to German company, explaining that it is the smallest, hardest bit in the history of tooling. German company bores it through the center with an even smaller bit and mails it back with a polite "*nein, danke.*"

Fable or not, it underscores prickly Teutonic pride. BMW considers itself an engineering firm, not a motor company, and has held itself stiffly outside the faddism of racer reps and annual shootouts — until now. Zero to hero, they went from never producing a superbike (yeah, shut up about the

R90S already) to rolling Soichiro over with the quickest, yet gentlest, yet *nastiest* sportbike ever bolted together.

It's motorcycling's first F-16, all power and maneuverability and joystick to your brain, yet incapable of achieving its performance without a battery of triple-redundant processing power. The onboard traction Führer allows four modes, each closer to the edge: RAIN, SPORT, RACE and SLICK. Track-day recommendation is RACE, while SLICK requires a special plug and is reserved for racers with radial-ply knee-pads. It's a power tool joined to the base of your spine with the reflexes of a home run hitter, the manners of an English butler and the punch of Max Schmeling.

The S 1000 RR, like a 5/8-scale P-51 Mustang replica, looks just right until you walk up next to it. Indecently diminutive as Speedos on wrinkly German tourists, seventeen-inch wheels just look wrong on Real Motorcycles, but on the snack-size RR they're as appropriate as Morris mags on a TZ750.

Then I sat on it. Ever seen an elephant on a shop stool?

But as those who turn down offers to ride OPM (Other People's Motorcycles) for the weekend probably don't deserve and almost certainly won't receive further such offers, I saddled up and bolted while my luck held. I needn't have worried. On this trip, BMW's mini-literbike was practically a rabbit's foot for me.

The RR and I started by vaulting the ferry line and heading for Kingston on the Olympic Peninsula. Snotty, rich kid crotch rockets don't usually attract much comment, but this one did. Harley bagger rider Dave and I chatted through the float about topics in common including sportbikes, customs, and wilderness horseback search and rescue, and he sneakily picked up my SBC coffee tab. Nice fella, like most riders.

On debarkation, Dave went around the outside on 101 and I took Route 3 down the inside toward my Hallmark Day lunch date with Mom.

Like its contemporaries among Big Boy hyperbikes, the S 1000 RR has monstrous radial-mount calipers. But unlike, say, Ducati's Streetfighter S, the RR has brake control feel gentle and sweet as dew on spring petals — not to mention mystically transparent ABS. It was only later that I realized that I'd resprained my left thumb under the RR's braking forces, whereas the unsubtle Duck punished me for every injudicious lever squeeze with a front wheel darkie and a savage, Streetfightin' punt to the junk.

Talking bikes with the attendant of a Poulsbo Stop & Go gained me a free look at a service station map and a tip to try the Seabeck Highway NW, a route highly recommended. Take Newberry Hill road west off Highway 3 and bear right at the tee, then left at Seabeck Bay. Scenic, nicely surfaced and twisty, SHNW was lightly patrolled and virtually untrafficked right up until you opened this magazine.

It's also where I made the sad discovery that RAIN mode exists on the S K RR mostly so guys like me can feel like heroes. Toggling it up to RACE mode scared me pale, so I left it there for the duration of sunny weather. It still showed itself the safest bike I've ever ridden.

In the past, I've landed on my head doing things much less dramatically stupid than exiting a corner marked "25 mph" at 96 mph with the front wheel hovering and the rear sliding. I checked my spec sheet and I'm not rated for that, but this bike does it easily — even with me aboard. Theoretically, of course.

You don't need speed to enjoy the Peninsula (unless you're trying to take your mind off the misery of being folded into an express envelope). On a spring day with the screaming blue yonder interrupted only by the splendid white peaks of the Olympic range, my home place vividly displays every color except brown, tan and grey.

Sunday morning traffic was parked at the churches, where the signs read "LIFE IS TOO SHORT TO BELITTLE" and "MOTHERS HEAR WHAT CHILDREN DON'T SAY." I had no comment. I was on my way to see Mom.

Checking the clock and mileage at Shelton, I turned inland toward I-5, atherosclerotic carotid of the Northwest, to make time. Nearing Vancouver after one too many rest area conversations starting "Wow, I didn't know BMW made a bike like that," I realized I'd run out of three things: time, fuel and pain endurance.

The Bavarians' vest pocket superbike is a miracle of packaging, but my body is not. I haven't been that size since middle school. My right knee is rated only ten percent disabled, but after a few hours on the Super One RoadRash it was 90 percent gone. Still, one doesn't keep Mom waiting. I ground my teeth, used light throttle and promised burnt offerings to the Rabbit Lord if my luck, knee and bladder held.

As I pulled into Portland's Golden Touch Family Restaurant, the bike's digital clock ticked the appointed 13:30 hours and the low-fuel warning flashed on. Crawling off the bike, I hobbled to the men's room, chomping ibuprofen and momentarily ignoring my cell phone caller, who turned out to be Mom. They were in their Model A roadster, thoroughly late and having a wonderful time. When your mother has her cardiologist on speed dial, you don't begrudge her an extra half-hour's wind in her still-red hair.

• • •

An endless stream of chattering strangers stopped by to inquire, not about the BMW but about the old Ford. It was an encouraging reminder that my folks are still cooler than I.

Roadhouse food more than compensated by family memories, the Rabbit's Foot and I continued south toward errands and friends. Near Jefferson, clouds clanked shut the sky and my bluebird of happiness flew off the handlebar. When moldy weather closes around my bike, I feel less ease, more caution. Twinges turn to pain and nostalgia to regret. "Why do I live here?," I wondered, leaning the bike into 50 mph of west wind and horizontal rain. Way too often, my home turf has no colors beyond grey. Sniveling about my summer gloves and missing Black Betty's grip heaters, I switched to RAIN mode and pounded on.

Business completed that evening, I had a plate of stuffed pork chops and fresh corn bread from Robin in Eugene and listened to her tales of playing kid games at the Manson ranch back when good-time Charlie was more of a guitar-playing hippie, less of a murderous crankster. I might write Robin's stories if I had the nerve but she tells them better, anyway.

Next morning after pancakes, I checked in with Bill the Chicken Whisperer to refine our version of history. With both his truck and his well offline again, I brought in milk and O.J. and left with a minty original box of Delta

Rockwell lathe tools. It seemed a lucky trade, even if they impinged on my minimal seat space. I paid for it later when the bumpy Benton County Scenic Loop pounded my tender vittles into gravy.

Northwest of Corvallis runs Kings Valley Highway, and this is how good it is: I lost an hour trying to shortcut over to it, but I was still determined to get there. It clouded over and rained hard on the way to Wren, but I was still Hell-bent and glory-bound for KVH. It is so magically delicious that the sun came out just as I entered Highway 223. That it pounded rain shortly thereafter failed to prevent it from being one of the best riding jags in my no-longer-so-limited experience, because that's how good it is, that road. And that bike.

Riding the RR over broken, greasy, heaving pavement in the rain felt faster and safer than most bikes feel in perfect conditions. RAIN mode isn't required for four-season riders; stick with SPORT and punch it into RACE on sun-kissed roads.

For all its red, white and blue racing livery glory, the bike didn't make me any more attractive. For that, you want a custom cruiser, the functional equivalent of dating super-models. You do it for the reflected attention and to make other men wonder what that's like.

Performance bikes are the porn starlets of motorcycling. After a while you start wondering why *all* the bikes won't do those things — but try it with a decent, mature bike and you'll get yourself slapped hard.

Once internalizing that the RocketRipper will stop like a windshield grasshopper, snap roll hard enough to strain your hips and accelerate harder than literally anything on the road, you might form the dubious ideation that you've transformed from a schlub with a bike payment to a middling superhero. This succubic vision strokes your ego through the night until you wake up screaming like Carl Lewis, "I'm the *fastest man in the world!*"

You're not. If at risk of fantasizing that you're actually fast just because you can burp the speed shifter when the dash light twinkles, do not buy this Beemer. Too much for your juvenile ego, it will launch you into the afterlife to the hollow echo of Darwin's laughter. While its computers may handily dampen slides, stoppies, wheelies and skids, they surely won't prevent you plowing a plastic-lined furrow if you freeze in a corner. The world's smartest table saw can't build you a house if you don't have skills. It'll just rip your fingers off.

If you're bigger and taller than your girlfriend, do not buy this bike. You may dance like Fred Astaire on it, but his little slippers are gonna blister your size 12s even if they are lined with lucky rabbit fur. Also, the beautifully welded aluminum swingarm will bump your heels.

There must be something to it, though. It cost me two days of limping around but the Rabbit's Foot got me to lunch on time, soldiered through driving rain like Bavarian cavalry, made friends and influenced people, never punished my feckless injudiciousness and didn't land me in jail. It will probably win a lot of races, if that's important to you.

As soon as they make them in men's sizes, I'll be first in line.

September 2010, Motorcyclist

DANCING WITH THE DEVIL

For those who set the road on fire to light the way for us.

In the end, we're fertilizer. We invent immortality so we can dream god-heroes to transport us beyond death and reassure us that we're more than that, more than meat with a punch line. We are each of us begotten in the radiant image of Adonai (sure y'are…).

We reassure ourselves that our cultures are immortal, despite the ruins we walk over; that our philosophies will resound down the epochs — and never mind the dearth of Zoroastrian evangelists chatting on Oprah.

Fertilizer we may be, but fertilizer on the hoof can always persuade itself it's something special and undoomed.

Anything but the same old shit.

•••

Like Casey Jones in the old song, Pete Conrad mounted to the saddle and he took his last ride to the Promised Land. Except he wasn't stoking the fires of the Cannonball Express like Casey Jones, or strapped into another titanium tuna can with another 200-ton bottle rocket shoved up his ass.

The retired astronaut went out for a gambol on his bike. He missed a corner and chucked it into a culvert, sustaining fatal injuries. Captain Conrad put his lights out in much the same way as another famous military man, 64 years earlier. T.E. Lawrence, aka "Lawrence of Arabia," also died in hospital following a late lunch of roadside dirt. The 1996 Harley-Davidson Conrad rode actually may have been a tick slower on the top end than Lawrence's 1932 Brough Superior SS100 but after all, Lawrence was a much younger man.

Commentators clucked over his bad judgment. Mission Commander Conrad should have worn a better helmet, should have watched his speed, should have taken a safety course. Most damning: at 76, he was old enough to know better. No one seems to consider that an aeronautical engineer and Navy test pilot who flew to the moon and back may have retained the confidence to take a big boy's chance without adult supervision.

Anyway, I'm guessing none of those precious little scolds ever worked among the hallway wailing and acrid piss pong of a nursing home.

•••

Wicked hangover this morning, the kind of cup you beg G-d to take from you and promise anything — any sacrifice, be it goat, son or birthright — in cheap barter for a moment's relief, or at least for the mess of pottage stirred from caffeine, ibuprofen, sugar, acetaminophen, sweet doughnut lard and pseudo-epinephrine. But there's no alcohol sloshing through my system; no oxy, ex or meth. Nothing so dull receding from my central nervous system, crisping lobes of liver on its way out the back.

Yesterday my new motorcycle, thunderous and demon black, took me up the mountain, closer to G-d, backward through time, skittering to the crumbling edge of a highway falling into the dark side of forever. The harder I flogged her, the more she tittered through her shiny black mask, and I'm the one with sore shoulders today.

The road to Paradise is crowded and over-patrolled, but there is another road, on another mountain. Strait and narrow, heaved and broken, often closed: you can go that way with friends, but you'll reach the end alone. Giggling, if your moment of grace is unexpired; steaming and bleeding in the other event.

Promise broken, then.

Pretty Wife and I traded pledges to stay away from stupid before she embarked for the Holy Land of Perennial Combat and I settled in to hold down our little suburban fort. Saddling up with the mousiest of good intentions, I waddled down Maple Valley Highway toward our Black Diamond link-up at a respectable, middle-aged canter. Wincing at the pain shooting up from the low bars into my wrists, and fairly nauseated by the effect of high footpegs on the squashed intervertebral disks in my low back and neck, I promised myself to dispense with sport motorcycles and settle into a more sedentary form of juvenile self-expression. Myspace maybe, or some other form of Internet porn.

The way to Windy Ridge wriggles up the backside of Mount St. Helens, steaming sullenly ever since her brush with fame after publicly blowing her top. The very Brittney Spears of northwest peaks, St. Helens inveigles a constant stream of suitors to mount her fecund flanks even as she plots her next sticky hot eruption, wondering to herself what happened to her smoothly curved figure and why sensible people keep their distance.

There are no suburban green street signs there, only yellow warning diamonds imploring your prudence. Pavement is cracked and broken, frost-heaved and potholed. The worst gashes are outlined in fluorescent pink traffic paint. At 50 mph in a corner marked for 10, the pink squiggles induce target fixation in the friendly manner of Coleman lanterns inviting moths to a neighborly barbeque.

Masquerading as our own youth if only for the bracing dose of stupidity that's in it, we broke the law for hours, each according to his personal gospel of survivability and the degree to which he'd been anointed with the fragrant oils of adrenaline.

For the first time in too long — first time since my last promise, anyway — I leaned out far enough over public pavement to conjure demons out of the ground and leave them standing flat-footed, staring after me and holding the bag of my mortal aches and pains and limiting fears, forgotten. Somewhere on that road lies a broken left peg feeler, looking for all the world like an edge-ground, black-anodized bone pin.

•••

When services let out, I was tired, sweaty, sore and 150 miles from home. Once more around the mountain, then.

Whinging once about the increasing unreadiness of my crumbling carcass to handle "what might come up," I received a summary benediction from my dauntless VA counselor.

"You can do whatever you need to do," Casey reminded me. "You just gotta understand you're gonna pay for it."

Sure and the piper came this morning, blaring bagpipe solos of burning knees, percussively crunching joints and the soaring arpeggios of tendinitis. She's a hard mistress, the murdersickle, and when the oil in my personal crankcase gets low, it overheats with the greasy stink of deep-fried squid…

Against my better judgment and my word, I spent a non-refundable chunk of my physical capital on that road. One dancing sunbeam leading me into triple-digit silviculture and I might have blown the whole wad.

Can that ever be worth it?

There's no financial payoff for a fast ride with friends, and no glory whatever in sacrificing your prized motorcycle on a cliffstone oubliette. Are you stupid enough to bet your life against that fleeting, fragrant whiff of immortality? Is it that important not to blink? If you believe you even have a choice, you probably do.

Nice guys don't finish last. They take extra laps while the cool guys blow up and crash out of the game. Lead thee not into temptation. Into the Valley of Death rode nobody sane. Take a step back from the edge, ride home at The Pace of Reasonable Men, and kiss your family.

Sometimes I don't. The devil stands behind me wearing toe cleavage pumps and designer décolletage. She strokes my hair while I bet, laughing at pot limits while I flop sweat, addled and hoopy and tracking like a SCUD.

Those are the times I have to push in the whole stack. On the day that I lose — and everybody loses, a chip at a time or the whole pile at a throw — she'll laugh again and raise an eyebrow at the Dealer.

Maybe she'll tip me a wink as they escort me out the back.

January 2009, Motorcyclist

ABOUT JACK LEWIS

Jack wears thick glasses, drinks Ardbeg if you're buying, owns three motorcycles and two chainsaws, and prefers slip-on shoes.

Editorial writing earlier in Jack's career resulted in the D.B. Houston Journalism Prize, SPJ Editorial Writing honors, Best of the Palouse citation, and WSU Philosophy Club Gadfly of the Year.

More recently Jack has contributed stories to *Operation Homecoming: Iraq, Afghanistan, and the Home Front, in the Words of United States Troops and Their Families.* NPR Selected Shorts and The New Yorker Online featured "Road Work," which was also nominated for a Pushcart prize.

In addition to Jack's regular contributions to *Motorcyclist* magazine, "Riding Home" was published in *The Devil Can Ride: The World's Best Motorcycle Writing.*

In 2011 Jack published *Nothing in Reserve: True Stories, Not War Stories,* which was selected as a Reviewer's Choice by Midwest Book Review.

Included at the back of this book is "Tools of the Trade," an excerpt from *Nothing in Reserve.* We hope you'll enjoy it.

COLOPHON

This book contains original material with all copyrights accruing to the author. Please do not distribute pirated copies. If you have received a questionable copy, please consider leaving a review at one or more online bookstores.

This book was typeset in Adobe Garamond Pro, with headlines in Lucida Sans. The title is set in Haettenschweiler and Book Antiqua.

Litsam titles are proofed through an innovative collaboration of readers and authors. The readers listed on the following page substantively improved this book by finding errors or offering editorial feedback. If you would like to know more about this new form of publishing, please visit Litsam.com.

Litsam
for the books!

THANKS AND APPRECIATION

Litsam wishes to thank:

Alex Wall, for suggesting the title "Head Check."
Marguerite Storbo and Michael Pierce for early feedback.
Lyle Gunderson for great copy editing.
David A. "Flash" Braun for remarkable technical editing.
Dennis Weatherly for last-minute error catching.
Larisa Harriger for editorial feedback.
Alon Tuval, Donn Christianson, and Jack Lewis for photography as noted.
Shasta Willson for photography except as noted, and for interior and cover design.

Jack Lewis wishes to thank:

Larisa Harriger, for Pants Before Noon.
Brian Catterson, for the running room.
Mom, who taught me to write.
Dad, who showed me that life is stories.
Paul Sturges, an ideal of quiet excellence.
Ann Thye, for encouragement beyond all reason.
My family, for unstinting support.
You, the reader, for being the point of the exercise.

TOOLS OF THE TRADE

We hope you enjoy this sample from Jack's previously published book Nothing in Reserve *(Litsam, 2011).*

For even the high lifted and chivalric Crusaders of old times were not content to traverse two thousand miles of land to fight for their holy sepulchre, without committing burglaries, picking pockets, and gaining other pious perquisites by the way.

Had they been strictly held to their one final and romantic object — that final and romantic object, too many would have turned from in disgust.

— Herman Melville, Moby Dick

It was hours before the first call to prayer when I woke up for the fourth time that night, burned my eyes on the Luminox dial, shoved old feet into cold boots and stood up quiet in the darkness, listening. I heard generators running.

I put a hand out to the right and found my rifle and body armor, another out to the left for the big MOLLE ruck that served as my nightstand. In the absolute dark of my blinds-drawn hooch, I could find my DCU blouse, bleached to a smeary light butterscotch, by the 0230 glow of my watch. I slipped it over my Under Armour tactical tee. On its best day, the issue cotton undershirt was only good for cleaning weapons.

Forty-five seconds later, I was dressed and shrugging into my "tool belt," an Interceptor Body Armor vest. The front was a MOLLE-strapped rack crowded with the khaki- and green-colored tools of my trade: bullet pouches, compass, fixed-blade knife, medical pack, whistle, night vision goggles, surgical scissors, switchblade knife, digital camera, multi-tool, more ammunition. It cantilevered enough weight out front to make my 40 year-old back creak, but it would be counterbalanced by a big rucksack soon enough.

You can carry more ammunition than you need — and damn, it's heavy — but the instant you need ammo, you can't have too much. Cartridges are to line soldiers as clamps are to cabinetmakers: a pain in the rear to tote and store, but indispensable during those few, vital, fast-moving moments when you really, really need them.

I hung a Surefire G3 Nitrolon flashlight from a lanyard around my neck, careful not to mash the end cap button. Firing up 200 lumens of xenon light inside my little tuna can would blast my night vision for half an hour.

Then I clipped my Colt M4 rifle to the tactical sling on my vest, and started my commute to work.

•••

Russ was already suited up and hopping around when I tapped softly on his door. Damn kid was always ready. There's no better tool in the world than a switched-on soldier.

A quick, preventive-maintenance visit to the stink box and off we schlepped, past boxcar-sized generator sets and sand-filled HESCO barriers to the crenellated parking field dividing the TOC bunkers from our hoochal area. A quick shot from my Surefire showed me where each of the soldier-swallowing potholes lurked, all the way across the 150-meter parking zone.

The next best thing to a good troop is a functional coffee-maker, and Russ had Starbucks Breakfast Blend gurgling through our globetrotting Mr. Coffee before I could growl, "Where the hell's my…"

Nothing cuts through the pasty phlegm of Iraq's "poo dust" like hot, fresh coffee. We sipped it quietly out of Styrofoam cups while we checked our gear.

Everything is disposable in a hostile fire zone.

•••

My big toolbox for the day was a PSYOP speaker pack. At 75 lbs., it was handy for broadcasting, not so handy to tote. I sighed as I pulled BA5590 batteries — each the size and weight of a brick — off the charger and added spares to my pack. On the far side of the bunker, Russ loaded up on visual product: handbills and posters and cards, oh my.

Finishing up our coffee, we stuffed gear into Elsa the Wonderhummer and rolled across the retired Saddam airbase to our supported infantry company. We reported at the appointed hour of 0330 and Apache's commander threw us aboard his XO's Stryker armored vehicle. We were only straphangers, but Apache's ground pounders were grunts orphaned on a cavalry base. They shared our doom-struck sense of humor. We got on well with them.

On any job site, first impressions are important. My speaker bag was too big to stow inside the crew compart-ment — if you wanted to stow any soldiers in there, that is. It always got lashed to the roof. Whenever we rolled with a new gaggle of guys, I'd one-arm press the speaker pack up to an air guard and casually ask, "Couldja grab this for me?" When it damn near sucked him over the side, I'd boost it up to him. Then I'd make a crack about us PSYOP types putting the "T" in S-O-F, and we'd all get along fine after that. I may have invested a bit too much shoulder cartilage in that little trick. The new troop commander emerged from his cluttered office, half-dressed with his armored vest on but no web gear.

"You all know what you're doing by now," he started. "Let's hear a word from Chaplain Goodall."

A hundred guys in green and tan armor, festooned with ammunition and buddy-aid kits, gave their attention to a barrel-chested chaplain with a fluty voice and a crooked, perpetual grin. Thirty-five years old with a couple of kids and an allegedly happy wife in Vancouver, the FOB Sykes chaplain was a prior-enlisted soldier and new school fundamentalist who had followed the Lord's call to Fort Lewis and ended up assigned to this cavalry squadron in a Stryker brigade.

"Okay, gather around guys," he said, fluttering his hands like a chorus line quarterback. "C'mon, bring it in."

The chaplain was going to call our next move straight from the playbook of G-d.

"The first thing I want to tell you men," the chappy began, "is that God doesn't have a problem with killing, as long as it's righteous killing and the killing is performed with justice and in the glorification of His name."

A few soldiers looked up, puzzled, as CPT Goodall plowed on in his sunny voice.

"God doesn't have a problem with killing bad guys. For Bible-believing Christians, God is all about killing bad guys.

"Now let's bow our heads and pray together.

"Most heavenly Father, Ye who shielded the Israelites in their travails and strengthened Joshua to blow down the wicked walls of Jericho, we ask You to make your holy presence manifest in the hearts of these your soldiers. Make a mighty shield to guard them in their missions, and blunt the swords of thine enemies…"

This went on for some time. Eventually, my neck got stiff and I straightened up to look around. A few helmets and patrol caps were still bowed, but most were staring blankly as though they could see straight through the hangar blast doors to the green image of a target waiting in the dark.

"…and let them strike another tremendous blow for peace and justice in Your name, Lord. This we ask in the strong name of your son Jesus Christ, who taught us to pray…"

That was our cue to chant the Lord's Prayer together. Black, white or Latino; Catholic, Presbyterian or Muslim — no surveys were taken. Like the Pledge of Allegiance, the Lord's Prayer was brand-independent ecumenicalism endorsed by the chain of command, now new and improved by a martial intro worthy of the most militant Pakistani *madrasa*.

Our huddle broke on the final "amen" as quickly as cheers drown the last note of the national anthem at baseball games. Lieutenants accosted the captain while sergeants broke off to check on their men and equipment, administering clipped imperatives about more temporal concerns:

"Pull those jerry cans off the back. It's a fire hazard, dumbass."

"Did you fill radios?"

"You can piss later. Yeah, alright, hurry up."

"Get that FBCB2 up *now!* You shouldn't've been fuckin' off in the first place!"

"How much ammo we got for the fifty?"

Soon enough, we were all sitting in the half-lit bellies of our assigned vehicles, running through checklists in our heads while subconsciously monitoring the radio speakers' jargoned mumble: "Apache Six-Seven, Six-Six."

"Six-Seven. Send it."

"Line up on the road. SP one-zero mikes."

"Roger." The first sergeant switched from command to troop net. "All vehicles move to the gate."

Cables groaned and ramps clanged heavily into place all over Apache's parking ramp. Supercharged diesels spooled up and soldiers on bench seats bumped shoulders as their armored transports lurched into motion.

Most Apache guys were dead sick of riding air guard, so I could usually talk someone out of his hatch without pulling rank. I put a dirty boot on the troop seat and hoisted my tired ass up into the air guard hatch. It was better than being inside if somebody puked up a festering gobbet of poo dust, unsanitized black water, KBR niblets and powdered green Gatorade.

You made a fine target silhouetted against the Big Sky moon of northwestern Iraq, but there wasn't much better than riding air guard in a Stryker blasting down deserted highways in the dark, senses turned up to 11, the only source of heat and noise and motion in all the world. Some bikers believe that only motorcyclists know why a dog hangs its head out the car window. I submit that they've never pulled air guard in the sandbox.

Testing my NVGs for the third time, I tugged a drive-on rag up over my nose and mouth and pulled out my first full magazine, laying it on the cold steel roof next to the rifle I held loosely by its grip, waiting for the VC's command to go "red-direct" as we left the wire. God willing, I would stuff it back into my ammo pouch at end of mission still pregnant with its lightning potential of powder, brass and copper-jacketed lead.

Deliver us from evil.

In any trade, tool prep separates retail hobbyists from the pros. Before we lifted off from Ft. Bragg, my team disassembled all our rifle magazines, cleaned and tested them, and reassembled them with 550 cord loops extending from the base plates. Beyond giving employment to our jittery fingers, we now knew we could reliably yank mags out of our pouches by the cords. We could also snap our empties onto a carabineer during firefights.

In a combat zone, nothing is expendable.

•••

After checking in with the Apache squaddies holding Tall 'Afar castle, a 1,400 year-old tool of the Ottoman occupation, we wound downhill through the cobbled streets to the road beneath its east-facing wall. Morning prayer call was starting by the time we dropped ramp and moved out on LPCs to our objective, a group of dwellings thrown together as haphazardly as a pile of stone puppies.

The staff sergeant leading the patrol had his mission, and we had ours. He proceeded to interview people with his HUMINT specialist while Russ and I set up a series of

rooftop locations to broadcast counter-terror and non-inter-
ference messages from our manpack's portable amplifier,
speaker and digital recorder. The grunts carried a battering
ram and a 12-gauge in case persons of interest didn't come
out when they knocked, and we broadcast recorded Arabic
messages in case others wouldn't go back in — persuasion
added to coercion.

"How do we know they're even listening?," Russ asked
at one point. Two hundred meters away, a crowd gathered,
pointing and yelling.

"Play Message Three."

Message Three was an order to disperse and go inside, or
be detained. Everyone went inside but the two military-aged
males who liked to yell. I pointed my rifle in their general
direction, just to scope them a little closer through the 4X
ACOG sight. The two fellas looked a little agitated. Then
they looked at me. Then they went inside.

Around mid-morning, the squad we supported finished
their door knocking. We quit our roof hopping and
rejoined them to finish out their patrol.

Moving along the river was a hands-on, squishy-boot
education in every needed thing that's missing in Iraq, and
every blight we hoped to remove. Tall 'Afar didn't exactly
have a garbage dump; instead, the whole town functioned
as one. Citizens pushed and slung everything from cars to
cans to kitchen slop over the edge, out the window, down
the hill. Woe betide those who lived low on the topography.

By the time it slumped to the river, Tall 'Afar's garbage
was a viscous stew of offal, flaps of plastic, moldy textiles
and sewage. Constantly outgassing, the boiling grey river
occasionally caught fire.

Our tools were rifles and machine guns. What we really needed were shovels. Wishing for a decent hardware store like Hardwick's, where I had worked back in Seattle, I stepped around a dog carcass and slipped on a chunk of fruit. Stumbling for a balance point, I heaved my ruck around and crunched my downhill boot through the ribcage of a rotting donkey.

Damn. Those were the best boots I had left.

From the river, we moved up across the crotch of the road where it started to rise out of the drainage. There was a large building there, like a warehouse or barn that I'd been wondering about. I grabbed Russ out of our Ranger file and pulled him toward it. One of the infantrymen told me they'd already searched the building.

"Staff Sarn't Salinas says we don't go in there today."

"Tell your staff sergeant that Staff Sergeant Lewis will be out in a moment."

"Whatever."

•••

It was dead quiet in the building. When we yanked the squealing steel door open to infiltrate the place, we walked into a working museum of woodcraft. Dust motes swirled through shafts of sunlight falling onto a monstrous iron bandsaw, wide board jointer, and a planer that could flatten totem poles.

Several benches were set up around a workshop bursting with finished and partially complete furniture, mostly cabinets and dressers. Narrowly dovetailed drawers were wrapped by chisel-cut mortise and tenon casework. Hand carvings embellished edges and panels, some surfaces further bedecked by punched metal detailing.

We were surrounded by the hope of life.

Russ watched me curiously as I walked around, quietly touching things. I moved the top wheel of the colossal bandsaw, stroked my fingertips over the jointer's worn outfeed surfaces. Decades of use had left them nearly devoid of Blanchard grinding swirls. Not a power tool in there was younger than me.

"Hey, Sergeant, look over here."

I walked across the shop to where Russ stood over a workbench. Except for the thick coating of dust, it looked like the joiner had laid down his tools and gone to lunch. Chai and deep-fried eggs, maybe, or falafel with goat's milk. Work locally, eat locally.

I plucked a hand tool out of a pile of curly shavings. There was a half-inch #39 dado plane lying next to it, but my eye was caught by a No. 5 Bailey pattern.

"Russ, ya know what this is called?" I grinned like I hadn't grinned in months. "This is a 'jack plane'."

"It's named after you, Sergeant!" Russ's eyes sparkled, reflecting the avarice in my own. "You should put it in your pack."

I frowned at Russ, then down at the tool in my hands. It felt right there, broken in but not busted up. The sole was conditioned, the iron had plenty of meat, and the tote tucked as smoothly into my hand as a river stone into King David's sling. Muscle memory kicked in. I field stripped the plane, popped off the cap iron and squinted straight on at the edge. The user kept a fair hone on his equipment.

"You should just take it, Sarge."

I stood there, thinking about it. We never took property. Souvenir hunting makes U.S. forces look bad and militarizes the populace. Not incidentally, stealing is wrong. But here was this wondrous thing — this fine tool deserving of use — just sitting there calling out to every tool jones I had, a pretty pruning hook in a world bristling with spears.

It was a red Marples. The finish was perfect.

Red Marples handplanes haven't been made for ages. They were never imported to the States. It's nearly impossible to score one in the U.S.A. Back at the hardware store, we had talked about them in hushed tones, plotting our acquisitions.

The voice in my head agreed with Russ. I'd probably never hold another red Marples in my own two hands if I left that one behind. That felt like justification enough.

There was room in my pack. It wouldn't hurt my knees any worse than the gear already in there. Hell, I could toss out a BA5590, call it a field loss and be at even weight.

Its owner was probably dead. At the least, he wouldn't be back here anytime soon. Overwatched by the guns of the U.S. cavalry on the hilltop, this shop stood at the edge of one of the nastiest insurgent neighborhoods in that whole benighted republic. That wouldn't change anytime soon. There was no electricity to power the big iron.

The Turcoman who pushed this plane surely didn't know what he had here. It was a plain working tool to him, bench clutter; a donkey to beat on until it failed, then unsentimentally chuck into the slough of despond down by the riverside.

I looked at that plane, snuggled into my hands, and wished for that simple thing as hard as I've ever wished for an object. Reassembling it, I carefully aligned the chip breaker a millimeter back from the edge. My weapon hung forgotten at my side as I took a few imaginary strokes. In my mind's eye, ribbons of Port Orford cedar sussurated off the frame of the Aleutian kayak project water-dancing through my desert dreams.

Then I set the red Marples carefully back on the bench, side down to protect the iron, and walked out into the sun.

When you take a man's money, you steal a piece of his time. If he has time enough left and uses it well, he can outbalance your pilfering with his skill. If you nick a man's tools, you remove hard-won extensions of his faculties, muscles and nerves. Though I might have convinced myself to take a trophy, I couldn't cut off the hands of a craftsman. That's not American justice.

That handplane would have called me thief every time I touched it. Maybe I'd have a red Marples someday, but not until I earned it fair.

If one day I am so blessed, every time I use it I'll think of a lean, dark woodworker holding his beard out of tool's way as he sweats over his grandfather's bench in an antique cabinet shop, on a battle-torn street, just uphill from where the river runs with fire.

Prosper well, my brother.

Tools of the Trade appeared in Jack's 2011 memoir Nothing in Reserve: True Stories, Not War Stories, *available as a paperback at many bookstores, Powells.com, Amazon.com and in multiple e-book formats. ISBN: 978-1935878025*

CPSIA information can be obtained
at www.ICGtesting.com
Printed in the USA
FSHW022011191218
54590FS